AF522638

OPPORTUNITY BECKONS

In the middle of difficulty lies opportunity.

ALBERT EINSTEIN

The difference between what we do and what we are capable of doing would suffice to solve most of the world's problems.

MAHATMA GANDHI

Edited by GURJIT SINGH

OPPORTUNITY BECKONS

ADDING MOMENTUM TO THE INDO-GERMAN PARTNERSHIP

RUPA

Published by
Rupa Publications India Pvt. Ltd 2017
7/16, Ansari Road, Daryaganj
New Delhi 110002

Sales centres:
Allahabad Bengaluru Chennai
Hyderabad Jaipur Kathmandu
Kolkata Mumbai

ISBN: 978-81-291-4520-8

First impression 2017

10 9 8 7 6 5 4 3 2 1

Printed at Replika Press Pvt. Ltd, India

To my parents,
Swaran and Daljit Singh

Für Deutschland kann ich sagen: Uns sind indische Investoren herzlich willkommen. Ich möchte sie ausdrücklich ermutigen, sich noch stärker als bisher in Deutschland zu engagieren.

Bundeskanzlerin Merkel zur Eröffnung des deutsch-indischen Wirtschaftsforums, 6 Oktober 2015

For Germany I can say: Indian investors are dearly welcome. I want to encourage them explicitly to become even more active in Germany.

Chancellor Angela Merkel at the inauguration of the Indo-German Economic Forum, 6 October 2015

We see Germany as a natural partner in achieving our vision of India's economic transformation. German strengths and India's priorities are aligned... our focus tends to be on economic ties. But I believe that in a world of seamless challenges and opportunities, India and Germany can also be strong partners in advancing a more human, peaceful, just and sustainable future for the world.

Prime Minister Narendra Modi at the inauguration of the Indo-German Economic Forum, 6 October 2015

Contents

Introduction

The visit of Indian Prime Minister Narendra Modi to Germany in April 2015, when India was the partner country for the Hannover Messe for the second time, was a game changer in Indo-German relations. The dynamism that Prime Minister Modi reflected at the fair, in his speeches and in his meeting with German Chancellor Angela Merkel, served to change the view of India in Germany. Suddenly India was everywhere and expectations rose high, and were carried over to the Hannover Messe fair in 2016, when President Obama was present on behalf of the US. Visitors to the 2016 fair said the Indian show was even more impressive than the previous year!

The change in perspective at the presentation of the Make in India initiative at the Hannover Messe and the vigour and dynamism displayed by Prime Minister Modi have served to set a new agenda for cooperation between the two countries. This cooperation was buttressed by a substantive meeting of the German and Indian leaders at the Inter-Governmental Consultations in October 2015, and was reiterated in two other meetings that they held during the same year.

I arrived in Germany in January 2016 basking in the gains of 2015 when Prime Minister Narendra Modi and Chancellor Angela Merkel met four times, and a new aura around India was created. Germany declared itself a steadfast and dedicated partner in the new Indian initiatives—Make in India, Smart Cities Mission, Digital India, Swachh Bharat Abhiyan, renewable energy, Namami Gange, skill development. Clearly it was now time for implementation, and to prepare for this we had extensive consultations before my arrival in Germany and immediately thereafter, with a wide variety of interlocutors, particularly among the business sector.

One of the salient points which emerged during my consultations was that the perspective in which India was viewed in Germany was still not conducive to a fulfilment of the political commitments that our leadership had made in 2015. While the Indian and German governments were in a firm handshake, businesses, academia, students, tourists and the media in Germany still had doubts about India.

This led us to think of ways to enhance the perception of India in Germany, and vice versa. Among the initiatives that we thought of was the creation of this tome where we have identified several themes in which India and Germany can do more, and where a common perspective can perhaps be outlined. A wider impact of this collection of essays is likely to enhance a serious perception building of India in Germany.

We sought essays from a wide variety of interlocutors, while trying hard to steer away from those who were committed Indophiles and India lovers. We wanted to reach a constituency which was open to an exchange of views, to get a frank discussion going and therefore, get many others to think about India. In order to complement this discussion, we sought essays from Indian opinion leaders on the same themes. As you progress through the book, you will see different perspectives from Indian and German opinion leaders, showing how each person views the Indo-German relationship in a particular area, and offers suggestions for its enhancement.

While the list of subjects is certainly not conclusive, I do believe it is illustrative and manifests the diversity which indeed exists in the Indo-German partnership. If there is one major perception that becomes clear, it is that our friendship has evolved into a partnership. The challenge of building a different perception takes up much of our time. As it succeeds, it leads to more positive assessments of India and of what it stands for. This is becoming perceptible within the German government, in Parliament and in some sections of the business community. A better understanding is still required in a wider section of the German media, universities, Mittelstand, tourism and the like.

This collection of essays looks to the future. It hopes to broaden the agenda of a deeper Indo-German partnership. I have emphasized what I consider the major drivers of the partnership between India and Germany. The idea was not to include many traditional areas of engagement. I am confident that as the overall engagement strengthens traditional areas of engagement will also obtain sustenance.

To attempt such a book so early in my time in Germany was indeed a challenge, but I could see that the Indo-German partnership was ready to redefine its depth and diversity. I attempted a nudge in that direction and received encouragement. I was advised not to wait but to take advantage of the fresh views on this bourgeoning relationship. When I discussed this topic with the Director General of the Confederation of Indian Industry (CII), Chandrajit Banerjee, he was spontaneous and prompt in agreeing that the time was right for such an effort, and offered his fulsome support.

Rajesh Menon, deputy director general, CII, was a solid pillar of support and when we discussed the themes, he promptly suggested the names of several people from India who could contribute and, what is more, ensured that the contributions reached me on time. My mother and my wife were equally keen that I use my early impressions of a bourgeoning relationship, and implement this idea.

On the German side, many interlocutors that I met received my request to write for this book at my very first meeting with them. I considered how we could diversify our ideas and look beyond India lovers in Germany, and focus instead on people who were contributing to the partnership but without much acknowledgement. To all the contributors from the Indian and German sides, I owe you a debt of gratitude for joining this ambitious project and for contributing so willingly and quickly.

My own team at the embassy was very helpful indeed, by coming up with ideas and pursuing our new agenda. I received able support from Dr Pradeep Rajpurohit, R. Madhan, P.S. Gangadhar, Vikram Vardhan and Bastian Chacko. Judith Gasch provided able coordination as did my secretaries Tej Krishan and Hemant Gautam, without whom this book would not have been written.

The responsibility for selecting the authors is entirely mine though the credit for the fulfilment of this project goes to many of the individuals I have mentioned, and some who I have not mentioned. The views, however, expressed in every essay remain those of the authors. While I may not endorse all the views expressed by the contributors, I believe that their contribution adds credibility and shows a progressive approach, which those interested in developing the Indo-German partnership could benefit from.

The chapters and contributions included in this book were completed in September 2016. The content therefore reflects situations and economic and/or political realities at that point in time.

Gurjit Singh
November 2016, Germany

Adding Momentum to the Indo-German Partnership

◈

Gurjit Singh

Gurjit Singh, Indian Ambassador to the Federal Republic of Germany

Gurjit Singh has been India's ambassador to Germany since January 2016. He joined the Indian Foreign Service in 1980, and has served in a number of countries in his thirty-six years of service. He is well known as a business-friendly diplomat and has implemented several developmental programmes and expanded India's reach in different countries. These countries in turn, have benefited from his dedication to culture, trade, investment, etc.

His first foreign posting was at the Indian Embassy in Tokyo, Japan, where he was in-charge of political, information and education matters. He became proficient in the Japanese language while he was there. After completing his posting in Tokyo, Mr Singh returned to New Delhi where he served on the East Asia desk. In 1988, he was posted to Colombo, Sri Lanka, as first secretary (political), during the period of the Indian Peace Keeping Force (IPKF), and its subsequent withdrawal.

With the advent of economic liberalization in India in the early 1990s, he was posted back to Tokyo, as head of the Commercial Wing, and was part of India's effort to attract foreign investment. At that time he wrote his first book, *The Abalone Factor: An Overview of India–Japan Business Relations*, which won him the Bimal Sanyal Award for Research by an Indian Foreign Service officer. The book was published in 1997 when Japan was the partner country at the India Engineering Trade Fair.

Subsequently, he was posted as deputy high commissioner of India to Nairobi, Kenya, where he was also the deputy permanent representative of India to the United Nations Environment Programme (UNEP) and UN-HABITAT, and contributed to the growing interest in environmental and urbanization issues.

He returned to New Delhi as director of the Passport Division, where he made a substantial contribution to the computerization of the division, and the setting up of systems which led to significant improvements in delivery. He was subsequently promoted and became director general (joint secretary), in-charge of Africa. He started a series of initiatives which eventually led to the holding of the India–Africa Conclave and India–Africa Forum Summits.

Thereafter, he was posted at the Embassy of India in Rome, where he contributed to the consolidation of the economic engagement between India and Italy, before being appointed as ambassador of India to the neighbouring African countries of Ethiopia and Djibouti. He was also India's representative to the African Union and the Economic Commission for Africa and Inter-Governmental Authority on Development (IGAD). In this capacity, he consolidated India's presence in Africa and the regional economic communities, and was instrumental in setting up the first India–Africa Forum Summit in 2008.

His significant work in promoting economic engagement with Ethiopia opened up many investment opportunities and brought his qualities as an economic diplomat to the fore. During this period his second book, *The Injera and the Parantha: Enhancing the Ethio-India Relationship*, was published with a foreword by then Ethiopian Prime Minister Meles Zenawi.

Subsequently, Mr Singh was appointed additional secretary in-charge of Africa and the African Union, and the Second India–Africa Forum Summit was held in 2011, during his tenure. The economic and human resource development-led initiatives introduced by him received strong support from India's African partners. This was the period when the India–Africa partnership bloomed and forged ahead.

In 2012, Mr Singh was appointed ambassador of India to Indonesia, Timor-Leste and to the Association of Southeast Asian Nations (ASEAN), making him the only Indian diplomat to have been ambassador to two regional organizations, namely, the African Union and ASEAN. During this period, he consolidated India's economic engagement with Indonesia and added significantly to the functional cooperation with ASEAN. His third book, *Masala Bumbu: Enhancing the India–Indonesia Partnership,* was published at this time, along with a comic book on

India and Indonesia titled *Travels Through Time*, written by him. This was a unique instance of a comic book written by a diplomat. Mr Singh also made a YouTube video to announce the start of his term in social-media savvy Indonesia.

Since January 2016, he has been the ambassador of India to Germany and in a short period, has implemented the major decisions taken by the leaders of India and Germany during their summit in October 2015. This intensified engagement has opened up many functional opportunities and a wider engagement between the two countries has systematically crystallized.

Gurjit Singh has frequently contributed essays and articles to journals and books, on issues related to economic development and trade. He also has an abiding interest in developmental economics and sustainable development, and was well-known in UNEP and UN-HABITAT. He was instrumental in India's support for the Africa Climate Policy Centre and the United Nations Economic Commission for Africa (UNECA) in Addis Ababa.

Mr Singh studied at the prestigious Mayo College, Ajmer, and obtained his Bachelor's degree in Politics from St Xavier's College, Kolkata. He is a postgraduate in International Studies from the School of International Studies, Jawaharlal Nehru University, New Delhi. He has also attended programmes at the Indian Institute of Foreign Trade, Indian Institute of Mass Communications and the Indian School of Business.

Mr Singh is an avowed cinema buff and is also fond of cricket and other sports. He is a Kenya Cricket Association qualified umpire. He enjoys travelling, experiencing different cultures and cuisines, and meeting people. His commitment to enhance outreach programmes in every assignment and to enlarge the agenda of engagement is well known. He is considered a business-friendly developmental diplomat.

He is married and has two children.

Adding Momentum to the Indo-German Partnership

Gurjit Singh

In June 2016, the German Bundestag considered a multiparty motion to expand cooperation with India in education and science. The essence of this motion was that by investing more than other emerging economies, India had been able to develop well, and this pace of development had in turn allowed India to play a key role in shaping the forces of globalization. The motion recognizes that more German companies were going to India while a larger number of Indian students were coming to Germany. It appreciated India as the world's biggest democracy, a reliable partner and its immense potential. Keeping this in view, it suggested that exchange programmes should take these new factors into account. Following a tap in Parliament, a consensus emerged that Germany was committed to the deepening of its partnership with India. A partnership which, inter alia, focuses on areas such as education, skill development, science and technology (S&T), and research, with the objective of creating a new paradigm of collaboration and cooperation.

This recognition of the Indo-German partnership was the result of two summit-level meetings held between India and Germany at the highest level. In 2015, Indian Prime Minister Narendra Modi and German Chancellor Angela Merkel announced a whole new agenda for bilateral cooperation with greater dynamism and motivation. Bilateral engagement between India and Germany is to be seen in a wider context and is to be intensified through a public, private and civil society engagement to reach its full potential. The transformation which was coming to the fore was that the economic functional relationship between the two countries would also be expanded manyfold, and it would not be confined to that.

With the launch of the Inter-Governmental Consultations process in 2011—which was successfully held once again in 2015—German engagement with India acquired multiple dimensions, leading to a more fulsome strategic partnership. The Inter-Governmental Consultations process generated momentum in the field of human resources development (HRD) and

Research and Development (R&D) as well as political and security issues. The new trio of cooperation beyond economic and HRD engagement included security cooperation, high technology partnership and a more appreciative defence engagement. These kept in view the rising German capabilities and desire to cooperate, as well as India's own openness and potential for greater opportunities.

To implement these new ideas, strengthen existing economic and functional engagements and create a wider politico-strategic partnership, it became imperative to focus on the implementation of the decisions taken between Prime Minister Modi and Chancellor Merkel, particularly following the landmark Inter-Governmental Consultations of October 2015. However, one of the problems that has emerged with regard to implementation is that despite positive feelings at the higher levels of government and in Parliament, a perception of anxiety and a 'wait-and-watch' approach seems to permeate the German landscape.

The commitments made at the level of leaders and governments and supported by the Parliaments of the two countries need wider acceptance so that decision-makers can become aware of the positive steps taken to grasp the opportunities in India's growth story. To tackle this perception, the Indian Embassy in Germany has undertaken several steps including wider social media outreach, closer engagement with the diaspora with a functional approach, publications in German, and greater contact with smaller newspapers and media houses in Germany, among others. This collection of essays is part of the same effort.

There is clarity in both India and Germany about their importance to each other. For India, Germany is its best friend in Europe and its biggest economic partner. India sees Germany as a stabilizing force and a country which plays a responsible role both within Europe and outside it. Germany, on its part, sees India as a responsible democracy on a growth trajectory and wishes to associate with it for both economic and political reasons.

The democratic and demographic dividend of India is attractive to Germany, which also values India's consistent foreign policy and commitment to shared values. In a rapidly changing world, a greater consultative engagement between India and Germany is emerging. This engagement has become even more important following Brexit (British vote to exit the European Union (EU), since Germany will now be India's main interlocutor in the EU. In some ways, Brexit has provided India and Germany with an opportunity to develop greater momentum in their partnership.

The Pillar of Economic Partnership

One of the cornerstones of the Indo-German partnership has been steady and robust economic engagement. However, while their trade and investments have increased in the last decade, the demands for their expansion are now more pressing. The potential for growth is clear but the challenges which need to be overcome before we can grasp the opportunity for expansion may seem overwhelming. Our strategy is designed to address these impediments. Often it is a perception gap rather than a real challenge. If India was akin to Germany in its infrastructure and technological base, the opportunity cost would not be so beckoning as it is now.

In any case, I do believe that every challenge is actually an opportunity, and this is what our economic perspective needs to recognize. Two essays, one by Dr Naushad Forbes, President of the Confederation of Indian Industry (CII), and the other by Ulrich Grillo, President of the Federation of German Industry (BDI), point to the opportunities that exist in the two countries, and how they can be seized. Even though there are more than 1,600 German companies in India, the success story of German companies has not been adequately articulated and is in need of wider and better understanding.

Mr Grillo has pointed out the greater attention paid to India following the launch of Make in India at the Hannover Messe in 2015, in the presence of Prime Minister Modi and Chancellor Merkel. He also conveys the greater hope German industry has that India will reform further and improve its ease of doing business. Since most German companies in India are in the manufacturing sector, they see the Make in India programme in a positive light and recognize the advantages that it would bring to the industry.

Mr Grillo recognizes that with the greater urbanization of India, there must be a fresh focus on renewable energy, skill development and other sectors where Germany and India share strong complementarities. He strongly calls for renewed vigour in the EU–India free trade agreement (FTA), and believes that the Indian opportunity truly beckons.

Dr Naushad Forbes, in his essay, emphasizes that there is a new India with a transformative agenda; a major economic destination which ought to be a preferred economic partner of Germany. He emphasizes manufacturing, particularly in automotives, infrastructure, defence, railways and aerospace, as new areas for expansion. Clean energy, urban development and skills are seen as the correct path which will allow India and Germany to find greater convergence in the years ahead. He also focuses on engaging with the Mittelstand, the champions of German manufacturing, to enhance the engagement with India.

The Indian Embassy's Make in India Mittelstand programme is one such initiative. Mario Ohoven, president of BVMW, in his essay 'Impulses for the Indo-German partnership 4.0' looks at the economic development in India as well as the new spirit of optimism which now permeates India. As the largest organized group of the Mittelstand in Germany, he says BVMW is indeed well placed to support more German companies in India, and points out that 1,307 'hidden champions' of the world are in Germany. We are looking forward to his help to find more champions of Germany in India!

With reference to Industry 4.0, Mr Ohoven focuses on innovation and examines the IT industry, the pharmaceutical industry, the Smart Cities programme and the support these can derive from Indo-German development cooperation. His essay clearly demonstrates that while there are opportunities, these need to be expanded in the context of Industry 4.0 so that Indo-German cooperation becomes more contemporary.

In my essay 'Opportunity 2.0 for the Mittelstand', I have pointed out the complementarity of a younger India with growing demand, and Germany with stagnating demand, and the opportunity of matching of skills and demands, particularly in the context of Industry 4.0. I have tried to show how much we are trying to persuade the German Mittelstand to take further steps and seek business opportunities in India. While twenty-six of the thirty companies of the DAX index at the Deutsche Boerse are engaged economically in India, of the mid-sized companies on the M-DAX only twenty-eight out of fifty companies are in India.

The lack of a coherent group approach, the abiding by self-financing attitudes, a cautious view rather than immediate grasping of opportunities, incomplete understanding of the Indian system and market size, and ultimately a dominance of extant perception of India being a challenge rather than an opportunity, are the kind of issues that we are systematically contending with.

In the euphoria of building up investment promotion and seeking foreign direct investment (FDI), the normal intercourse of trade and commerce is often neglected. As all of us focus on seeking more investment, we need to remind ourselves of our trade linkages. The complexities of trade policy were left on an automatic mode more in Brussels than in Berlin. I am firmly of the view that trade often contributes to investment and needs nurturing. The absence of an India–EU bilateral trade and investment agreement, despite several years of negotiation, remains a hindrance, but I often wonder whether Indian companies have not already factored in the non-tariff issues which have affected their entry into Europe.

Some of the issues do remain, particularly with regard to free movement of people, pharmaceuticals and agricultural commodities, for instance. Meanwhile, Europe remains interested in having its wines and cars get easier access into India. The lack of progress in the India–EU agreement and a possible reduction in the areas where it can make a critical difference, has led to trade finding its own solutions.

Be that as it may, the expansion of trade between India, and its largest EU partner, Germany, has not been satisfactory. There has been no dearth of Indian participation in German trade fairs, and while Indian participation at Hannover Messe attracted the largest attention in 2015, it is noteworthy that India has participated in nearly seventy trade fairs in Germany. These were mostly supported by the Indian Ministry of Commerce and related ministries, and the Export Promotion Councils.

The importance of Germany in the Indian trade engagement has remained undiminished, and India has moved from an India pavilion approach to sectoral participation in an effective manner. While there certainly hasn't been any dearth of trade promotion efforts by Indian agencies, trade expansion has not kept pace with expectations. The target of 20 billion euros by 2012 set up in 2007, is yet to be fulfilled even in 2016. Greater innovation, diversification in product lines, import substitution and turning trade opportunities into investment, are needed to be grasped.

These issues have been analysed with special reference to the regional context, by Timo Prekop, managing director of the German Asia-Pacific Business Association OAV and Dr Jayanta Roy, senior economic adviser to Deloitte, who have given some direction to growing Indo-German and Indo-European trade. Undoubtedly, India and Germany need closer interaction on policy pertaining to regional trade agreements, given the size of their bilateral trade. Dr Roy has pointed out that while India's strength lies in the IT and services sectors, many of the barriers in India and Germany are precisely in these sectors and need to be resolved.

On the German side, the perceived barriers are mainly for investment rather than for trade but, as we improve on the ease of doing business in India, these are likely to get resolved. The German side also believes that in trade negotiations India has a protectionist view but understands that the agreement with the EU will not move unless the free movement of skilled Indian services-related workers is allowed, and market access for manufactured goods, pharmaceuticals as well as agricultural projects is improved. With a better understanding, Mr Prekop concludes, a lot can be done to boost trade between India and Germany.

The Indian Embassy in Germany, of course, takes full cognizance of the importance of trade and in 2016, it focused on fresh market surveys in areas where India has potential which has not been tapped fully in Germany, for example, where Germany was importing from other countries and not so much from India. Thus, market surveys in areas like textiles and garments, chemicals and organic chemicals, food products, beverages and agricultural products, IT, engineering goods, electronic components, auto components, iron and steel, gems and jewellery were conducted by our mission in Berlin and consulates in Frankfurt, Munich and Hamburg.

When we look at development cooperation, then we see the diversity of German cooperation with India. At the same time, the large amount of development cooperation that we have needs to be translated into business opportunities for German companies. They must also begin to work to make consortiums with Indian and other companies to tap into the larger opportunities in India rather than remain confined to niche areas where they are real champions.

Germany is working with India to establish a high-speed railway which is likely to run from Chennai to Bengaluru and Mysuru. The feasibility study and the railway will be financed by German support. Talks are also on for Germany to support a speed upgradation corridor around Delhi. The redesigning of a station to modern standards like the Hauptbahnhof in Berlin, are also envisaged. These offer ample scope for business to business (B2B) enhancement and a consortium approach.

Similarly, renewable energy is a major area of engagement. This emanates from the common desire to contribute to the amelioration of the climate change situation in the world, and help India fulfil its ambitious Intended Nationally Determined Contributions (INDCs). The joint effort for renewable energy, particularly solar energy, has come into greater focus since 2015 when India became one of the largest recipients of development assistance from Germany. This issue has been looked at closely by Tobias Zech, Member of Parliament (MP) from the German side, and Dr Leena Srivastava, vice chancellor of TERI University, who has co-written a paper with Sapan Thapar, a fellow at the same university. The importance of this sector in adding greater momentum to our partnership has thus been well brought out.

The energy transition has been positively assessed by Professor Srivastava as an unparalleled exercise under the Indo-German energy programme. The clean technology sector is likely to grow and require a greater cohesive policy so that there is transfer of technology as well as transfer of successful business practices and social impact.

Professor Srivastava also believes that this is an area where an exchange of experience and best practices can be shared as it will contribute to a better climate in the world. Mr Zech, on the other hand, while recognizing that India is perhaps a partner for the future, compliments both sides for a determined push for a renewable energy engagement and correctly calls for German companies to grasp the opportunities offered by the Indian market.

He believes that such an investment could become an employment generator and make a positive social impact in India. I particularly like his view of connecting development cooperation to business opportunities, which is often missing from the Indo-German narrative. The International Solar Alliance, which was initiated by India as part of the climate change discussions, has become an important engagement. However, Germany, though an important partner of India in this segment, is not directly associated with the alliance. There is room here to develop a wider partnership which will add momentum to the alliance.

Other areas of development cooperation include water resources and sanitation where Germany is supporting Namami Gange, particularly in Uttarakhand. German companies are also working with Indian companies for Indian projects for water and wastewater management as well as sanitation. This contribution to the Swachh Bharat campaign and to larger infrastructure development is also linked to the Smart Cities initiative. Germany decided to support three smart cities soon after the first list of twenty smart cities was announced by India. The chosen cities of Bhubaneswar, Coimbatore and Kochi are unique in that they are not major hubs of German activities, whether academic or economic.

In fact, these three cities could become future nodes of engagement with Germany. Dr Michael Beckereit, chairman of the German Water Partnership, and Naina Lal Kidwai, chairman of the India Sanitation Coalition, have looked at this issue from both sides to show the diversity of opportunity and demand. The Smart Cities initiative has been looked at by Pedro Miranda, global head of Siemens, Smart Cities, and Ravi Parthasarathy, chairman of the CII National Mission on Smart Cities, who have pointed out the conceptual validity of the idea and the possibilities of new opportunities.

Dr Beckereit has pointed out the salient features of the German engineering capacity in the water sector and the work that they do to connect partners and clients, thus bridging the gap between development cooperation and business. One of their biggest focus areas is India and the Indo-German water partnership is a significant contribution to find German solutions to Indian challenges. They see potential in water management, water supply and irrigation as well as wastewater management, but correctly emphasize that German Mittelstand companies often cannot face the competition of large international consortiums which bid for the same projects in India. Thus, the German water partnership offers a coalition route of accessing the Indian market.

Dr Naina Lal Kidwai focuses on the sanitation aspect of the water engagement as a priority linked to the Swachh Bharat campaign. She appreciates the focus on the German partnership, the closed-loop approach and calls for utilizing collaborative platforms that promote a multiplicity of players and levels, particularly through public–private partnership (PPP) models. Her argument that for the vast resources that are required for this sector in India a greater cohesion of business with development cooperation would be necessary is one of the salient points that this book promotes.

With reference to the Smart Cities programme, Ravi Parthasarathy has pointed out how it brings together various initiatives and financing mechanisms and offers business opportunities for development cooperation to provide basic and other infrastructure in a smart way. He identifies transportation, sustainable energy, and water and waste management as significant areas of engagement between India and Germany, which could lead to employment generation, productivity, better living conditions and the like.

He strongly supports the consortium approach with a long-term view and has discussed the financing options available. It is helpful that the company that he chairs, Infrastructure Leasing & Financial Service (IL&FS), is a consortium partner of Siemens on whose behalf Pedro Miranda has also contributed an essay in which he has focused on intelligent urban infrastructure and how German activities can be utilized. He has focused on how their consortium can reach out with its capabilities to garner more opportunities in India.

Corporate social responsibility (CSR) is not an area which is commonly discussed between India and Germany. While Indian companies in India follow the CSR rules quite meticulously, what German companies do in this area is not so well known. Azim Premji, chairman of Wipro, has written a perspective essay on the philosophy and implementation of CSR, while Bernhard Steinrücke, director general of the Indo-German Chamber of Commerce, has written about the CSR activities of German companies in India. Mr Premji describes how education and ecology have led their CSR efforts, and focuses on a community-based approach. He calls for a closer understanding by German companies of how Indian companies see their social responsibility and sustainability initiatives through a common approach.

Mr Steinrücke's essay describing what major German companies do in India shows a level of commitment, but perhaps the commonality of approach that Mr Premji has so vividly brought out is an area of future cooperation. It is good to see these essays together because CSR ultimately also has to be seen as a supplementary development finance alternative. And if it can fulfil national programmes and objectives, then it is playing an even more useful role.

Smart cities, water resources and renewable energy are today among the priority areas for German development cooperation with India, and will be a significant contributor to the enlargement of the partnership. The momentum that can be built out of this will transform them into business ideas and attract FDI, with more B2B contact to supplement the government-to-government (G2G) link of the developmental activity.

To my mind, there are many opportunities to build consortiums for bringing together these initiatives, and having German companies work with Indian and other companies to avail of the larger business opportunities that are outside development financing modules. Such opportunities, when grasped, will open up areas for FDI and technical collaboration, and also provide greater B2B contact between Indian and German companies.

The Pillar of Human Resource

Other focus areas of the book are expanding the horizon on research, science and technology (S&T), education, skill development, innovation and start-ups. India and Germany have been cooperating on S&T since 1974, and while this cooperation has progressed well it now needs a more equitable building of partnership and joint research.

The Indo-German Science and Technology Centre, the launch of German satellites by Indian space vehicles and cooperation at the German research centre DESY are steps in the right direction but need multiplication. We have noted that in a debate in the plenary session of the Bundestag on 19 June 2016, all major parties in the German Parliament supported a resolution for enhancing cooperation with India in education and science. They recognized that joint promotion of research projects would be another pillar of Indo-German cooperation. And all these areas would be expanded, including vocational training, particularly through the iMOVE programme, to help India's vocational system cope with demographic and socio-economic challenges.

They all supported 'A new passage to India programme' by the German academic exchange service (DAAD) to exchange students and academics in all subjects between Germany and India. This programme is now supported by the Indian Global Initiative for Academic Network (GIAN) project, which is a scheme for foreign faculty to participate in teaching in Indian institutes.

Exchange programmes in education between India and Germany have become even more meaningful as many Indian universities now have ties with German universities which have also shown enthusiasm to reciprocate. About forty such arrangements are in place, and the quantum of such exchanges is now at a level which is not easy for the embassy to monitor. It is now easier to support new initiatives and allow them to come to fruition on their own, for example, the IIT-TU9 initiative and other programmes under the Indo-German Partnership in Higher Education announced during the Inter-Governmental Consultations in October 2015.

There is interest on the German side to establish programmes with Indian universities and Indian Institutes of Technology (IITs) and Indian Institutes of Management (IIMs), but our effort has been that we should expand this engagement and get newer institutions and universities, so that the number of institutions interacting with their German counterparts is increased. A similar diversification is noted since both countries have agreed to support an International Centre for Advanced Studies in Humanities and Human Sciences. Somehow the non-S&T cooperation between Indian and German institutions does not work with the same passion as it does with others.

Of the 401 universities in Germany, 211 have got Indian students, whose numbers have increased from about 4,000 to 12,000 over the past three years. Given the rising number of Indian students and academics and their greater interaction, the Indian Embassy has undertaken several initiatives including the Indian Professionals Forum, the Indian Academics Network and the Indian Students Portal.

These were all launched in the first half of 2016 and focus on engaging with the Indian diaspora in Germany on a sectoral basis depending on their professions. While these are new initiatives, they have helped us find out what Indians are doing in Germany, whether they can help in fomenting closer cooperation with Indian institutes and building greater relationships. No doubt these initiatives have helped expand our engagement with the Indian diaspora.

We have an essay by Professor Reimund Neugebauer, president of the Fraunhofer Institute, on the theme of expanding research, and S&T in the India–Germany partnership. He has emphasized the multi-stakeholder model under which Fraunhofer and Indian institutions became close partners in their effort to drive innovation. Fraunhofer also has strong public sector cooperation in India, and in order to provide a deeper impact on technology is collaborating with Indian central organizations. At the same time, Fraunhofer is developing strong links with academic institutions, which has created real value for the India–Germany partnership.

From the Indian side, the former director general of the Council of Scientific and Industrial Research (CSIR), Dr R.A. Mashelkar, who has been at the forefront of many S&T related initiatives, has contributed an important essay. He is full of praise for the idea to collaborate with Fraunhofer as well as the Humboldt Foundation, the Max Planck Institute and the Indo-German Science and Technology Centre.

Dr Mashelkar notes that Germany's key competency in high technology and India's demand for it can create an effective partnership and points out several opportunities for German companies based on research and technology. I agree with him when he says that the partnership that we establish in research and technology is something for the future.

With regard to education, Professor Andreas Pinkwart, Dean of the HHL Business School in Leipzig which has several engagements with Indian institutions and also Indian business schools, has given his impressions of how this engagement has evolved. He has referred to the strategy of the German government for the internationalization of science and research, and believes this is a good response to Prime Minister Modi's statement that Germany is a natural partner for India. He also believes that following Brexit, there is additional impetus for Indo-German cooperation in education and research.

From the Indian side, Professor Pradeep Mathur, director of IIT-Indore, who is behind the IIT-TU9 initiative, has given his view on the same topic. He feels that in education, academic and student exchanges are good partnership builders. He notes that while the growing number of students in German universities is a good sign, it is the coordination among top German and Indian institutions that will be the key to achieving excellence, and moving the Indo-German dialogue on research and education in the right direction.

Closely linked to education is skill development which is necessary to increase employment in India. The country, with 800 million young people, is looking to make the Make in India programme a success so that more employment can be generated and its young people can be gainfully employed. Skill development and emphasis on manufacturing go hand in hand, since one without the other becomes a weak link. Thus, the Make in India programme, we have equally focused on skill development in India, particularly adopting the dual education system of Germany as relevant.

There are indeed many German companies in India which organize training programmes and, as in Germany, run these for three-year periods. I have had the opportunity to observe some of these training programmes. However, the intake in them is relevant to their employment needs, and not so much to the overall demands of India. In any case, the Indian requirement is for an employment generation situation and not a near-full employment situation as required in Germany.

At the 2015 Inter-Governmental Consultations (IGC), Prime Minister Modi and Chancellor Merkel welcomed closer cooperation in the area of vocational cooperation and skill development by supporting policy reforms in the apprenticeship system, including dual-system pilot projects in selected industry clusters. Prime Minister Modi also commended German companies in India which incorporate skills development programmes in their business strategy and thereby contribute to the development of their own enterprises as well as to the human capital base of India. He encouraged others to follow their example.

These ideas have been taken forward and Mark Hauptmann, member of the Bundestag and a vibrant supporter of economic engagement with India, has given his views on how skill development is at the core of our engagement. He has enumerated the various G2G and B2B initiatives in skill development, linked vocational education with competency standards and emphasized inclusiveness. He is clear that German models need to match the requirements of the Indian system.

Dr S. Ramadorai, former vice chairman of TCS and the former chairman, National Skill Development Corporation, has spoken about the Indo-German partnership and the opportunities it opens up, besides the national skills qualification framework which is contributing to standardization. In an interesting cross-cutting approach, he refers to the role of the Mittelstand, Fraunhofer, Industry 4.0 and innovation, which are covered in other essays in the book, as providing great opportunities for Indian organizations to link with German ones, and calls for building similar institutions in India. The essays by Mark Hauptmann and Dr Ramadorai clearly indicate the importance and potential of skill development to build momentum in the Indo-German partnership.

While working on this book, it became clear to me that Industry 4.0, start-ups and the like were all issues related to innovation, and it was time that we also looked at the possibility of an innovation partnership through a better realization of the potential on each side. In this area, we received an important contribution from Stephan Vopel and Murali Nair of the Bertelsmann Foundation, about a study they commissioned on innovation in India. The results of their study clearly show the emerging trends and opportunities for German companies.

They have compared the innovation led by MNCs with that of Indian companies and identified the potential for German companies in India. The study reveals that Mittelstand companies in Germany are technology leaders but face a shortage of next-generation IT talent, which could be an opportunity for closer cooperation between India and Germany on innovation and research.

From the Indian side, Nisha Dutt, CEO of Intellecap, has written about the possibilities of the new developments in Indian entrepreneurship finding resonance with German partners. She has identified the key movements on 'conscientious entrepreneurship' and emphasized that India is no longer solving problems of developing countries alone but is creating solutions globally. These are enabling new intellectual efforts taking into account the decentralization and availability of capital, and the growing demand for an inclusive view across the board.

She has emphasized how Germany's Mittelstand and India's young employment pool could create an effective partnership, and has suggested ways to do so. I believe that the innovations, start-ups and new entrepreneurship modules will provide another dimension which will add momentum to the Indo-German partnership.

The Pillar of Strategic Partnership

While functional and economic cooperation has been discussed at length, strategic issues in the Indo-German engagement have not been adequately studied. Despite talks about the common adherence to democracy and its values, our common participation in the G-20 and G-4 and our desire to have an equitable world order, somehow there is a lack of urgency and depth in these discussions.

India and Germany are both democracies, yet their strategic vision and security cooperation do not get the same importance that they attach to other countries which have greater priority. Since India and Germany are truly strategic partners, their strategic partnership certainly needs to be developed. Given Germany's inhibitions and restraints, areas like civilian nuclear cooperation are not on the agenda. However, as G-4 partners we have a common commitment to many values and an equitable world order, and need to discuss a strategic vision which is beyond our extant ideas.

Our democratic and federal principles, polities and the commonalities which emerge from them have been well considered in two complementary essays, one by Dr Hans-Gert Pöttering, former president of the European Parliament and current chairman of the Konrad Adenauer Foundation, and the other by former Indian ambassador to Germany, Kishan S. Rana. Dr Pöttering believes that parliamentary democracy is a key factor for stability for both India and Germany, and we could form a Euro-Asian axis for peaceful development as partners. He has presented interesting ideas on the common challenges that we face.

His essay looks at turning our concerns into fruitful partnerships including intensive dialogue between politicians and experts on civil societiy as well as dialogue between youth. His conclusion is that India and Germany will be important pillars in the multilateral system, which is precisely the idea that this book set out to explore. Interestingly, former ambassador to Germany Kishan S. Rana has compared the democratic and federal systems, and seen contrasts and commonalities between them. The decentralization of power, the growth of civil society reforms in our socio-political system to create remarkable ambitions for creating a shared reality, and the commonality of democracy offers a basis and scope for future collaboration.

Comprehensively speaking, this collection of essays will help towards enhancing the perception of India in Germany. But the subject itself requires attention, particularly where the media and popular perceptions are concerned. Thus, we have Nicole Bastian, foreign editor of the business newspaper *Handesblatt,* writing on widening understanding between the two countries. She has emphasized the importance of media and popular engagement to buttress the overall India–Germany partnership. She also believes that strong economic exchanges between the two countries have still not led to knowledge of each other, and like China, which came into German focus because of strong economic interaction, perhaps the time for India is now coming. She does mention that there are far too few German correspondents in India, and there aren't any correspondents from India in Germany.

With the growing strength of the internet and social media, perhaps Indo-German encounters can become stronger. Senior journalist Ashok Malik presents another view. He believes that in India there is greater interest in Germany than in the EU as an entity, and says greater attention needs to be attached to tourism, travel exchanges of students and journalists, and other popular activity. He sees these as inadequately harnessed by both sides in their effort to enhance the perception of one country in the other. As leaders in their respective regions, he believes that India and Germany need to do more to increase their popular understanding of each other.

As part of our strategic partnership and enhanced security cooperation, issues like cyber security, maritime security, fight against terrorism, disaster management and other non-traditional threats come to the fore. In the absence of direct strategic threats which could be considered as common, it is non-traditional security (NTS) which is common to India and Germany but often not given its due.

During the IGC in 2015, one of the most underplayed but significant agreements was on security cooperation, and this is an area whose implementation we have strongly focused upon. Our joint working groups in this area have started to function with greater regularity, functional exchanges have started and a closer understanding including the possibilities of joint defence equipment production based on our more open investment policy for the defence industry have emerged as significant areas of future potential.

There are two interesting essays on security cooperation. Noted analyst Dr C. Raja Mohan, director, Carnegie Endowment for International Peace, and Jürgen Hardt, MP and foreign policy spokesman of the ruling CDU/CSU parliamentary group, have emphasized our shared values and what can be done to enhance our security cooperation based on these values.

In his essay 'Definitive Notes from an Uncertain Trumpet', Dr C. Raja

Mohan emphasizes that despite seeming differences, Indian and German interests have often coincided. He introspects on Indo-German security cooperation in the twentieth century and particularly in the Cold War years, and then talks about their renewed engagement. While assessing the challenging global situation, he urges both sides to take leadership and have a warmer security partnership.

He believes that the era of benign neglect is over and India and Germany are among the rising nations that can fill the emerging power vacuum. Both countries have shown considerable keenness and movement towards level-headed foreign policy interventions on non-traditional threats. He has no doubt that Delhi and Berlin are now ready to construct an enduring security partnership.

This coincides with what Jürgen Hardt, German MP, believes. He points out that the Indo-German bilateral relationship is focused on many areas, but rarely on cooperation in foreign and security policy which today's world demands. He says the Indo-German partnership, which is based on shared values and interest, will find greater opportunities in bilateral partnership, international forums and, in the case of India, with the EU. He advocates communication beyond formal processes so that India and Germany can talk to each other whenever the need arises to find responses to emerging challenges, and effective multilateralism with a stronger bilateral connection.

In a wider articulation of our strategic partnership, Dhruva Jaishankar of Brookings India talks about how India and Germany are realizing a strategic conversation and the importance of Delhi and Berlin is growing in the international arena. He says the time is right to take the partnership to a truly strategic level, focusing on terrorism, maritime security, cyber security and internet governance, among other things. He calls for a strategic relationship beyond the narrow walls of security.

In the concluding essay, well-known editor and opinion leader Theo Sommer has written about 'Vision Germany–India'. He points to the shift of power and wealth, the emergence of unseen emergencies and the need to move beyond 'compartmentalized cooperation'. He talks about strategic diplomacy pinched with realism, touching upon our democratic federal credentials, and our strong economic linkages, and points to a situation beyond what we currently talk about so that the strategic partnership becomes substantive.

He believes that India with its young population, commitment to the rule of law, shared vision of democracy and human rights, a vibrant society with stability in the region and the status of a responsible power, provides a firm foundation for a joint Indo-German vision of the future which, he cautions, must remain realistic.

An overall reading of this book will give the impression that while there is a lot happening in the India–Germany partnership, much of this is still a work in progress. We certainly wish to take the Indo-German relationship from an economic partnership to a wider strategic partnership which includes public, private and civil society collaboration. As we tread on that path, we will realize that this is truly an effort to script future history.

Expanding Economic Partnership

◈

Naushad Forbes
'A Dynamic Economic Partnership'

◈

Ulrich Grillo
'Indo-German Business Ties: A Partnership with Potential'

Dr Naushad Forbes, President, Confederation of Indian Industry

Dr Naushad Forbes is the co-chairman of Forbes Marshall, India's leading steam engineering and control instrumentation firm. He chairs the steam engineering companies within the group.

Dr Forbes was a lecturer and consulting professor at Stanford University from 1987 to 2004, and developed courses on technology in newly industrializing countries there. He received his bachelor's, master's and PhD degrees from Stanford University.

Dr Forbes is on the board of several educational institutions and public companies. He is an active member of CII and has chaired the National Committees on Higher Education, Innovation, Technology and International Business.

A Dynamic Economic Partnership

Dr Naushad Forbes

In April 2015, Indian Prime Minister Narendra Modi and German Chancellor Angela Merkel shared the stage at the launch of the prestigious Hannover Messe where India was the partner country. An impressive performance highlighted the creative arts of India, and an innovative digital lion unveiled the strength of its manufacturing sector.

'For people in India, Germany is a valued partner and an enduring symbol of technology and innovation, quality and productivity,' the Indian Prime Minister stressed at the event. Chancellor Merkel was just as forthright at the Indo-German Business Summit where she stated, 'We can certainly learn a lot from a country which is still willing to explore, has an innovative power and still has to fight to secure prosperity... We need this fresh wind blowing from India to stay successful ourselves.'

India's presence as a partner country at Hannover Messe for the second time reflected the close and warm friendship between India and Germany as well as their potential for economic cooperation. Germany is very special to the Indian mindset as prominent German intellectuals and thought leaders have helped rediscover India's rich cultural past and knowledge reservoir. Intellectual and philosophical engagements between the two countries have surpassed India's interaction with other European nations, and Germany has emerged as a vibrant centre for Indic studies. As Rabindranath Tagore noted, 'Germany has done more than any other country in the world for opening up and broadening the channel of intellectual and spiritual communication of the West with India.'

With this strong foundation, economic engagement between India and Germany is based on shared respect and common cultural paradigms. In fact, economic and commercial interaction can be the bedrock for the evolving strategic partnership between the two countries, and there is huge untapped potential that can be leveraged in the coming years to benefit both sides.

India and Germany inked their first trade agreement in July 1950, even before diplomatic relations were established in 1951. Germany was a close partner in India's development drive in the initial years after Independence in 1947, and helped set up the Rourkela steel plant and IIT-Madras. Top German companies, such as Mercedes-Benz, Siemens and Bosch, are deeply embedded in the Indian manufacturing environment, and their systems and processes have percolated down the supply chain to build greater synergy between the manufacturing sectors of the two economies.

Businesses on both sides have evinced strong interest in leveraging the opportunities from convergence of the two economies. German companies have entered India with a long-term vision and sustainable models to take advantage of the Asian country's large consumer markets, competitive cost structures, and skilled workforce. At the same time, Indian industry has derived benefits from Germany's technology transfer, proximity to European markets, and high level of productivity. The small and medium enterprises (SMEs), known as Mittelstand in Germany, have emerged as a key source of strength for bilateral economic engagement and a role model for Indian industry.

Overview of Trade and Investment

From 2007–08 to 2011–12, the total exchange of goods between India and Germany rose from $15 billion to $23.5 billion, a growth of almost 60 per cent in just five years. However, due to the backlash from the global economic crises, bilateral trade has remained somewhat subdued since then, and registered less than $20 billion in 2015–16. It is notable that Germany is India's second largest export destination in the European Union (EU), accounting for about a fifth of total exports to the region. Germany is also the top preferred source for India's imports from the region, contributing more than a quarter of the total goods purchased from the EU.

Indian exports to Germany touched $7.1 billion in 2015–16, a data point that has remained largely around the same level for the past five years. Importantly, the contraction in exports to Germany in 2015–16 was significantly lower than India's overall export performance, indicating that Indian goods are in continued demand in Germany. India's export basket is widely diversified and primarily comprises manufactured goods. Top Indian export products include textiles and apparel, chemical products, leather and leather goods, machinery and electronic equipment, auto components, pharmaceuticals, and iron and steel products, among others.

Germany's exports to India have also moderated over the last five years, and reached $12 billion in 2015–16. The key German exports to India include electrical generation equipment, automobiles, machine tools, bearings and gear equipment, organic chemical products, etc.

The investment story is robust in both directions. German companies directly brought in about $8.5 billion worth of funds into India between April 2000 and December 2015. It is estimated that over 1,600 Indo-German collaborations and more than six hundred joint ventures (JVs) between Indian and German companies are under way in 2016. Germany also ranks third among foreign technology collaborations in India, testifying to Indian interest in Germany's advanced capabilities as well as to that country's desire to transfer know-how for India's development.

The large EU economy is also a preferred destination for Indian companies, many of which have engaged in mergers and acquisitions (M&As) as well as greenfield investments across sectors such as pharmaceuticals, Information Technology (IT), automotives and machinery, among others. About two hundred Indian companies are believed to be active in the German industrial environment. These companies understand that engaging with Germany adds to their technological and process capabilities, provides access to vibrant EU markets, and builds their international visibility. In turn, Indian companies provide their strengths of working in challenging circumstances, business acumen, and understanding of complex markets to the German economy. In general, the India–Germany FDI flow has been successful and productive for both sides.

The New India

At a time when India is undergoing rapid transformation, the two partners must work together to elevate the contours of their engagement. In 2015, the Indian economy emerged as the world's fastest growing major economy with a GDP growth rate of 7.3 per cent. Aided by a strong and proactive reform agenda, India is established on a firm upward growth trajectory bolstered by strong macroeconomic fundamentals including prudent levels of fiscal deficit, inflation and current account deficit.

The *Financial Times* FDI monitor showed that India topped the world in greenfield FDI with $63 billion worth of new FDI projects in 2015. The International Monetary Fund (IMF) expects India to continue growing at a pace of 7.5 per cent for 2016 and 2017, remaining steady at the top of the world's fastest growing large economies.

There are several reasons why India has emerged as a top economic destination of the future. The demographic profile of the country with a growing population of young people will continue to drive savings and investments, while also providing a large consumer base and workforce for the world. According to studies, by 2030, India's consumer spending could be close to $13 trillion. Another factor is the infrastructure mission that the country has embarked upon, with huge capacity creation across sectors such as transport, communication, power and urban facilities.

Third, the government has fast-tracked reforms relating to key areas of the economy such as investor facilitation and administrative processes, attracting FDI, reform of public expenditure, and the financial sector, among others. In taxation, it has committed to introducing the landmark Goods and Services Tax (GST) and bringing down the corporate income tax rate. In addition, prudent macroeconomic management has encouraged the Reserve Bank of India, India's central bank, to progressively reduce interest rates by 150 basis points from 2014 to April 2016.

This is supported by a range of initiatives taken by the government to channelize investments. The Make in India campaign unveiled at the Hannover Messe, as well as Digital India, Smart Cities, Clean India, Skill India, and Startup India are among the economic forces unleashed through strategic action plans. These programmes provide significant opportunities for the rest of the world to leverage India's growth story for their success.

As a preferred economic partner, Germany has a major role to play in the Indian development narrative.

Sectors of Opportunity

Manufacturing

German manufacturing is globally renowned as one of the most competitive in the world. The country has prioritized innovation and excellence, which along with its high-quality skilled workforce and enabling institutions, ensures its continuing leadership of global manufacturing. Its sophisticated products, at the cutting edge of technology, made Germany the world's largest merchandise exporter until it was overtaken by China a few years ago.

The Make in India campaign is a signature initiative that seeks to make India a manufacturing powerhouse. The strategies under this campaign include ease of doing business, creation of requisite industrial infrastructure with world-class facilities and connectivities, building global linkages through

FDI, and fostering technology, innovation and design. Additionally, twenty-five sectors have been identified for special promotional policies.

Indo-German manufacturing engagement has been robust over the years as German companies have built up capacities in India across sectors such as automotives, pharmaceuticals, machinery, electronic equipment, etc. With the convergence of competitive Indian technical skills and futuristic German R&D, the two countries should venture together into advanced manufacturing areas, termed as Industrie 4.0, such as robotics and automation, the Internet of Things, and additive manufacturing.

In particular, the opening of the defence manufacturing and railway production sectors to FDI offers many new opportunities for German manufacturers. The defence equipment sector alone is expected to generate $30 billion to $40 billion worth of revenue in the medium term for the private sector. Aerospace is another sector with potential for bilateral engagement. India's upcoming industrial parks, manufacturing clusters and corridors are also destined to enhance external linkages in line with its free trade agreements across Asia. German companies can establish specific country clusters within this ecosystem.

The private sector of Germany, led by numerous SMEs, or Mittelstand, are central to the country's manufacturing prowess. Family-owned businesses in Germany are highly successful entities, able to adapt to global trends and produce for the world. India as an emerging economy aspiring to build up its own manufacturing sector can derive support from the advanced machine tools and automotive sectors that are the leading industries for Germany's Mittelstand and family businesses, as well as other manufacturing sectors.

Infrastructure

A number of cross-cutting areas have been taken up in India to create a facilitative climate for infrastructure investment. These include faster and time-bound approvals and clearances, new models for public–private partnerships to better distribute risks, and establishment of a National Investment and Infrastructure Fund for term finance. Infrastructure Investment Trusts (INVITS) and Real Estate Investment Trusts (REITs) have been initiated to attract large-scale investments in infrastructure.

The Indian Railways envisages an investment of $120 billion over the next five years on capacity expansion, station redevelopment and a high-profile, high-speed rail project. In the roads and highways sector, the target is to accelerate the speed of construction of new roads to 30 kilometres a day in the next two years. The real estate sector and urban development are progressing under the 100 Smart Cities campaign and the mission for 'Housing for All' under which 20 million new homes are planned. There are also scaled-up targets for ports and airports which are being rapidly actioned. The idea to promote waterways will revitalize India's rivers, reduce transport costs, and promote sustainability.

Germany is a leader in waterway transport as well as port and airport infrastructure, and its expertise would be immensely valuable in building the arteries of the new India. Likewise, India's railway endeavour can benefit from German partnership in training and new capacity. German infrastructure companies can come together with Indian companies in consortium mode to develop projects.

Skill Development

India is seeking to emulate the German model of skill development and apprenticeship through its Skill India mission, targeting the skilling of 400 million people by 2022. Key partnership projects between the two governments are under way to build capacities in India, including projects for trainers and apprenticeship cooperation. Germany's engagement in building an institute to guide skill development in India will emerge as a cornerstone for our endeavours. India also needs to step up mechanisms such as joint working groups, to fast-track outcomes.

Digital India

Digital India seeks to empower Indian citizens with the power of the internet. Since its launch, the campaign has delivered notable results. It has attracted $16 billion worth of investment proposals. Sixteen greenfield electronics manufacturing clusters have been approved. The digital mission has gained from German participation in electronics manufacturing as well as scientific cooperation. Germany is a preferred destination for Indian scientists and engineers and numerous partnerships have emanated from joint research projects. The IT and digital space can be a vital area of future cooperation.

Clean Energy

The rapid expansion of India's renewable energy sector, led by the government's ambitious target to scale up from about 35 GW installed capacity in early 2015 to 175 GW by 2022 has generated high global interest. The target, the largest renewable capacity expansion programme in the world, comprises 100

GW from solar, 60 GW from wind, 10 GW from biomass and 5 GW from small hydro systems. The government is also drafting India's first Renewable Energy Act to provide comprehensive policy support to the sector.

Today, India ranks among the top five nations globally with over 25 GW of wind capacity, and is in the top ten with 5.25 GW of solar capacity. India is also leading the activities of the International Solar Alliance, a global inter-governmental organization dedicated to the promotion of solar energy across 121 member countries.

Germany has emerged as a country of interest for India in its renewable energy mission. Several Indian companies have set up manufacturing facilities for energy equipment in Germany, and German companies likewise are undertaking production in India. In fact, Germany is one of two partner countries for Re-invest 2017, the national renewable energy investment summit being held in India from 15 to 17 February 2017. The scale of future cooperation is immense and India will be a big market for Germany in this sector.

Urban Development

India's Smart Cities Mission, designed to energize cities to take care of the rising urban population, plans to modernize 100 identified cities of which twenty cities have already commenced work. Further, upgradation of 500 cities is envisaged. This is expected to entail an investment of $150 billion, including a high proportion from private sector projects. German companies engaged in consultancy, project management, finance and construction must scale up their activities in India through targeted partnerships with municipalities.

Small and Medium Enterprises

The German SME sector, which has enterprises that are considerably larger than those in the Indian SME sector, is a model for India. Both governments are seeking to promote cross-border linkages including sourcing, investments and mergers and acquisitions among their respective vibrant and dynamic enterprises. Indian start-ups have drawn global interest as innovative new participants in the emerging knowledge economy, and it is expected that there will be more than 11,000 new tech entrepreneurship ventures in India in the coming few years.

Recognizing the alignment of interests, the Make in India Mittelstand initiative has been launched by the Indian Embassy in Berlin to facilitate investments by German SMEs into India. The partnership of the SME sectors of the two countries promises to be an exciting future development.

To Sum Up

India's development path and the strengths of the German economy can together shape a unique partnership opportunity for businesses in the two nations. Proactive common interventions from the governments and industry sectors of the two nations can unlock an extensive range of shared areas of cooperation. Going forward, the two sides can work on the areas and issues identified by businesses. The India–EU Broadbased Trade and Investment Agreement under negotiation must be fast-tracked and implemented urgently to deliver benefits to stakeholders as quickly as possible.

For Indian companies, challenges in obtaining visas, export controls and non-tariff barriers present hurdles to scaling up their activities with regard to Germany, particularly in sectors such as pharmaceuticals, services, trade, and high technology. German companies operating in India face challenges in land acquisition, administrative processes and clearances and taxation, among others.

While these are addressed at the intergovernmental level, businesses must continue to examine areas of bilateral cooperation. Germany is the EU's largest economy, and the world's second largest outward investor and third biggest trading nation. India is the world's third largest economy in purchasing power parity terms, the fastest growing major economy and the second most populous country, with a massive developmental mission ahead. Closer integration of these two regional economic leaders is inevitable and can only gain momentum.

The convergence of a resurgent India and a progressive Germany can be a defining economic partnership for the future, bringing prosperity and gains to both sides as well as to the rest of the world.

Ulrich Grillo, President, Federation of German Industries (BDI) (2013-2016)

Ulrich Grillo was born in Cologne in 1959. After a traineeship at Deutsche Bank AG, he studied Business Administration. He then worked for Arthur Andersen & Co. Ltd, A.T. Kearney Ltd and the Rheinmetall Group. In 2001, he joined the executive board of Grillo-Werke AG and has been its chairman since 2004.

From 2006 to 2012, Grillo was president of the WirtschaftsVereinigung Metalle Düsseldorf/Berlin. Since January 2013, he has been president of BDI. He was confirmed for another two years in this position in November 2014. He is a member of several supervisory and advisory boards.

Indo-German Business Ties: A Partnership with Potential

Ulrich Grillo

Germany and India have long been close economic partners. In recent years, this relationship has gained further strength. The rise of a strong consumption-oriented middle class in India, the modernization of Indian industry, as well as India's increasing integration into global value chains, has made India an important partner and market for German industry.

The growth outlook for India is very positive. The Asian Development Bank (ADB) is expecting India to grow by 7.6 per cent in 2016 and 7.4 per cent in 2017. Growth is expected to accelerate up to 7.8 per cent in 2018. With a growth rate of 7.8 per cent, India will be one of the most dynamically growing countries within Asia and the fastest growing major emerging economy globally.

In addition, India provides a huge market of 1.2 billion people. Considering these indicators, India is expected to become the biggest consumer market in 2022. And as opposed to many other countries in the region whose populations are shrinking—or are about to shrink in the immediate future—India offers a steady and promising outlook on this front. India's population growth is expected to start declining around 2060.

The recent pick-up of growth rates is reflected in the trade statistics of India and Germany. Whereas the trade volume has been declining since the beginning of the decade and amounted to only 16 billion euros in 2014, a rise to 17.3 billion euros could be observed in 2015. From 2014 to 2015, Indian exports to Germany rose by 6.5 per cent, and German exports to India rose by 9.6 per cent. As a point of reference for these numbers, it is useful to turn to the 1990s, when the Indian economy started opening up. Back then bilateral trade stood at only about 2.7 billion euros.

Today, Germany is India's most important trading partner within the European Union (EU). From a German perspective, the biggest share of exports is machinery, accounting for about a third of German exports to India. Besides machinery, durable goods such as electronics, metal goods, chemicals, automobiles and automobile parts are exported to India. India, on the other hand, exports goods such as textiles, chemical products and electronics to Germany.

In addition to the bilateral trade volume, the number of German companies in India (and vice versa) has also increased over the past few years. From 2000 to 2013, German foreign direct investment (FDI) in India rose fivefold to about 7.7 billion euros, making Germany the seventh largest investor in India. At present, about 1,800 German companies have offices, production sites or R&D facilities in India. Inter alia, German companies are teaming up with their Indian counterparts in order to develop resource-friendly and efficient high-tech products.

German companies are thus contributing to a more sustainable economic development of India. Indian investments in Germany have risen even more sharply, though the investment level is still much lower: between 2000 and 2013, investments by Indian companies in Germany rose tenfold to about 0.5 billion euros. In view of this number, there certainly appears to be a lot of untapped potential for Indian investors in Germany.

Key Factors Contributing to the Good Relationship

The German industry's involvement in India dates back to 1867, when Siemens began laying the world's first undersea cable from London to Kolkata. Almost 150 years later, the economic partnership between India and Germany has been built on treaties such as the bilateral trade treaty of 1955 or the strategic partnership agreement of 2000. But apart from such formal agreements, it is structural determinants that make India and Germany natural partners. One of the key factors contributing to their efficient bilateral relationship is the similarity in the structure of the Indian and German economies.

The backbone of the economies of the two countries is the family business that makes long-term-oriented investments. In Germany, 91 per cent of all companies are family-controlled businesses (excluding public companies). They provide for 56 per cent of employment in Germany and generate 48 per cent aggregate turnover in Germany (all ZEW data). Three-quarters of these family businesses have revenues of less than one million euros. The situation is similar in India, where family businesses account for about 90 per cent of companies, many of which are small- to medium-sized. Large and internationally well-known companies such as Tata, Mahindra and

Mittal are also controlled by families.

Moreover, India and Germany both believe in the importance of a strong industrial base. In Germany, a significant part of added value is generated by the manufacturing sector. To improve the industrial base in India, Prime Minister Narendra Modi launched the Make in India campaign and put industrialization high on India's political agenda.

In addition, both countries complement each other at the level of resources: German companies are innovation leaders as regards hardware and machinery, whereas Indian IT companies are at the forefront of software development, drawing on a wealth of highly skilled IT engineers. Considering the ongoing efforts to manage and shape the fourth industrial revolution ('Industrie 4.0 in Germany), that is, the digitalization of the entire value chain, it is in the IT field, Internet of Things (IoT), and smart manufacturing that India and Germany have great potential for fruitful cooperative endeavours.

As Germany is facing a demographic challenge, it is actively seeking to attract highly skilled workers from abroad. Future cooperation between Germany and India could potentially be deepened by such professional exchanges, which could enable the building of bridges between the two countries on a personal and professional level.

Germany and India are among the leading economies in their respective regions and in spite of their own strengths and challenges, should benefit from maintaining and expanding their established links of mutual learning and cooperation.

Prominent Projects of the Partnership

How well the Indian and German economies are matched is apparent from their numerous prominent joint projects in the past few years. One example is the 'Year of Germany in India' project held in 2011 and again in 2012. True to the motto 'Germany and India: Infinite Opportunities', bilateral relations between the two countries received a fresh impetus with this project which had the 'Urban Mela' as its centrepiece. This was a roadshow touring the Indian cities of Mumbai, Bengaluru, Chennai, New Delhi and Pune.

In particular, urban development, one of the areas where India and Germany have huge potential to work together, was a focal topic of the Year of Germany in India project and partnerships between businesses were fostered. Many German companies, including Bajaj Allianz, BASF, Bosch,

Deutsche Bank and Siemens, showed keen interest in India by supporting this project. Hubert Lienhard, the current chairman of the Asia-Pacific Committee of German Business (APA) and president and CEO of Voith, also actively shaped this project with his ideas.

In 2015, India's position as Germany's official partner country at the Hannover Messe gained much attention. Prime Minister Narendra Modi, who was accompanied by a massive business delegation, opened the fair and promoted his Make in India campaign in Germany. After some years of slower growth in India and therefore, the rather modest growth of German companies in the country, India's participation in the fair was watched closely by the local industry which saw India gaining new dynamism under Prime Minister Narendra Modi. While many industries in India have sustained overcapacity due to the Indian economy's lower-than-expected growth rates between 2010 and 2013, the expectation is that once these capacities are utilized, India will once again become a focus of German business.

The importance of their partnership can also be observed in the fact that India and Germany run inter-governmental consultations every two years. For Germany, India is one of only four non-EU countries (in addition to China, Israel and Brazil) with which this format has been established, highlighting the desire for close cooperation. The consultations offer an important opportunity to bilaterally improve the business frameworks for German companies in India and for Indian companies in Germany. During their consultations in October 2015 for instance, India and Germany agreed upon a 'fast track' arrangement to support German investments in India. Many companies have already used this mechanism successfully.

Key Challenges for German Businesses in India

Although some German companies are already profiting from the renewed dynamism of the Indian economy under Prime Minister Narendra Modi, key challenges remain which are discouraging other German companies from entering the country.

Among the major obstacles, infrastructure deserves mention. With some facilities hardly connected, or even non-existent, infrastructure constitutes a grave concern, particularly the lack of a consistent energy supply as well as missing links in the transport network. In addition, red tape, excessive bureaucratic hurdles, as well as high corruption levels challenge German businesses. The Berlin-based non-governmental organization (NGO)

Transparency International ranked India 76th out of 168 countries in its 2015 Corruption Perceptions Index, indicating the difficult framework that businesses are forced to operate within in the country. The complex tax systems as well as limited and difficult access to public tenders and a lack of skilled labourers are additional obstacles for companies in India.

Assessment of the Modi Government from a Business Perspective

After Narendra Modi assumed office as prime minister following the landslide victory of his Bharatiya Janata Party (BJP) in the parliamentary elections in May 2014, many German companies pinned their hopes on India's economic development going by Narendra Modi's success in turning around the economy of the state of Gujarat during his term as its chief minister from 2001 to 2014. Looking at the current growth outlook for India and the new lease of life for the country's markets, these hopes were justified. However, many companies had hoped, and are still hoping, for more far-reaching reforms from the BJP government, probably underestimating the difficulties of India's layered political set-up.

The introduction of a common Goods and Services Tax (GST), land reform enabling larger infrastructure projects, and a more flexible labour law are among the items on the wish list of German companies. These are widely regarded as reforms that could give an enormous stimulus to GDP growth in India.

However, even though the big reforms might not be politically feasible at this time, the smaller steps undertaken by Prime Minister Narendra Modi are leading the economy in the right direction. The initiatives grouped under the umbrella of Prime Minister Modi's flagship campaign Make in India address important issues. Skill India strives to address the problem of a lack of qualified personnel.

Digital India, for instance, has the important aim to increase internet connectivity in the country—a huge challenge given India's sheer size. In addition, investment limits have been raised by the government and initiatives have been undertaken in order to improve India's 'Ease of Doing Business' ranking and eliminate corruption.

German businesses have indeed observed that bureaucratic procedures have been speeded up and that officials have become more responsive to the demands of companies. As mentioned above, the 'fast track' mechanism in particular has had a discernible positive effect so far. Still, India is only at rank 130 of 189 in the Ease of Doing Business Index 2016, indicating that more effort is needed here.

German companies, however, emphasize that campaigns such as Make in India may work to the advantage of German companies even though the prime goal of the campaign is to promote India as a production hub. High localization requirements and the difficulty that international companies face in accessing public tenders are some obstacles in this respect.

The EU–India Free Trade Agreement

The India–EU free trade agreement (FTA)—the Bilateral Trade and Investment Agreement (BTIA)—should be vigorously pushed by both sides to remove any remaining barriers to bilateral trade and further improve Indo-German and India–EU relations. As in the case of Germany, India's trade volume with the EU received a major boost in 2015. In that year alone, bilateral EU–India trade volume totalled 77.5 billion euros, up from 72.7 billion euros in 2014. However, even though there is an upward trend in trade statistics, trade with India is below potential.

Besides reducing barriers to trade and therefore, stimulating the mutual exchange in goods and services, the political signals from the BTIA would be huge. At a time when globalization seems to be in retreat, nationalism stirred and borders closed, the successful conclusion of an FTA between two global economic powerhouses such as Germany and India would certainly be seen as a welcome reminder of the benefits of open markets.

The thirteenth EU–India summit, held in March 2016 after a regrettable hiatus of four years, was important. Still, the positions between the EU and India on the trade agreement seem far apart. However, regardless of such differences of opinion, both sides urgently need to put the BTIA high on their political agenda. For the EU it is also crucial to stay in the race of rapidly evolving regional trade deals in Asia, such as the RCEP (Regional Comprehensive Economic Partnership). The FTAAP (Free Trade Area of the Asia-Pacific), which neither the EU nor India are part of, could prove a window of opportunity. It could remind both countries of the importance of having strong trading partners for whom the borders are open.

Opportunities for Future Indo-German Cooperation

Once investment obstacles are removed and the Indian market remains on track towards developing into an even more dynamic business environment, there will certainly be more cooperation between India and Germany in a number of areas.

India is facing rapid urban development—significantly more rapid than many other countries. Until 2040, another 315 million people will be added to the urban population in the country. This acceleration of urban growth will raise new questions concerning sustainable transport and energy systems, housing and healthcare supply, to name just a few. German companies stand ready to partner with their Indian counterparts and work on innovative and sustainable solutions to these challenges. Already, German companies are involved in the '100 Smart Cities' project set up by the Indian government to upgrade Indian cities in a sustainable and citizen-friendly manner.

Another area where the potential for collaboration is huge is renewable energy. With Energiewende in Germany, German companies are at the forefront of innovation with respect to making the production and consumption of these products more climate-friendly, as well as using renewable energy sources. In India, on the other hand, energy demand is increasing rapidly on a daily basis. Since the year 2000, energy demand has almost doubled, and this trend is expected to continue at an accelerated pace.

Today, 70 per cent of India's energy comes from coal (OECD/IEA 2015 estimate). India does, however, have the resources to increase renewable energy. Solar power, for instance, where India has huge untapped potential (estimated at around three times the total power capacity installed in India today), is one area that Prime Minister Narendra Modi has pushed in the past two years.

India and Germany have also worked together closely on skill development and vocational training over the past few years. Many German companies are very active in building up functional training programmes in India, adapted to the local conditions. This cooperation might help India to counter the lack of skilled labourers. Nevertheless, in order to fully reap the benefits of the cooperation, more support is still needed by the Indian government and Indian companies to accept and implement similar systems.

The Road Ahead

The future of Indo-German economic partnership is promising. A similar economic structure, complementary resources and common challenges make India and Germany natural partners. The mutual interest of companies from both countries could be observed during the Hannover Messe in 2015. This momentum must not be allowed to ebb without exploiting the opportunities it provides. India and Germany therefore need to work together to abolish any remaining trade barriers and improve the frameworks for businesses in both countries. The EU and India need to join hands and energetically work on the negotiations for the EU–India FTA.

Once the setting is ready, trade and investment flows will live up to their potential. In areas such as urban development, sustainable transportation, energy efficiency and renewable energy, German and Indian companies will be able to work together even more closely than at present, solving problems with innovative products and technologies. German industry stands ready to partner with their Indian counterparts in this process.

The Bridge of Democracy

◈

Hans-Gert Pöttering
'Germany and India: A Euro-Asian Axis of Democracy and Peaceful Development'

◈

Kishan S. Rana
'India and Germany: Comparing Democracy and Federalism'

Dr Hans-Gert Pöttering, Chairman, Konrad-Adenauer-Stiftung, is a German politician (Christian Democratic Union of German—CDU) and was the longest serving member of the European Parliament since its first direct election in 1979 till his mandate ended on 1 July 2014 after thirty-five years of uninterrupted membership. He has held a number of leading positions in the European Parliament and European People's Party throughout his political career. From 1999 to 2007, he was chairman of the European People's Party-European Democrats Group in the European Parliament. From 2007 until 2009, he served as president of the European Parliament.

Dr Pöttering has published widely on various issues of European affairs. His autobiography titled *Wir Sind Zu Unserem Glück Vereint—Mein Europäischer Weg* (2014) has been translated into various languages. Currently, Dr Pöttering is Chairman of Konrad-Adenauer-Stiftung, a position he has held since 2010.

Germany and India: A Euro-Asian Axis of Democracy and Peaceful Development

Dr Hans-Gert Pöttering

Germany and India enjoy an enduring and engaging relationship that is mutually beneficial and deeply rooted in our shared values, common interests and clear commitment to democracy, global development and peace. This connection has helped the two nations bond on their common perceptions, aspirations and expectations from the emerging world order. The relationship has matured based on recognition and respect for one another's strengths, capacities and achievements. Clearly, Germany–India collaboration is a win–win project with both sides recognizing and focusing on the advantages and the ever-widening zone of possibilities for cooperation.

Parliamentary Democracy: A Key Factor of Stability and Strength During the Modern History of Both Countries

Germany

During the years of the establishment of our modern democracy in Germany seventy years ago, the world was still reeling from the shock of the atrocities and unthinkable cruelties of Nazi tyranny perpetrated before and during World War II. That was the period when the international community of nations designed and approved the establishment of the United Nations and its institutions, built on the core value of human dignity and the global values of freedom, justice, tolerance and solidarity, in order to contribute to a more humane world.

In the same spirit, a few years later, in 1952, six European nations laid the cornerstone of the European Union (EU), by uniting economically and politically within the framework of the European Coal and Steel Community. The democratic system in West Germany was established in accordance with the global values shared by the United Nations and the young European Community.

This democratic system not only served as an instrument for decision-making and governing, it had also to guarantee the core values on the basis of the rule of law. Furthermore, the authors of the German Constitution, the 'Basic Law' of the new Federal Republic of Germany, took into account the lessons learnt from the failure of Germany's first democracy. In the so-called 'Weimar Republic', weak democratic institutions, elements of a semi-presidential system and a deficient electoral system of proportional representation, led to a divided parliament and this, amongst others, paved the way for Hitler's accession to power in Germany.

The new German parliamentary democracy has been designed as a strong pluralistic system. Thus, it has been able to protect itself against political interference from the extreme left and the extreme right, and produce a stable vibrant democratic life, with only a few plebiscitary elements. Member-based democratic political parties with their distinct programmes became key actors in the democratic process. The various parties provided the electorate with different options for political development and offered solutions for economic and social problems.

The systematic promotion of civic education has helped citizens develop a strong identification with the democratic state and systems. The state has aimed at empowering and motivating citizens to actively participate in democratic dialogue and decision-making by holding accountable their elected representatives on the local, regional and national levels. Additionally, the German political foundations, ideologically connected with the different democratic parties but funded from the state budget, have played an important role in educating citizens on thematic and procedural issues in political life, and in making them qualified to take over leadership positions in the democratic institutions.

This strong and stable parliamentary democracy, supported by the great majority of citizens in West Germany, became the basis for economic rehabilitation and the so-called 'economic miracle' in the 1950s and 1960s. It was also responsible for the establishment of a strong social security system resulting in social peace and stability, and for the reacceptance of Germany in the international community and the developing European Community.

India

During the same period, India succeeded in developing its democratic system after gaining independence from British colonial rule and overcoming the initial period of violent conflict. Based on the core values of freedom and tolerance promoted so convincingly by national hero Mahatma Gandhi, the newly independent India was able to establish a strong parliamentary democracy.

In spite of its overwhelming diversity of ethnic groups, religions, cultures and languages, and in spite of huge economic and social challenges, India succeeded in creating a vibrant democracy. Moreover, this parliamentary system provided its different regions with comprehensive rights of self-governance under its federalist union system—a striking similarity between Germany and India.

A second feature that both democracies share is strong political parties that follow the rules of the parliamentary and constitutional system. Political diversity in Germany today is based on the six dominant political parties, and it remains to be seen whether the right-wing populist party, Alternative für Deutschland, founded in 2013, will succeed in entering the German Bundestag in the 2017 federal elections.

India's politics juggled a much greater number of parties and, due to its huge diversity, numerous regional parties, too. The fundamental rights guaranteed by the Indian Constitution include the right to equality, freedom, freedom of religion, cultural and educational rights, the right against exploitation and the right to constitutional remedies. The German Basic Law asserts a commitment to human dignity, free development of personality, protection of physical integrity and personal liberty, freedom of faith, assembly and expression. The promise that the two political systems have made to their people is strikingly similar. Their faith is rooted in their non-negotiable affirmation of core democratic principles.

Being Partners

In the decades following World War II, both Germany and India strengthened their roles in the global community and became leading players in the development of regional communities such as the European Union and the South Asian Association for Regional Cooperation (SAARC). The collapse of the Soviet Union led to a rearrangement of international relations, and a new world order.

While Germany, due to the challenges brought about by the reunification and the subsequent extension of the European Union, focused its policies on Europe and the Euro-Atlantic partnership, India, although preserving good ties with Russia, developed strong relations with the Western democracies and redirected its economic policy towards a stronger market-oriented approach. However, the key to growth and development in both countries was their stable parliamentary democracy.

Since then a lot more has changed. Over the last twenty years, we have witnessed a profound reshaping of the world with the rapid rise of Asia. India, thanks to its policy of economic liberalization during the last two decades, today is surpassing China's slowing growth and is well positioned to lead Asia's continuing rise in the coming decades.

Germany, being one of the main advocates of the European integration process, has risen to become one of Europe's major economic driving forces. This provides a solid platform for the two nations to strengthen their economic ties. Already today, Germany is India's most important trading partner within the European Union. In 2014–15, bilateral trade amounted to almost 16 billion euros.

In 2011, India became the first non-European country, besides Israel and China, to have regular institutionalized high-level meetings on a government level with Germany. Indo-German relations today are based on a dense network of relations between economies, institutions, academia, civil society, and individuals.

A special focus is being given to cooperation in the area of sustainable development leading to joint projects on topics such as river cleaning, renewable energy, energy efficiency and sustainable urban planning. Members of the respective Parliaments regularly meet their counterparts, as do judges, and representatives of the states, regions and cities. We at Konrad-Adenauer-Stiftung are committed to deepening these relations through our programmes, and by bringing together decision-makers from both countries.

Joint Challenges

Today, parliamentary democracy worldwide is facing difficult times. Some European countries are witnessing a decreasing interest in politics in general, a decline in voter turnout in general elections and a loss of party members. But surveys also show a certain loss of trust and confidence in politicians and decision-making processes. The perceived gap between political decision-makers and citizens is widening, nurturing populist movements which have no responsible solutions for existing problems. This phenomenon became a reality in some European countries, in the US and nowadays even in Asia.

Against this background, political education is crucial for preventing disenchantment with politics. The mission of Konrad-Adenauer-Stiftung worldwide is civic education. As chairman of Konrad-Adenauer-Stiftung and former president of the European Parliament, I would like to stress: We all know that democracy needs a sound constitution. More importantly, we know that a democracy needs democrats. Nobody is a born democrat. Our citizens need to learn to be democrats. This is where political education is needed. The sole purpose of political education, of teaching political processes, is to empower individuals for standing up for democracy as responsible citizens and assuming an active role in politics and society.

Regarding India, high approval ratings are recorded vis-à-vis the Indian democracy and its institutions. According to experts on India, the success of Indian democracy can be traced back to its ability to include minorities and disadvantaged groups, for instance by creating new federal states for linguistic groups or reserving seats in Parliament for representatives of Scheduled Castes. However, fragmentation of the political spectrum on the regional level needs to be addressed carefully.

The promotion of inclusive political measures irrespective of ethnic affiliations and the fight against popular rhetoric are important instruments to help prevent fragmentation within society. The future of Indian democracy will very much depend on the following factors: Will elected officials succeed in delivering on reforms promised and, therefore, solidify economic growth? Can this economic growth have an inclusive and beneficial effect on the entire population?

Yet, in my mind, the greatest external challenge for our parliamentary democracies at this time is international terrorism. Radicalization and the increase of terror attacks are a problem for the entire globe. As recent events in Germany, Europe and elsewhere show, this danger is likely to persist. It will be our utmost priority to improve international cooperation on aspects such as intelligence sharing and deradicalization programmes.

Moreover, for democracies like Germany and India, the terrorist threat is even more dangerous as open, pluralistic, rule-of-law, based countries constantly have to carefully strike a balance between freedom and security. In contrast to authoritarian regimes, security measures to help prevent and fight terrorism need to be based on legal grounds in democracies. To find this equilibrium will be a key task for both our countries.

Another shared interest of both nations is the stability and security in the Indian Ocean region. The critical sea trade route that connects the Middle East, Africa and South Asia with the broader Asian continent to the east and

Europe to the west is of crucial importance in terms of trade and energy supplies to India and Germany. Diverse security challenges ranging from piracy, drug smuggling and natural disasters, to concerns over energy security affect the region.

Turning Mutual Concerns into Fruitful Partnerships

The similarities in the challenges as well as the beliefs, values and political systems of the two countries should lead to even stronger cooperation between the two countries. But what would this cooperation look like? In terms of domestic challenges for our democracies, there are several fields of cooperation which in my view could turn out beneficial to preserving and strengthening our common values.

Germany and India could further improve their dialogue on the core issues of concern to their citizens. It would be important to identify issues which, due to their complex nature, are prone to populist misuse in political debates. Members of political parties, party leaders and leaders of political youth organizations from both countries should exchange ideas and views about these issues, learning from each other.

Multimedia information tools—including tools compatible with social media—could provide citizens of different ages, educational backgrounds and life situations with interesting and understandable orientation and information on these issues. This information could be disseminated by different institutions and organizations—the public, political parties and civil society.

Furthermore, I strongly support an intensive dialogue between politicians and experts from the two countries in order to deal with the question of value orientation of leaders in politics, business and civil society. In the last decade, Konrad-Adenauer-Stiftung has intensified its dialogue programmes that seek to foster an exchange between decision-makers from Germany and India and further deepen relations on the parliamentarian, economic and academic levels. For instance, in 2015 we invited a delegation of the Bharatiya Janata Party (BJP) to the Party Congress of the Christian Democratic Union (CDU) in Karlsruhe, Germany.

One of the outcomes of this visit was that the BJP joined the International Democrat Union (IDU)—an alliance of Conservative, Christian Democrat and like-minded parties—in 2016. Through creating networks between politicians and experts from various fields, the understanding for India and its decision-making processes has grown in Germany—and I believe this has been the case vice versa. I see these exchanges as crucial for the future of bilateral relations and would like to invite the German and Indian public to reach out to their counterparts on the other side by building up personal connections.

Also, I find it very important to build a dialogue between the youth of India and Germany as they hold the future of the two countries in their hands. Together with its Indian partners, Konrad-Adenauer-Stiftung supported the first-ever survey-based youth study in India which sought to explain the aspirations, perceptions and attitudes of Indian youth. A new study is in the making. For both societies, it is crucial to understand how we can motivate the new generation to assume an active role in politics and shape a democratic future. Indeed, supporting future Indian leaders has long been a priority for Konrad-Adenauer-Stiftung—we award scholarships to young Indian students and scholars every year to study and research in German universities. These scholarship holders are important stakeholders for the future of Indo-German relations.

The current external challenges of parliamentary democracy also provide important opportunities for cooperation between the representatives of the Indian and German governments and political parties in order to strengthen the international acceptance of their positions and to limit the influence of those who are contributing to the destruction of our fundamental values. It is imperative that Germany and India join forces to combat international terrorism and hence, protect our shared values.

German–Indian cooperation is particularly strong with regard to the joint fight against terrorist groups. It is important to point out that joint activities go beyond mere sharing of intelligence. German and Indian investigation agencies have been cooperating to come up with an effective strategy to investigate terror-related incidents. Both countries have had discussions to develop concrete plans to deal with future terror-related challenges.

In 2015, Chancellor Merkel and Prime Minister Modi agreed to step up cooperation on counter-terror measures. A joint working group on counter-terrorism shall henceforth meet on a regular basis. In the face of the evolving threat both countries face, one can expect this cooperation to grow much deeper in the years to come.

Concerning security in the Indian Ocean, strategic defence cooperation between Germany and India is going to be vital over the next few years. India's strategic location and shared concerns with Germany in this regard make it an ideal partner. Germany considers India a pivot for the stability in Asia. In 2008, Germany and India had a common naval drill when their navies carried out a joint exercise off the coast of Kochi. As a large quantum of Germany's imports and exports are seaborne, stability on the oceans is crucial for us. Herein lies an opportunity for greater German–Indian strategic defence cooperation in the years to come.

Joint Pathways

With Germany's growing global role and the rapid rise of India over the past two decades, both countries are important players in an emerging multipolar international order. A common set of values of democracy, freedom, liberty and respect for human rights has led us to committing ourselves to a shared vision of the emerging international order. One of these common beliefs is the need for adaptation of the international security structures to the power relations in the twenty-first century. For example, Germany and India have joined forces to work for the refinement of the United Nations Security Council to reflect the prevailing international environment.

German–Indian ties have evolved and strengthened and today have come to represent the success of democracy. Over the coming years, there is great potential for the Germany–India economic partnership to develop into a much larger bilateral initiative. Cooperation in renewable energy resources and transfer of technology is going to be the key to joint progress. Cooperation in research and technology should go hand in hand with our joint efforts to combat climate change.

Without a doubt, India and Germany—together with Germany's partners in the European Union—will be the important pillars in a multipolar international system. India is a player of major importance with respect to climate protection and global poverty reduction. Only with India—playing a key role in South Asia—will the international community reach the Agenda 2030 targets, a policy field ranking high on the German political agenda.

The fact that both India and Germany are devoted to liberal democracy under a constitutional order, bolstered by judicial independence and a federal system of government, gives them the language and grammar to construct a Euro-Asian axis of democracy, peace and prosperity.

Kishan S. Rana, former Ambassador of India to Germany, Kishan S. Rana has authored and edited several books, including *Inside Diplomacy* (2000); *Asian Diplomacy* (2007); *Diplomacy of the 21st Century* (2011); *The Contemporary Embassy* (2013); *Diplomacy at the Cutting Edge* (2015).

Bio: BA (Hons) and MA in Economics, Delhi University. Indian Foreign Service (1960–95); worked in China (1963–65, 1970–72). Ambassador/High Commissioner: Algeria, Czechoslovakia, Kenya, Mauritius and Germany. Served on Prime Minister Indira Gandhi's staff (1981–82). Foreign languages: Chinese and French.

Professor Emeritus, Diplo Foundation, Malta and Geneva; Honorary Fellow, Institute of Chinese Studies, Delhi; Archives By-Fellow, Churchill College, Cambridge; Public Policy Scholar, Woodrow Wilson Centre, Washington, DC; Guest Faculty, Diplomatic Academy, Vienna; Commonwealth Adviser, Namibia Foreign Ministry, 2000–01.

India and Germany: Comparing Democracy and Federalism

Kishan S. Rana

The constitutional structures of India and Germany offer parallels, some superficial, as well as deep and profound differences that provide illuminating contrasts. In both countries, the end of World War II in 1945 brought transformative change, in effect political rebirth. Germany emerged from the ashes of the defeat of Hitler's Third Reich, while India shed the shackles of 200-year-old British colonialism. Both nations chose democracy as their constitutional form of government, in vastly different circumstances.

For post-World War II West Germany, then under occupation by the Allied Powers, that choice was virtually mandatory, but one that was accepted with joy by its people. East Germany, under Soviet occupation, became one of Moscow's East European satellites. The Federal Republic wrote its hopes for unification into its laws, but as years passed, no one really believed unification would happen. For India too, democracy was an obligation, sacrosanct for the fathers of the freedom movement, their unshakeable promise to establish rule by the people, for the people, of the people.

Comparing Democracy Systems

Post-1945, the circumstances confronting the two states were superficially similar, but also hugely different. Both faced economic and social development and reconstruction challenges, but for Germany it was a matter of restoring its past strength, while India had the more daunting task of building a new modern state, and overcoming extended, pervasive colonial exploitation and neglect.

The German Constitution, called the Basic Law, was partly a construct of the Allied Powers, France, the United Kingdom (UK) and the United States (US), while India's Constitution was a homegrown product, borrowing and adapting selectively from other countries; it was forged after a comprehensive two-year debate by its Constituent Assembly in 1948–49.

It would take a volume to compare the democracies of India and Germany, and perhaps a second one to examine the federal principles and practical governance arrangements that each has evolved. Let me put aside any notion of a deep examination, and offer instead a few thoughts, selecting just a few themes as pointers to the way the two countries have fashioned and operated their political systems, to give expression to democracy and federalism.

The most obvious difference between the two countries is the electoral method, though some comparable outcomes exist behind this difference. Germany uses the proportionate representation (PR) method, with a relatively high threshold of 5 per cent of the total vote that a party must cross, in order to qualify for seat allotment. Some observers regard the PR system as uniquely democratic, as parties get seats in direct proportion to their share of the total vote share.

Under the classic UK-inspired 'first-past-the-post' voting system that India and many others use, a party can win nearly the same percentage of votes as the winning party, at the province or national level, and still end up with a distinct minority of seats. But in defence of that system, one might say that such aberrations even out in different constituencies across the country, and over time.

In contrast, a consequence of the PR system is that with multiple parties in the contest, it is almost impossible for a single party to win a majority, which makes coalition governments almost inevitable. In India, coalition governments are also now the norm in New Delhi (and often inevitable in the states as well), because of fragmentation in the body politic, and the emergence of regional and caste-dominated parties. This has in effect produced the kind of political plurality that the PR system engenders.

A special feature of German democracy is that political parties are assigned a special place in German Basic Law, which is rather unusual. The framers wanted to ensure that no charismatic leader might in the future carry out a 'constitutional coup' as Hitler did in 1933, when he usurped democracy to become a dictator. This has produced interesting consequences.

While German political personalities contest elections through their own campaigns, as in any democratic system, what really matters is not their own constituency result, but the share of the total vote that all their candidates muster in the entire election; based on that percentage, seats are assigned to their party. Those declared elected are the ones on the 'party list'. Thus leaders from small but politically important parties such as the

Free Democrats (FDP) or the Greens may sometimes not manage to win a majority in a single seat, but they gain seats in the federal or state parliaments (or in the other elections) by virtue of their party's vote share, plus their rank on the party list.

This has a special consequence, in that sometimes colourless party apparatchiks get into parliament without having won a majority in a constituency, or having faced the searing winds of a real election. (Something similar happens in the Rajya Sabha elections in India, for which the votes are cast by the members of the state assemblies, on the basis of the dictates of their party. Based on the party strength in the assembly, each party knows how many votes they can muster, leaving out the complexities of 'cross-voting.') Another unexpected consequence of the German electoral system is that teachers are often the only professionals with the spare time to take up politics; the Bundestag has an unusual number from this profession.

The German system throws up another special feature: civil servants are encouraged to join and support political parties of their choice; they can even take leave from their government jobs to work in party offices. The rationale for this feature, almost unique in democracies, is the same as mentioned above, that is, a conviction that a political process open to wide participation would safeguard the system. Does that make for partisanship among officials? Not in practice. German officials understand their responsibilities and act with balance. The Basic Law also mandates that political parties must adhere to the democratic foundations of the German state; if they are found in violation of this requirement, the Constitutional Court may abolish that party.

Consider another dimension: The 'family connections' that dominate Indian politics do not exist in Germany; nor do political dynasties. The spectacle of a popular leader who wins an election, accompanied into the state assembly by a cohort of close relatives, including sons and daughters-in-law, is mainly a Global South phenomenon, particularly in India. So too, alas, is the wide prevalence of electoral corruption; this makes the task of election commissions supervising elections in India increasingly difficult.

A major issue for large federal democracies is the management of the election cycle. At one end we see the US, with a rigid timeline for the federal and state electoral process that is cast in stone. At the other end is the UK system and its adaptations elsewhere, under which the government in power can call for an election at a time of its choosing, with the caveat that polls must be held after a stipulated maximum time period, often five years.

In countries where governments are answerable to their parliaments, the key is to ensure that the rulers enjoy the 'confidence' of these representatives of the people. How can one ensure near-fixed terms for governments under such parliamentary democracies, while respecting parliament's right to demand accountability?

Germany found an ingenious method to square this circle, with its 'Constructive Vote of No Confidence'. That method simply reverses the traditional no-confidence vote, meaning that instead of voting a government *out* of office, the legislature votes in a new government (after every election, the first task of a government provisionally appointed is to win a confidence vote).

This ensures that in any situation, there is always a government that enjoys majority support. This provision does not ensure that elections outside the normal cycle never take place, which has become a rarity, as German experience of the past six decades has shown. Indians have recently shown new interest in such a formula. If such a method is adopted in India, through an amendment of the Indian Constitution, the basic constitutional framework would really not be affected.

A practical point may arise, that is, political parties that are out of power may not support any measure that curtails the traditional confidence vote or seems to give advantage to the ruling party or coalition. Theoretically, such an amendment might pass muster before a general election, but only if the issue is debated in depth, and real consensus is created in support.

This idea might conceivably gain traction since most political parties recently seem to be coming around to the view that a continual cycle of state and national elections, as India now witnesses, has become a major political distraction. In March 2016, Prime Minister Modi suggested that the Election Commission should find a way to ensure that state assemblies can serve out their full terms, and that he is in favour of simultaneous polls for the Lok Sabha and state assemblies.

It would be impossible to maintain such a system without some mechanism that ensures that ruling governments do not seek fresh elections as a matter of political choice. It remains to be seen if such far-reaching change can appeal to political parties that are not renowned for seeking common ground. The first requirement is extensive public discussion in India; this is yet to take place.

Another dimension of democracy that can be compared is the way the two countries have developed their institutions. First, consider the political parties mentioned above. German parties that are deemed to be of national status all operate what are called 'political foundations', each named after a party stalwart—Konrad Adenauer Siftung for the Christian Democratic Union (CDU), Freidrich Ebert Siftung for the Social Democratic Party (SPD) and so on. Very unusually, they are paid a sizeable annual grant out of the federal budget; the government in power sets the total size of that grant, while actual disbursement takes place on the basis of an established, predetermined formula.

These foundations undertake two kinds of activities. At home, they engage in 'political education', in effect helping to build up their own support base, especially among the youth. Abroad, they act as implementing agencies for some of the technical cooperation projects implemented out of the federal aid budget. They maintain offices in foreign capitals around the world; each of them concentrates on selected functional actions, for example, the Adenauer Foundation on entrepreneurship development, the Ebert Foundation on trade unions, and so on. These overseas offices also feed their party offices with reports on developments around the world.

This German model has no parallel in any other country and in my view, is virtually impossible to replicate. But what Indian political parties might perhaps learn from Germany is the tight professional élan with which German parties are organized.

Second, consider the growth of political think tanks in the two countries, especially those covering foreign affairs. India has seen extraordinary growth in its number of think tanks in the past fifteen years; some are now also established in cities outside New Delhi, which dominates the Indian foreign affairs landscape. However, most of the Indian think tanks are tiny and underfunded, but they struggle on nevertheless, with a fine, growing output of research, conferences and international partnerships.

In contrast, German think tanks are much better organized and well funded, but in terms of agility and innovative actions, those in India can probably give them some pointers. For example, in the past decade, Indian think tanks have established 'Track Two' (i.e. non-official) dialogue with over thirty countries, covering economic, social and even political issues.

Third, about four decades back, many foreign Indologists spoke of the 'de-institutionalization' in India; that was a proxy term for their political critique, often focused on Prime Minister Indira Gandhi's policies. This term has lost currency after the 1991 economic reforms launched by Prime Minister Narasimha Rao, and the subsequent Indian resurgence. The continuing vigour and dynamism of the Indian Parliament, the courts, and a multitude of other national institutions has shown the hollowness of that de-institutionalization thesis.

Fourth, in both countries, civil society organizations including NGOs are thick on the ground, fecund and innovative. In India, much of this is truly a people's movement, with the famous ones such as Self-Employed Women's Association (SEWA), Kailash Satyarthi's Children's Foundation, Sisters of Charity and Barefoot College at one end, and countless small entities that quietly work on education, rights enforcement, social problems, women and child issues, and development.

Much of this vigour has emerged in the past three decades; Indian official agencies now accept and fund such NGOs, treating them as vital partners in the last-mile delivery of services, often performing much better than government agencies. What India still lacks, however, is homegrown civil society organizations with a wide, international footprint. Is it not strange that all the renowned international NGOs are based in rich countries?

One might think of more items to include in a wish list of India–Germany democracy experiences. The year 2016 marked the twenty-fifth anniversary of India's economic reforms. Two facts of these twenty-five years are striking. Each of the seven governments that have ruled India in this time, representing different political coalitions, has carried forward the reform agenda, some more vigorously than others. But at the same time, each of the opposition parties has usually played a blocking game, save in some situations where a minor opposition group has supported the government from the outside.

As for the main opposition, each has vigorously contested those very policies that they had themselves espoused, when they were in power. It is unnecessary to blame any party, because almost all of them have played the same cynical game. In Germany, 'Grand Coalitions', bringing together the two principal political parties, the CDU and the SPD, have ruled at different times, in 1966–69, 2005–09, and 2013 to the present. In the *Länder* (states), these coalitions have been more common.

The moral in this for India is simple: sometimes national issues are of such importance that it might be better for the principal political parties to try and work jointly, even to the point of forming a 'government of national unity', than to engage in knee-jerk political contests. Aren't national challenges in India sufficiently profound for this to be considered as a political option? This may appear far-fetched, given political polarization in India, but should it not at least be discussed and considered?

Federalism Contrasts

Federalism is at the core of German democracy, in ways that one unfamiliar with the country might not imagine. Consider this: Until Prussian statesman Otto von Bismarck unified the country in the nineteenth century, Germany had been a collection of kingdoms, princely domains, dukedoms, and other quasi-autonomous entities. Their unifying element was a language, in its different dialects, plus a powerful cultural sense of German-ness. Unification came from free choice by these entities that opted for, or were pushed into, coming together. It is, therefore, not surprising that the sixteen German *Länder* (states) enjoy a degree of intrinsic autonomy that is rather different from the situation of the twenty-nine Indian states, for which federalism remains a top-down process.

In Germany it was the *Länder* minister-presidents and the *Länder* assemblies that drafted the German Basic Law, which came into effect in May 1949. It was based on a 1948 initiative taken by a six-power conference, consisting of the three Western occupying powers—France, the UK and the US, plus Belgium, Luxembourg and the Netherlands. These six were co-signatories to the German Constitution.

For an Indian, several features of this German federalism are striking. For one, it is a decentralized constitution; the 'residual powers', addressed in Article 30 rest with the *Länder*, that is, the federal government only has the powers directly specified. This goes back to the country's history from medieval times. In contrast, India's founding fathers and the 1948–49 Constituent Assembly were preoccupied with safeguarding the nation's unity, at a time when many loud voices in the West estimated that the chances of India's survival were slim. Accordingly, they created a centrist federal structure, with residual powers held by the centre.

Consider the nomenclature India uses: New Delhi is home to the 'central' government, not the 'federal' government (the latter word is seldom used in India). Yet, since the proclamation of the republic in 1950, power in India has very gradually shifted to the states, partly in recognition of the reality that New Delhi cannot run a country of India's size and diversity in centrist fashion, and partly as a result of the emergence of regional parties that have decisive clout in both the Lok Sabha and the Rajya Sabha.

Since 2014, Prime Minister Modi has given voice to a state-driven perspective, under his 2014 slogan 'cooperative federalism', amended a year later to 'cooperative and competitive federalism'. This captures the country's mood, also reflected in the recommendations of the Eleventh Finance Commission that has vested more funds with the states. It is now also clear that it is the states that are the true locus of economic reform actions, be it on critical land acquisition issues or the reform of labour laws.

In Germany, one might say that subtle and limited evolution has been in the reverse direction, essentially reflecting the realities of governance of a major advanced state, confronting a web of domestic and external challenges. For instance, a federal-level police force has been created in recent years to deal with terrorism threats.

Additionally, German federalism is self-regulating. There are no governors to oversee the actions of the *Länder*. Nor is there anything that remotely resembles India's Article 356, which is evoked from time to time to establish central rule in states, under the rubric of 'President's Rule'.

This has been one of the most controversial features of the Indian Constitution, frequently contested in the courts. How do Germans manage without such a device? The same way that another federal country like the US manages this; it also does not have a mechanism through which a federal government usurps the rights of provincial governments. The latter are deemed to have the competence to manage their affairs; the constitutional or supreme court is the final arbiter.

In some ways the most remarkable feature of the German system is that its Upper House Bundesrat is not just a 'House of States' in name, (Rajya Sabha in India). The Bundesrat is actually composed of the minister-presidents of the sixteen German *Länder*, who are its members, accompanied by *Länder* ministers in proportion to their size. At one stroke, the constituent subunits gain political weight in the federation. Observers note that over the past sixty-odd years, through evolution in practices, the *Länder* have gradually gained additional powers over federal legislation. How different would India be politically if only the states had a real presence at the Centre?

Unfortunately, the Indian Parliament's 'House of States' seldom reflects an authentic state or provincial perspective in its debates. With even a local residence requirement now waived, perhaps half or less of the Rajya Sabha MPs truly identify with the states they represent. How different this is from the vision of the constitution makers. Just imagine: If the Rajya Sabha was composed of chief ministers of the twenty-nine Indian states, how much more powerful would these provincial satraps be in the Indian system?

Final Thoughts

As an Indian, I have come to admire the comparative moderation, sense of propriety and respect for values that are hallmarks of the German political system, including its federal arrangements. This makes for a system that is largely self-regulating in many respects, though recent growth in right-wing parties that cater to, and even amplify, xenophobia gives one pause for thought. Overall, Germany reflects a maturity that the Indian system is yet to attain. The Indian system is not only highly contested, but is also witness to practices that do not truly contribute to the real strengthening of the governance system.

Behind these differences is a deep, shared reality. In both countries, elections are a vigorous, open and sometimes unpredictable manifestation of the will of the people. This reality subsumes differences in the levels of economic prosperity, education and social circumstances that starkly separate India and Germany. The electoral process is as unscripted, autonomous and independent in Germany as it is in India. The Indian voter has repeatedly shown a level of discernment and understanding of the national interest that is no different from what one witnesses in Germany or in other rich countries that practise true accountability to the public and responsible governance. This essentially is what democracy is all about.

Creating a Common Strategic Vision

◈

Dhruva Jaishankar
'India and Germany: Realizing Strategic Convergence'

◈

Theo Sommer
'Vision Germany–India'

Dhruva Jaishankar is fellow for foreign policy at Brookings India. He was previously a transatlantic fellow and programme officer for Asia at the German Marshall Fund in Washington, a research assistant with the Brookings Institution, and a news writer and reporter for CNN-IBN television in New Delhi.

He has been a visiting fellow at the S. Rajaratnam School of International Studies in Singapore and a Brent Scowcroft Award fellow with the Aspen Strategy Group. Jaishankar is a regular contributor to the Indian and international media, including *The Indian Express*, *Foreign Policy*, and *The Times of India*.

He holds a bachelor's degree in history and classics from Macalester College, and a master's degree in security studies from Georgetown University.

India and Germany: Realizing Strategic Convergence

Dhruva Jaishankar

India and Germany are both emerging as important international leaders in the twenty-first century. India has seen its economic growth rate accelerate over the last quarter-century, and in that time it has doubled its share of global GDP. India's growing resource base and market are beginning to manifest themselves in an expanding commercial and diplomatic presence around the world.

Germany, meanwhile, has grown in political and economic importance, particularly in Europe. Its exports, manufacturing, and technology base have seen its economy make significant progress even as much of Europe has slowed or stagnated. International leaders and policymakers are increasingly turning to Berlin for major decisions regarding the European and global economy, and even on matters of European security.

The relationship between India and Germany has been described by the two governments as a 'strategic partnership' since 2001. Indeed, just as Germany's leaders have started to turn their attention to India, successive Indian leaders have recognized that Germany can play a role in transforming India in a manner in which few other countries can.

But is the Indo-German relationship truly strategic in nature? That would require close consultations on issues that define both countries' national interests, as well as broad-ranging cooperation and coordination on security, commercial and developmental issues. Despite enhanced diplomatic contacts, economic relations, and socio-cultural ties, the relationship arguably does not yet qualify as such.

What, then, can be done to realize strategic convergence between the two countries? Answering that question requires assessing bilateral relations to date, analysing some of the difficulties in forging closer strategic ties, identifying areas of convergence, and considering possible ways to forge a strategic relationship in the truest sense of the term.

Lows and Highs

The Cold War Era

Bilateral relations between India and Germany, in their current form, can be traced back to the 1950s, when the Federal Republic of Germany emerged after World War II and a newly independent India began to find its place in the post-war international order. Diplomatic relations between New Delhi and Bonn were established in 1951, with India being one of the first countries to recognize the new republic. Indian Prime Minister Jawaharlal Nehru visited West Germany in 1956 and again in 1960, marking some of the earliest high-level contacts between the two countries.

Strategic relations between India and both West Germany and East Germany saw some interesting developments during the Cold War period. In the aftermath of World War II, West Germany became an important source of defence technologies for India. For example, the German aeronautical engineer Kurt Tank came to Bengaluru in 1956 to help design India's first indigenous fighter aircraft, the HF-24 Marut. The later Cold War era also saw the sale by West Germany of submarine torpedoes and second-hand aircraft for India's aircraft carrier, as well as the licensed production in India of West German Dornier aircraft, which were manufactured in Kanpur.

However, even though India recognized the economic and technological importance of West Germany—and therefore, initially refused to recognize East Germany—relations between Bonn and New Delhi soured in the 1960s. Nehru chose not to criticize the construction of the Berlin Wall and West Germany soon cleared defence agreements with Pakistan for aircraft and tanks. West German relations with India only improved with the election of Chancellor Willy Brandt, whose social democratic policies and Ostpolitik approach to East Germany were welcomed by then Indian Prime Minister Indira Gandhi.

Meanwhile, India's relations with East Germany proved equally complicated. For many years, India did not have formal diplomatic ties with East Berlin, although an East German trade mission was established in India in 1954. East Germany and India did, however, cooperate in recognizing Bangladesh, a step that East Berlin felt would help in normalizing diplomatic ties with New Delhi. India finally established diplomatic ties with the German Democratic Republic in 1972.

Attempts at defence–technological tie-ups between India and West

Germany during the later Cold War years had their benefits but also resulted in unwelcome scandal, in particular a controversy involving Kiel-based German shipbuilding firm Howaldtswerke-Deutsche Werft (HDW). After India signed a contract in 1981 for submarines, it emerged in 1987 that a 7 per cent commission had been included to secure the contract. This eventually led to the firm being blacklisted by India. Among other negative implications, which affected broader India–West Germany defence ties, the controversy raised the costs for India's acquisition of spare parts for the submarines already acquired.

The Post-Cold War Era

Despite the difficulties at both ends during the Cold War, the early 1990s saw a series of structural shifts that enabled better relations between India and Germany. The fall of the Berlin Wall in 1989 and German reunification a year later meant that India no longer had to equivocate between Bonn and East Berlin. The collapse of the Soviet Union in 1991 also ensured that India was no longer bound by Cold War considerations of its own, creating an opportunity for New Delhi to forge new kinds of relationships with other international actors. India's economic liberalization efforts that same year also helped in making the Indian economy more open and dynamic, creating new commercial possibilities for German and international firms.

For much of the 1990s, Germany was preoccupied with the mechanics of unification and European enlargement, while India had to confront a series of domestic challenges. Bilateral relations improved in the aftermath of India's 1998 nuclear tests. In 2000, the two countries' foreign ministers agreed to an 'Agenda for German–Indian Partnership in the 21st Century'. This laid out the objectives of broadening and increasing the frequency of high-level contacts; highlighting security and disarmament; expanding economic relations, media contacts, and environmental cooperation; and cooperating on reforming the United Nations Security Council.

High-level diplomatic contacts between India and Germany soon increased visibly in their frequency and substance. Between them, three Indian prime ministers—Atal Bihari Vajpayee, Manmohan Singh, and Narendra Modi—together made five visits to Germany between 2003 and 2015. German Chancellors Gerhard Schröder and Angela Merkel reciprocated with an equal number of trips to India between 2001 and 2015, while German President Joachim Gauck embarked upon a significant state visit in 2014. These regular high-level interactions assumed greater structure as intergovernmental consultations, and led to the establishment of several high-level working groups covering issues such as industrial cooperation, high technology partnerships, and counter-terrorism.

The importance of India as a commercial partner for Germany was reflected in its privileged position as a partner country at the 2015 Hannover Messe. German and Indian attempts at lobbying for permanent membership of the United Nations Security Council, along with Japan and Brazil as part of the G-4 group of nations, lay dormant for many years. But they gained renewed attention with a meeting of the G-4 leaders on the sidelines of the UN General Assembly meeting in September 2015.

Security cooperation between the two countries in the post-Cold War period received a fillip with the signing of a bilateral Defence Cooperation Agreement in 2006. This has been followed by regular defence secretary-level talks, and meetings involving the heads of the two countries' armed forces. In 2008, the two countries took part in naval exercises off the western coast of India, involving an air defence ship, frigate, and tanker from Germany, as well as two frigates and training ships from India.

Such initial military-to-military contacts were accompanied by renewed German efforts at pushing forward military sales and joint defence production with India. That year, Bernd Mützelburg, German ambassador to India, articulated Germany's willingness to transfer high-technology weaponry to India as part of a 'partnership of equals'. The 2000s saw licensing arrangements for German anti-submarine sonar and for the continued production of Dornier aircraft in India, as well as the delivery of diesel engines for India's submarines, surface naval vessels, and Arjun tanks.

Interests, Alignments and Capabilities

For all the forward movement since 1990–91, the strategic dimensions of the India–Germany relationship have faced certain structural obstacles. One has simply involved different threat perceptions and priorities. Germany's post-1990 security priorities initially revolved around European enlargement, including intervention in the Balkans. Many people in India at the time saw Germany and the North Atlantic Treaty Organization's (NATO) humanitarian motives as an excuse to justify the pursuit of traditional strategic interests, and believed that Western intervention in the Balkans set a dangerous precedent for external involvement in India's disputes.

Following the 2008 Georgia War and the 2014 Ukraine crisis, the prospect of Russian belligerence grew in immediacy in Europe. New Delhi partly interpreted these events as an outcome of Western meddling in Russia's sphere of influence. An additional security concern for Germany in recent years relates to the consequences of the massive refugee inflow from Syria, Afghanistan, and North Africa. This has stoked anti-immigration sentiments in Germany, which may come directly or indirectly at the expense of closer relations with India.

For India, the post-Cold War international environment saw rather different priorities, with the immediate external security preoccupations relating primarily to China and Pakistan, both nuclear-armed neighbours with which India is involved in disputes over large tracts of territory. Beginning in the late 1980s and early 1990s, concerns about terrorism and insurgency supported by elements of the Pakistani state assumed political and national security prominence. Germany traditionally adopted an even-handed approach to India–Pakistan affairs, and its emphasis on human rights has not always gone well with New Delhi.

Moreover, lax export controls in Europe—including in Germany—contributed to Pakistan's nuclear development in the 1970s and 1980s. This was to have important consequences for India's security in the post-Cold War period. The other major Indian external security priority has related to China. Although both India and Germany enjoy significant commercial relations with China, Germany's enthusiasm has not necessarily been tempered by the security concerns shared by India and other Asia-Pacific powers.

A second and related reason for strategic divergence involves the two countries' existing security alignments. For Germany, security involves a considerable degree of cooperation with other European and transatlantic partners, whether through NATO or the European Union. There are no regular, working-level contacts between India and NATO, and the idea of deeper European Union security cooperation—while supported by some in Germany—is as yet stillborn. India, for its part, prefers bilateral security arrangements, although it is gradually moving towards greater trilateral coordination, particularly with like-minded partners.

Nevertheless, India's presence outside US-led alliance structures and its lack of institutionalized contacts with NATO—even on areas of overlapping interest—has so far prevented more fruitful security cooperation and coordination with Germany. This has been particularly applicable to matters relating to Afghanistan. Both Germany and India have shared similar objectives concerning Afghan stability and reconstruction, but often found themselves working at cross-purposes, with Berlin occasionally deferring to Pakistani sensitivities.

Finally, India and Germany often suffer from mismatched capabilities. Differences between the two economies can lead to complementarities and, as such, greater opportunities for cooperation. However, different capabilities in the security sphere are often unnecessarily complicating. India's military has had to grapple with a range of scenarios from nuclear conflict to counter-insurgencies. Its army is an extraordinarily large volunteer force, its air force has to maintain air superiority in its region, and its navy is gradually growing in resources and reach. Germany's military remains comparatively small, featured conscription until 2011, and is operationally limited.

This mismatch further complicates joint exercises and military-to-military contacts, as well as the possibility of joint operations. These factors are unlikely to change given that public opinion in Germany remains predominantly pacifist. A 2015 public opinion survey indicated that a vast majority of Germans—69 per cent—believed that Germany should limit its military role in world affairs.

A Path Forward

Taken together, the differences between the interests, alignments, and capabilities of Germany and India suggest only a modest future for bilateral strategic relations. But that need not be the case. The two countries are rising economies, federal democracies, navigating complex issues of identity, and committed to the rule of law. And their leaders realize that strategic convergence between the two requires, in addition to frequent high-level consultations and mutually beneficial defence–industrial cooperation, a clearer way of translating shared values into outcomes. In the security sphere, this is most readily apparent in three domains—counter-terrorism, cyber security, and maritime security.

Both Germany and India understand the immediacy of the threat posed by terrorism. Although the number of large-scale attacks in Indian urban centres has declined since the 2008 Mumbai attacks, the frequency of terrorist incidents in India has increased in recent years. Similarly, after a decline in the mid-1990s, Germany has witnessed a sharp rise in the number of terrorist incidents since 2013.

The greater frequency of small-scale but lethal terrorist attacks by poorly trained individuals inspired by movements such as the so-called Islamic State of Iraq and Syria (ISIS) poses a new threat to law enforcement authorities in both India and Germany. Addressing such a challenge requires bringing to bear a complex set of issues, particularly for liberal democracies such as Germany and India that seek to preserve the rule of law.

A second area of possible convergence relates to maritime security, which is assuming greater importance for both countries given its importance for international commerce. German vessels have fallen victim to piracy in the Indian Ocean, and since 2008, German forces have helped protect merchant vessel shipping as part of the European Union (EU) Naval Force Operation Atalanta. Around the same time, India also began anti-piracy missions in and around the Gulf of Aden.

The resulting operations by the two countries, along with several other countries, have led to a sharp decline in piracy in the vicinity since 2013. But fears of complacency and the possibility of similar security challenges compromising other key sea lines of communication make this an area for further cooperation between Germany and India.

Finally, cybers ecurity and internet governance offer another area in which Germany and India find themselves confronting similar challenges. Both countries have certain limitations to freedom of expression which translate into the online space—including in the Constitution in India's case and in the Strafgesetzbuch in Germany—and both share concerns about securing critical infrastructure. Efforts at sharing lessons learned on counter-terrorism, maritime security, and cyber security are all under way. But by elevating their importance and highlighting these areas of convergence, the two countries may be able to better set an agenda for a stronger strategic relationship.

A true strategic relationship will, naturally, have to move beyond the narrow confines of security. It will require deepening trade relations, for example, which remain rather underwhelming. Trade with Germany constitutes just 3 per cent of India's total trade, and both exports and imports have declined over the past five years. Strategic convergence will also require cooperating on the future of energy, an area in which Germany possesses considerable strengths, and where India has possibly the highest future demand of any country.

And finally, it will require consolidating people-to-people relations. The Indian-origin community in Germany—which is now over 100,000-strong and comprises over 60,000 German nationals and more than 40,000 Indian passport holders—is a valuable conduit for bringing the two countries closer together.

Ultimately, a true strategic relationship will require a realization in Berlin that India's rise is good for Germany. For its part, New Delhi must appreciate that a good relationship with Germany matters more than ever.

Theo Sommer, Former Editor, *Die Zeit*, was born in 1930 in Konstanz. He attended Manchester College in Indiana and the University of Chicago, then earned a PhD from the University of Tübingen with a thesis on 'Germany and Japan Between the Powers, 1935–1940'.

Sommer began working as a journalist in 1949. After holding the posts of foreign editor, deputy editor, editor-in-chief and publisher of the German newspaper *Die Zeit*, he became an editor-at-large in 2000. Since 2004, Sommer has also been the executive editor of the Times Media publications: *The Atlantic Times*, *The German Times*, *The Asia-Pacific Times* and *The African Times*. He has written extensively on foreign affairs, security policy, East–West relations and the rise of Asia. He also served as chief of planning staff for the German Ministry of Defence between 1969 and 1970.

Vision Germany–India

Theo Sommer

Leonardo Di Caprio's Western fur trapper Hugh Glass in the 2015 film *The Revenant* is not the only revenant in 2016. Geopolitics and realpolitik are back; spheres of interest and influence are once more contested by the great powers; nationalism is again rearing its ugly head; globalization seems to be going into reverse; concepts such as deterrence and containment are making a comeback; thoughts of war, even nuclear war, are weighing anew on the minds of global leaders. Crises have become the new normal.

'We live in a time of extraordinary change,' US President Barack Obama declared in his last State of the Union address in January 2016. 'We are living in a world that in many ways is falling apart,' says Klaus Schwab, founder of the Davos World Economic Forum. Our unravelling world conjures up William Butler Yeats' lament: 'Mere anarchy is loosed upon the world, / The blood-dimmed tide is loosed, and everywhere / The ceremony of innocence is drowned. / The best lack all conviction, while the worst / Are full of passionate intensity.' In the face of terrorism, civil wars, waves of migration from failing states, only Shakespeare's lines from *The Tempest* appear more pertinent: 'Hell is empty and all the devils are here.'

Three facts compound the problems emanating from this woebegone state of affairs. First, the dominant trend of our epoch is a historic shift of power and wealth from the occident to the orient, from the transatlantic to the transpacific region, from Europe and America to Asia; five centuries of white man's dominance have come to an end. Second, all the major powers and power groupings are in a state of transition. Third, the time is out of joint, but there is no one who can single-handedly set it right.

The political system of the United States is polarized and paralysed to the point of dysfunction. Its politicians have lost the ability to resolve problems constructively through rational dialogue and pragmatic compromise; a fatal predicament that will endure no matter who wins the presidential election—Hillary Clinton or Donald Trump. At the same time, the refugee crisis strikes at the heart of the European project. For the first time in half a century, one can no longer exclude the prospect that the European Union (EU), battered by economic malaise, the migrant emergency, terrorism and Brexit (Britain's vote to exit the EU), will collapse and fall apart.

Russia, too, is a country in transition. Economically, it is in free fall. Politically, it has turned out to be a spoiler, not a shaper. China, too, is in the throes of fundamental change. In Daniel Twining's graphic phrase, due to its authoritarian brittleness and the developmental challenges it faces China has become the 'People's Republic of Uncertainty'. As Beijing won't relent on its aggressive policies in the South China and East China Seas, its grandiose scheme 'One Belt, One Road'—the southern maritime and the northern Central Asian Silk Roads connecting the Far East with Europe—strikes many observers as a grand design to expand China's sphere of influence.

The Middle East is experiencing an extraordinary level of violence and turmoil. In Syria, Iraq, Yemen and Libya, the state system is fraying. Apart from Tunisia, the Arab Spring has ended in dictatorial winter. Islamic State (ISIS) is imposing its writ on Mesopotamia. Saudi Arabia and Iran are engaged in intense proxy warfare. The conflict between the Israelis and Palestinians, although no longer central to the region, continues to fester; another intifada seems more likely than any diplomatic settlement, two-state or otherwise.

Afghanistan's future after the International Security Assistance Force (ISAF) is perilous at best. Thus, the Levant area in the eastern Mediterranean stands at the very beginning of a long phase of turbulence—a 'Thirty Years War' like the partly sectarian, partly power-driven conflict that devastated and depopulated Europe in the seventeenth century. At the same time, the Chinese vs Chinese tug-of-war over Taiwan, the dangerous Korean tinderbox and the steadily increasing tensions between China and the US are rightly causing global concern.

Our world with its emergencies, crises and unforeseen wildfires is 'no one's world' (Charles Kupchan), a 'G-zero world' whose members don't share values, standards and priorities (Ian Bremmer). Global hegemony is no longer possible. While Washington will remain pre-eminent for decades, it will no longer predominate. Nor can any other nation don the cap of the world's policeman.

Looking at the world as it is, not as we might wish it to be, looking at the global flashpoints and at the political as well as societal upheavals everywhere, one cannot help feeling that our leaders should welcome another revenant: realpolitik. Which means: secure your defences but don't eschew dialogue. Contain where necessary and cooperate where possible. Keep your humanitarian principles in mind, but don't make them the sole benchmark for securing your interests. Avoid bluster and blame. Learn to live with differences among nations while simultaneously building on common interests.

Our diplomats have coined a new term for this: 'compartmentalized cooperation'. It is a method for dealing with friends as well as with rivals and adversaries. You disagree where your interests diverge, but you join hands wherever they coincide. Turning red-hot conflicts into frozen conflicts rather than bull-headedly pursuing your maximum objectives is considered the wisest course of action. Strategic patience is considered a virtue, not a vice. Avoiding disasters has to be accorded absolute priority. De-escalatory diplomacy is the order of the day.

II

What, in this volatile, uncertain, unpredictable and ambivalent world, could be a realistic vision for the future relationship between Germany and India? Before answering this question, I would like to take a brief look at the history of our bilateral relations.

Indo-German relations have their roots in the humus of culture and linguistics; politics and trade followed much later. Friedrich Schlegel's book *Sprache und Weisheit der Indier* (Language and Wisdom of the Indians), published in 1808, became the cradle of German Indology, which in turn gave crucial impulses to Indian Indology. The traders followed the scholars. To serve their interests, the two Hanseatic cities, Hamburg and Bremen, established consulates in Bombay (now Mumbai) and Kolkata (now Kolkata) in 1844. Interest in ancient India outweighed interest in modern India for a long time after World War II. Politics was a latecomer.

This was primarily due to British colonial rule, which the Indian subcontinent shook off only in 1947. India achieved independence in 1947 and the Federal Republic of Germany was founded two years later. In 1953, the two countries established diplomatic relations. During the Cold War, Jawaharlal Nehru's policy of non-alignment was seen as tilting towards the Kremlin, so the German–Indian political relationship remained tenuous and tinged by mistrust.

In the economic field, though, there were the first beginnings of cooperation. To be sure, bilateral trade remained relatively modest; in 1985, the value of Indian imports from Germany amounted to only 3.4 billion d-marks while the value of Indian exports to the Federal Republic was barely 1.1 billion d-marks. But there were a number of spectacular cooperative projects even in the epoch of Indian socialism (anchored in the Indian Constitution as late as 1976 by Indira Gandhi).

The Rourkela steel mill, built by a German consortium, was a showcase venture leading to intensive cooperation in the developmental field. For several decades, India topped the list of Germany's aid recipients; all told, it received more than 10 billion euros from Bonn and Berlin; in 2014 alone, India received 1.2 billion euros.

However, the end of the Cold War changed the status quo. Non-alignment lost its meaning in a world in which blocs had dissolved. When first the Soviet empire and then the Soviet Union disintegrated, India had to reorient its foreign policy in the new global configuration. Likewise, its *swadeshi* philosophy—a policy of import restrictions, stringent protectionism and sealing oneself off from the world market—no longer made any sense.

Japan, South Korea, Taiwan, Hong Kong and Singapore had shown that there was a better way, and Deng Xiaoping's China, having started reforming the economy and opening the country to the world in 1978, stormed powerfully ahead of India. India, the world's largest democracy and the second most populous nation on earth with 900 million inhabitants at the time, followed suit in 1991.

After a severe economic crisis which pushed the country to the cusp of insolvency, it had no choice. Since then, however, it has taken a giant leap ahead. For the first time since Independence, Indians can believe that the present is a launchpad into the future and not just an extension of the past.

Manmohan Singh, minister of finance at the time and prime minister from 2004 to 2014, opened up many sectors to private investment, incrementally welcomed foreign capital, cut customs tax rates and reduced import limitations. Since then, India has changed beyond recognition. In many regards, the country has become an unsung success story.

The stifling Hindu 'rate of growth'—3 per cent—is a thing of the past; it has increased to an impressive 6 per cent, 8 per cent, and in some years 9 per cent. India's GDP has risen to $2.09 billion, and per capita income to $1.805. Foreign trade has steadily grown to $755 billion. Foreign currency reserves once again stand at $314 billion. While half of India's population still lives in abysmal poverty, famine and starvation have been banished. About 250 million people have achieved middle-class status, and 20–25 million join their ranks every year. India's economy is now the seventh largest in the world.

India's phenomenal economic rise is mirrored in our trade relations. Today, Germany is India's most important trade partner in the EU. The volume of bilateral trade rose to 16 billion euros in 2014–15. Some 3,000 German companies do business in India; an increasing number of Indian firms do business in Germany. Germany is one of the ten most important foreign direct investors ($8 billion since April 2000).

There are also numerous indirect investments. India ranks twenty-fifth in the list of Germany's trade partners, while Germany ranks eighth as a supplier of goods to India, and fifth as a buyer of Indian goods. However, the share of Indo-German trade amounts to barely 1 per cent of Germany's total trade volume, so there is plenty of room for improvement.

Political, cultural and scientific relations between India and Germany have become ever closer during the past fifteen years. The 'Agenda for German–Indian Partnership', agreed on in 2000, and the Strategic Partnership established in 2004, bolstered by the India–EU Strategic Partnership of the same year, has become the basis of frequent, regular and intensive contacts: exchanges of high-level visitors, government consultations every two years, numerous agreements relating to cooperation in such sectors as energy, economy, vocational training, culture and science, security, agriculture, environment, climate change, urbanization, water and waste management. Multifaceted ties benefit both countries.

Deutschlandjahre events have been held in India, and 'Days of India' in Germany. India has been the guest of honour country at the Frankfurt Book Fair and the partner country at the Hannover Trade Fair. These events are evidence of India's resurgence and renewal, and have given bilateral relations between India and Germany a strong push.

III

The past is a prologue. So what is the vision for the future, building on the progress made so far? Visions do not pertain to the nitty-gritty. The obvious does not need spelling out. The fact that both India and Germany are democracies is not a guarantee for an across-the-board congruence of their interests. Both are federation states which invites comparisons and, beyond that, cooperation between individual federal states, yet does not assure it.

Business organizations such as the Bundesverband Deutscher Industrie (BDI) and the Confederation of Indian Industry (CII) are in close contact, boosted not least by the Indo-German Chamber of Commerce; their concerns, however, diverge as much as they overlap.

In all areas, sustained exchange of information about issues and opportunities is of the essence. Parliamentary exchanges are a valuable instrument in this process. So is the Indo-German Advisory Group, whose German co-chairman I was from 1996 to 2005. The Indo-German Advisory Group was founded in 1991, the year India started reforming and opening up to the world. Bringing together representatives of government, political parties, industry, banking, academia, science, the media and NGOs, it has become an important platform for frank dialogue during the past twenty-five years. Its function should be enhanced rather than curbed.

Visions should not be weighed down by unrealistic expectations such as the aspirations of the G-4 (Germany and India, Brazil and Japan) to secure permanent seats in the United Nations Security Council (UNSC). A change of the 1945 Charter would require a two-thirds majority in the General Assembly, including the support of all permanent members of the UNSC. Achieving the consent of regional rivals appears difficult enough for India, Brazil and Japan.

It is next to impossible for Germany, since the rest of the world will never agree to a third European nation getting a UNSC seat with associated veto power. Ignoring this truism, Germany has been barking up the wrong tree for more than two decades. While it should no longer press the issue on its own behalf, it would be well advised to altruistically support India's demand.

Another example of unrealistic expectations is the ambition to introduce Hindi in the teaching schedules of German high schools. Indians learning German—the official language of six European countries—acquire access to about a hundred million German speakers using no other national tongue; while Germans studying Hindi would learn a language of people speaking mostly English anyway. It would be far preferable to provide generous scholarships for the study of Hindi to a small group of specialists who really need it— academics, diplomats, culture ambassadors.

Priority, in my view, should be given to the continuation and reinforcement of collaboration in fields where partnership has already been established and successfully practised in the past: development, improving India's still lamentably insufficient infrastructure (airports, ports, high-speed rail connections, roads), skills development, water and waste management, clean and renewable energy, education, urbanization.

Joint research in science and technology and collaboration in sectors such as software development, biotechnology or robotics also holds immense promise. It goes without saying that establishing a level playing field is a necessary prerequisite when it comes to investment, opening up of markets, norms and standards and taxes—reciprocity, in other words. As many multinational companies diversify away from China, India can only benefit if it reshapes its economy by completing the reforms started in 1991.

Preventing or at least mitigating climate change is another vital task that should be tackled rapidly and intensively in order to narrow the gap between the two countries' approaches and responses to the looming threat of global warming.

Equally important, however, is an intensified effort to give meaning and substance to the term 'strategic partnership'. Germany should embolden India to sharpen its foreign policy profile as an emerging force for peace and stability around the world, transitioning in the process from 'strategic autonomy' to multiple partnerships. In particular, it should encourage New Delhi to accept the EU as an indispensable partner; in this context the speedy conclusion of the stalled free trade agreement (FTA) negotiations with the Brussels community would send a positive signal.

In return, India ought to be able to rely upon German cooperation in the G-20 group of nations; on German support for its foreign policy conduct in the South Asian subcontinent, especially its efforts to reach a durable accommodation with Pakistan; on German endorsement for providing a liberal counterweight to Beijing's authoritarian capitalism as well as for its attempt to balance China's 'One Belt, One Road' (OBOR)initiative by opening up its own route to Central Asia from Chabahar in Iran to Kabul; and, finally, on German backing for its rapprochement with the United States and for India's own pivot to the Asia-Pacific.

IV

For seven decades, the Germans have followed with passionate fascination the exciting race between the two Asian giants, India and China. Which of these great nations will reach the goalpost first—the dragon or the elephant? At this juncture, China is ahead in the race for prosperity, India is ahead in the freedom race. Can the elephant catch up economically?

Will it limit its geopolitical ambitions to its regional bailiwick or will it become a responsible stakeholder worldwide? A stabilizing force in the reconfigured Asian-Pacific order? A supporter of reforming the world organizations founded at the end of World War II or the co-sponsor and promoter of parallel structures—Shanghai Cooperation Organization, AIIB, OBOR, BRICS? And will it recognize the United Europe of States (note: not the United States of Europe), whatever its current trials and tribulations, as a crucial pole in the emerging multipolar world, or will it continue to take its brief largely from British Euro-sceptics now turned into Brexiteers?

India is an old civilization with a young population; a vigorous democracy. It is a country where the rule of law is unquestioned, although the judiciary is deplorably understaffed and overburdened, with millions of cases pending in various courts. It is a country that shares Western notions of human rights; a vibrant society, a pillar of stability in the region. It is a nuclear power, and a responsible one at that. Its economic progress is stunning. Its culture is one of the richest on earth. This constitutes a firm foundation for a joint vision of the future.

The Germans wish the Indians luck and success in the historic undertaking of modernizing their country. They are keeping their fingers crossed that India's drift into modernity won't engender extremism; that the inexorable change will take place without causing harrowing trauma; and that burgeoning prosperity will vitiate the strains and tensions of a polity characterized by colossal linguistic, religious and tribal diversity.

One final thought, though. The vision of the future must remain realistic. Our partnership will have to prove its value by managing practical problems and attaining practicable solutions. We won't profit from grandiose dreams and ambitions.

Realizing Security Cooperation

◈

Jürgen Hardt
'Sharing Values and Interests'

◈

C. Raja Mohan and Pratinav Anil
'Definitive Notes from an Uncertain Trumpet'

Jürgen Hardt, Member of Parliament, was born in 1963 in Hofheim am Taunus (Hessen). From 1982 to 1986, he served as officer candidate and naval officer (sub-lieutenant), ship security officer and technical diver with the frigate *Augsburg*.

He studied economics in Heidelberg and Cologne and was the federal chairman of the Association of Christian Democratic Students from 1987 to 1989. From 1992 to 1998, he was head of the Social Policy Department and Secretary-General Peter Hintze's office at the Christian Democratic Union (CDU) party headquarters. After that he became the European policy desk officer of the CDU/Christian Social Union (CSU) parliamentary group in the German Bundestag. From 2001 to 2009, he was the head of corporate communications at Vorwerk.

Since 2009, he has been a member of the German Bundestag, and since April 2014, he has been the Federal Foreign Office coordinator of transatlantic cooperation in the field of intersocietal relations, and cultural and information policy. In September 2015, he became the spokesman for foreign policy of the CDU/CSU parliamentary group.

Hardt is a member of several Bundestag bodies and holds many parliamentary posts, including the Committee on Foreign Affairs, the Committee on the Affairs of the European Union, and the Defence Committee.

Membership of other bodies: North Atlantic Treaty Organization (NATO) Parliamentary Assembly; Organization for Security and Co-operation in Europe (OSCE) Parliamentary Assembly (OSCE PA); substitute member of the Parliamentary Assembly of the Council of Europe; substitute member of the Inter-Parliamentary Conference for the Common Foreign and Security Policy; and the Common Security and Defence Policy.

Sharing Values and Interests

Jürgen Hardt

Discussing Indo-German relations today, business, trade, high-tech, IT and environmental protection spring to mind. Hardly anyone considers cooperation in foreign and security policy. However, in today's world with its dramatic increase in the frequency and concurrence of international crises and conflicts, this is one of the most important fields.

Events taking place in Asia or the Middle East today have a greater direct impact on us in Germany and Europe. Moreover, our countries constantly face new challenges such as Britain's planned withdrawal from the European Union (EU), the impact of which also needs appropriate responses. These responses are easier to arrive at when working together with strategic partners in the world. India and Germany are such partners—a partnership worth expanding.

Indo-German Relations

India was the first country to make peace with Germany after World War II and one of the first to establish diplomatic relations with the new Federal Republic of Germany, on 7 March 1951. Our relations have further intensified since India's programme of economic liberalization was initiated in 1991. Germany is India's largest trade and investment partner and, for Prime Minister Modi, a preferred partner in development and modernization, which invests more in its security infrastructure than any country in the world.

The South Asian country is one of the most dynamic economies in global competition. Besides economic affairs, another strategic interest for Germany lies in scientific and technological cooperation. India's companies are not only leading in information technology (IT) and software industries, but also in the field of biotechnology, space and satellite research. Moreover, India is considered an important international partner in the area of global governance.

Both countries can look back on their cooperation which started in the

1990s. An Indo-German advisory group was set up at the end of the twentieth century to present proposals for the deepening of bilateral relations. The political dialogue between both countries has intensified since the mid-1990s and Germany has become increasingly aware of India's growing geopolitical role in the international arena. The Agenda for the Indo-German Partnership, adopted in May 2000, provided the framework for both countries to intensify their cooperation in business, science, technology and culture.

Then German Defence Minister Rudolf Scharping initiated a strategic dialogue with India in 2001, agreeing, among other things, to hold talks between the military staff of the two countries, and to provide Bundeswehr training courses for Indian officers. In 2006, both countries signed an agreement to strengthen their security policy cooperation.

In 2007, Germany sought to involve India and other emerging economies more intensively in the G7/8 countries' advisory and consultation mechanisms via the Heiligendamm Process. Within the framework of the G4, Germany and India expressed their interest in permanent seats in the UN Security Council. While India has long been one of the most important contributors of troops for UN peacekeeping missions, Germany ranks among the UN's most important donor countries.

Finally, India and Germany have formal intergovernmental consultations between their cabinets—the last one was held in New Delhi in October 2015. Federal Chancellor Merkel attended the consultations in New Delhi with four federal ministers, six state secretaries and a high-ranking business delegation. Essentially, the consultations gave rise to a total of eighteen memoranda of understanding, from vocational training to security.

South Asia as a Geostrategic Region

South Asia offers business opportunities as well as regional and global challenges, which is why engaging in the region is becoming more important. South Asia is still not free from conflicts due to closely interwoven old and new security risks. Unresolved conflicts in Jammu and Kashmir or at the Durand Line between Afghanistan and Pakistan, the illegal proliferation of nuclear technology, a broad spectrum of ethnic and religious insurgencies with links to terrorist groups operating regionally and globally, combined with organized crime and the unpredictable impact of climate change, have turned the region into a powder keg.

Making matters worse are the proliferation of nuclear weapons technology by Abdul Qadeer Khan, the 'father' of the Pakistani atomic bomb, and the regional and global networks of Islamic terrorist groups, such as Lashkar-e-Taiba, which have links to Al-Qaeda and were responsible for numerous attacks in India and Afghanistan.

Moreover, China is continuing its expansion in South Asia, not only as a business partner, but also as a political influencer with intensive relations with Pakistan. China's influence is growing constantly in the Indian Ocean, and Beijing is enticing countries in this region with cheap loans and infrastructure measures to promote its projects as part of a 'new Silk Road' or 'Maritime Silk Road'.

Alongside regional developments, India, like Germany and the EU, is affected by global challenges, including cyber threats and terrorism—particularly resulting from a resurgent Islamism—as well as smuggling and piracy. Piracy off the Somali coast poses a major obstacle to the sea route through the Gulf of Aden.

Shared Values and Interests

Indo-German relations have gained momentum since the 1990s. Both countries are united by a range of shared values and interests, making them predestined to enjoy a strategic partnership. For Germany, the basis of these relations does not lie only in their shared history after World War II, or in India's economic importance. Its geostrategic role, expertise in cutting-edge technology and the potential of its professionals in areas like cyber challenges also make India an important partner.

Furthermore, Germany and India share many common interests and values in the areas of democracy, the rule of law and human rights. This was demonstrated in October 2015 by the fact that in their concluding statements, the heads of government of both countries emphasized their concerted efforts to achieve sovereign equality of all states, and articulated their commitment to respecting their territorial integrity and their desire to diplomatically resolve conflicts in eastern Ukraine and Syria, among others.

Cooperation in Strategic Partnership

One approach holds that regional security is a priority for the affected countries and not for extra-regional world powers. Neighbouring countries must find ways to coexist. In past decades, the attempted involvement by extra-national powers has seldom been advantageous.

But such an approach does not guarantee success. Not only the UN, but also international formats of all regional powers, including extra-national world powers, are more than sufficient to establish the framework for talks and find solutions, for example, the Normandy format, which was revived following the crisis in Ukraine, shows that successes like this can be achieved.

Moreover, many challenges of the present can only be addressed through cooperation—arms control, pacifying international conflicts such as those in Syria and Afghanistan, global challenges such as terrorism, piracy, money laundering and organized crime, as well as energy security and efforts to combat climate change, must be tackled together.

We are witnessing the world moving closer together each day. With our communications technology and modes of transport, crises and conflicts are getting to us ever more rapidly from far-flung parts of the globe. Strategies for our changing world are increasingly needed to solve these problems.

Cooperation in International Forums

The basis of common action and one of its most effective instruments is close cooperation in international forums such as the G20 and the UN, as well as other multilateral forums to tackle current and newly emerging challenges. To make the work of the UN even more effective, both Germany and India are working together to achieve reforms in its structure and methods. At the G4 meeting in New York in October 2015, all the group members reaffirmed their commitment to an extensive expansion of the Security Council with a permanent seat for each of the four nations. However, there has been no appreciable progress since the UN's 2005 pledge to implement a reform 'quickly'. A binding time frame for Security Council reform would, therefore, be a necessary next step.

Furthermore, India is involved in many UN missions also supported by German military. For instance, India has contributed troops to UNIFIL (United Nations Interim Force in Lebanon) in Lebanon and to the UN peacekeeping force MONUSCO in the Congo, as well as to UN missions UNMIS/UNMISS in the Sudan and South Sudan, and the UN mission UNMIL in Liberia. Joint involvement in UN missions proves India is a reliable partner.

India, Germany and the EU also support each other in other international forums, for example, as strategic partners of the Association of Southeast

Asian Nations (ASEAN), Germany and India lend their support to the establishment of a strategic partnership with the EU. Both countries are committed to expanding possible synergies and opportunities for cooperation within the framework of their respective efforts to cultivate regional links.

India and the EU

Important cooperation between India and Germany in the area of foreign and security policy takes place via the EU. Although, from an Indian perspective, bilateral interactions with individual European member states such as Germany, the UK and France may be considered more profitable than relations with the EU, working at the EU level is a worthwhile endeavour owing to its concentration of resources. While many Europeans are aware that negotiations with a sometimes not-easy-to-handle EU can be extremely arduous and complicated, the debate surrounding Britain's withdrawal from the EU gave rise to the European member states' desire to develop more efficient processes and mechanisms.

India already maintains good relations with Brussels, however. These relations lay dormant for far too long, before the summit between Prime Minister Modi and the presidents of the European Council and the European Commission injected fresh impetus into this relationship in May 2016. The summit not only discussed a comprehensive Bilateral Trade and Investment Agreement (BTIA), but also renewed the 2010 joint declaration on the fight against terrorism.

Both the EU and India intend to take greater action towards combating extremism and radicalization and to redouble their efforts to prevent recruitment by terrorist groups, inhibiting their financial flows and weapons smuggling. An agreement was reached to liaise more closely in monitoring financial transactions, as well as in judicial and police cooperation and measures against states supporting terrorists. Essentially, this paved the way for the establishment of EU–India working groups on issues like cyber threats, counter terrorism, anti-piracy and the non-proliferation of nuclear weapons and disarmament.

Bilateral Security Cooperation

Indo-German intergovernmental consultations are undoubtedly the most important engagement at the bilateral level. Armaments cooperation is an important common interest at these meetings. Additionally, exchanges with India in cutting-edge technologies are of great interest to Germany. German Federal Minister of Defence von der Leyen and Indian Minister of Defence Manohar Parrikar sounded out the possibility of future armaments cooperation between the two countries at a meeting in May 2015. The focus was on India's interest in industrial cooperation for submarines. After all, India plays a major role in ensuring stability in the Indian Ocean by fighting against piracy.

Germany and India already liaise closely in many areas at a bilateral level. Security issues are also becoming increasingly important at such expert dialogue levels. The second round of cyber consultations was held in Berlin in October 2015. Since India is not only undergoing a process of extremely dynamic economic development, but is also the world's largest democracy, bilateral cooperation in international cyber policy has immense potential for business, development, good governance, security and the international order.

Key topics of the consultations included cyber security and capacity-building in this area. India has a great deal of expertise in this field which can benefit both countries. It also has specialists that Germany urgently needs. Other important issues on the agenda included internet governance, norms for responsible state action in cyberspace and measures to combat internet crime. Once again, this cooperation demonstrates that Germany's and India's actions are based on the same premises and mindsets.

Both countries are committed to creating a peaceful, secure, open and cooperative cyberspace where human rights are respected. India and Germany agreed to take steps to consolidate this format and to conduct such cyber consultations on an annual basis allowing Indian experts to offer their advice in drafting the new white paper for German security policy. This underscores the importance both countries attribute to this political field and to their common efforts in this regard.

Numerous other political exchanges between Germany's and India's heads of state, members of government and parliamentarians have also been taking place outside the context of intergovernmental consultations and forum meetings. For instance, with India as the partner country, Prime Minister Modi opened the Hannover Messe with Federal Chancellor Merkel in April 2015, and followed this with an official visit to Berlin. Federal President Joachim Gauck chose India as the destination for his first state visit to Asia in February 2014. The Indo-German Parliamentary Friendship

Group of the German Bundestag travels to India regularly, and foreign and security policy plays an important role in its discussions.

Scope for Intensifying Security Cooperation

Considering Indo-German cooperation, issues such as economic cooperation and common trade appear, at first sight, to be a priority. But the partnership between Germany and India goes far beyond this. The cooperation between the two countries in foreign and security policy is already considerably more intensive today than many think.

With its extremely dynamic economic development, and being the largest democracy in the world, India plays a geopolitically decisive role regarding stability both within and beyond the region. Considering its various territorial, political, religious and social conflicts, South Asia will continue to rank among the regions with a high crisis potential in the future, especially when India's situation regarding China and Pakistan and their relations with one another is taken into account. Ensuring the situation in South Asia does not continue to deteriorate will be a decisive factor.

Simultaneously, it is important to realize that the regional security situation has already improved. The risk of a nuclear conflict between India and Pakistan, a spectre that was raised in the 1990s against the backdrop of permanent tensions, has been greatly lessened thanks to following the initiatives of Prime Minister Modi. Today's security policy challenges lie more in domestic conflict hotspots in the respective countries. India's foreign policy focus has also shifted. South Asia is no longer merely an important region for the country's own national security, but is also an indispensable market for India's economic development, giving rise to new political perspectives.

It would be a mistake to be satisfied with the current level of cooperation. Looking at the range of challenges in South Asia, it is in both Germany's and Europe's interests to intensify the security cooperation with India. There are many points of reference for supporting security policy cooperation bilaterally in South Asia.

To continuously improve security in the region, it is extremely important for India, in its transition from a 'balancing' to a 'leading' power, to continue pursuing a course of seeking peaceful dialogue, especially with its neighbours Pakistan and China, despite differences of opinion—whether these differences are over territorial issues or cross-border crime. Bilateral and international forums can be key in resolving conflicts.

Additionally, Germany should continuously campaign for the establishment of regional institutions for security policy cooperation in South and Central Asia—based on the European model of the Organization for Security and Cooperation in Europe (OSCE). Today, there aren't any organizations such as the ASEAN Regional Forum (ARF) or the Shanghai Cooperation Organization (SCO) in Central Asia for jointly tackling the many regional security policy challenges.

Germany is in favour of effective multilateralism with binding rules for member countries. India also has a long tradition of setting up multilateral institutions, started by its first Prime Minister Jawaharlal Nehru in the 1950s. Regarding the Responsibility to Protect (R2P), it is, of course, important to achieve a balance between national sovereignty and the principle of non-intervention in domestic affairs.

The two countries' efforts in the UN will continue to be informed by the desire to implement reform and the objective for both India and Germany to attain a permanent seat on the Security Council. To further improve cooperation within the remit of this forum, it would be conceivable, looking at joint UN missions, to continue coordinating military processes and allowing soldiers and officers to learn from each other within the framework of joint exercises.

At the European level, supporting the cyber, counter-terrorism, anti-piracy, non-proliferation of nuclear weapons and disarmament working groups would be important for achieving a more intensive cooperative partnership. These groups work on issues affecting India as much as Germany and the EU.

At the national level, it would be desirable to prioritize foreign and security policy within the framework of intergovernmental consultations, and to consolidate this in a regular format outside the context of the consultations. Simultaneously, efforts should be made to ensure Indo-German expert dialogues dovetail European working groups. Regarding the challenges in the cyber sphere, it would be desirable, beyond the existing cooperative frameworks, to intensify exchanges in the IT sector at the state level and to allow experts to gain insights into the working methods of the other country through exchange programmes.

In all these areas, it is crucial to become even more aware of the value of this strategic partnership and that—going beyond formalized processes—officials of the two countries talk to each other regularly. This way it will be possible to find responses to challenges that are perhaps not even considered yet.

A strategic partnership can also offer both countries new opportunities in other fields, for instance in the context of Britain's planned exit from the EU. Britain always had particularly excellent relations with India and its withdrawal from the EU could have far-reaching consequences. The EU will continue to be an economically important region for India even without Britain, and will remain a fixed point of reference with respect to foreign and security policy issues. Therefore, Germany should seize the opportunity now to further intensify its already excellent relations with India, by becoming Europe's new bridge to South Asia.

Bilateral relations between Germany, the EU and India could become the symbol of future political values and concepts of order that the German and European political establishment associate with the world's largest democracy.

C. Raja Mohan

Pratinav Anil

C. Raja Mohan, Director, Carnegie Endowment for International Peace, is a visiting research professor at the Institute of South Asian Studies, National University of Singapore (NUS), and consulting editor on foreign affairs for *The Indian Express*.

Mohan has taught South Asian studies in Jawaharlal Nehru University, Delhi, and the Nanyang Technological University (NTU), Singapore. He has published widely on India's foreign policy, the Asian security order and nuclear arms control. His most recent book is *Modi's World: Expanding India's Sphere of Influence* (New Delhi: HarperCollins, 2015).

Pratinav Anil is a graduate from Sciences Po Paris, and is currently pursuing a master's in International Relations at the London School of Economics. He has worked at the Gandhi Peace Foundation, (New Delhi), Centre de recherches internationales, Paris, and Carnegie India, New Delhi.
His writings on Indian foreign policy have been published by *The Indian Express* and *The London Globalist*, and he is currently co-writing a book on the Emergency in India (1975–77) with Christophe Jaffrelot.

Definitive Notes from an Uncertain Trumpet

Dr C. Raja Mohan and Pratinav Anil

To many observers, India and Germany are like chalk and cheese, naan and wiener, speaking different languages in different continents with few shared interests. A closer investigation shows a number of occasions when their trajectories have intersected. The nationalist elite of the two countries, for example, harboured aspirations to collectively upend the world order in the first half of the twentieth century, while their successors contented themselves with more prosaic matters such as trade and security links in the second half of the century.

This chapter begins with a review of Indo-German security cooperation during the two world wars. It then looks at how Jawaharlal Nehru and Konrad Adenauer navigated the early Cold War years with a surprisingly broad relationship. The third section captures the renewed engagement between the two nations after they drifted apart in the years after Nehru. In the final section, we assess how the changing global power distribution and growing international demands on them to take leadership are nudging Delhi and Berlin towards a closer security partnership.

India and Germany in the Two World Wars

In the run-up to World War I, there was a convergence of ideas and objectives. Nationalist sentiment was on the rise in India. The German Reich was at war with the British Empire, and their foreign ministry, the Auswärtiges Amt, reasoned that an enemy's enemy was a friend. Radical Indian nationalists across Europe and the United States were growing impatient with the Indian National Congress's peaceful methods. 'The time will soon come when rifles and blood will take the place of pens and ink,' proclaimed the newly formed Hindu Association of the Pacific Coast.

Soon after the outbreak of the world war, Har Dayal, the leader of the American-based Hindu Association of the Pacific Coast, met with Alfred Zimmermann, the German secretary for foreign affairs, and the Berlin Committee was born. Over the next three years, in what came to be known as the 'Hindu–German conspiracy', German money and arms, and Indian pro-independence propaganda literature were smuggled into the neutral United States—their final destination was Karachi, from where a grand insurrection was to begin. Communication channels were set up through which Ghadr and Bengali *bhadralok* revolutionaries liaised with German spooks, and German-funded schooners with Indian revolutionaries docked at the Socorro Island in Mexico and Hilo, Hawaii.

With German backing, a provisional government of India was set up in Kabul in August 1915. The efforts of the so-called Hindu–German conspiracy were largely unsuccessful—dubbed by one of its participants as a 'wild goose chase'—and the outcome was impounded ships, disillusioned revolutionaries, and imprisoned conspirators. Nevertheless, the conspiracy left a lasting legacy by opening political links between Germany and Indian nationalists.

In World War II as well, India's anti-colonial struggle and Anglo-German rivalry brought about German–Indian cooperation. Indian nationalist Subhas Chandra Bose smuggled himself across the Soviet Union into Berlin, meeting with then German Foreign Minister Joachim Ribbentrop and Chancellor Adolf Hitler, both of whom expressed interest in his idea of developing a fifth column of Indian soldiers fighting on Britain's side in Europe.

The Indian troops who rallied around Bose received military training by German elite commando forces near Hamburg. About 17,000 Indian prisoners of war in Germany and Italy were freed, and a quarter of these troops joined Bose's Free India Legion in 1942. Meanwhile, German troops, who were aiding the Faqir of Ipi to fight the British in Waziristan, coordinated with other Indian fighters in and around the subcontinent. However, the tide of the war began to turn in the Allies' favour, and German priorities turned away from their global ambitions, receding back into their neighbourhood.

Bose himself shifted his priorities to Japan and Southeast Asia. Despite this, Bose's Free India Centre and Free India Radio, both based in Berlin, remained symbols of the proximity of the two nations, which had aligned with each other in times of upheaval. The two world wars marked the first major instances of security cooperation between Germany and the Indian national movement, and also the significant constraints on it.

Nehru and Adenauer: Surprising Proximity

The defeat of Germany and its partition, and the division and decolonization of India, set the stage for a new phase of bilateral engagement. Independent

India became the first country in the world to end the state of war with West Germany, in January 1950. India and West Germany established diplomatic ties in March 1951, largely due to the strong rapport shared by their founding fathers, Prime Minister Jawaharlal Nehru and Chancellor Konrad Adenauer.

The two leaders—both of whom also held their country's foreign ministry portfolio—shared similar interests as they navigated the Cold War era. They sought to maintain a degree of autonomy, secure their national sovereignty, and industrialize their respective countries—one devastated by the two world wars, and the other by imperial rule. The Federal Republic of Germany established diplomatic contacts with India as soon as it received permission from the Allies to reopen the German Foreign Office in 1951.

The first German ambassador to India, Ernst Wilhelm Meyer, had a great affinity with Nehru and his non-aligned vision, and when his superiors at Bonn asked him to condemn India's decision to establish an East German trade mission in Delhi, he refused. Meyer argued that it was unwise to nettle Nehru when Indo-German relations were in their infancy. Nehru's visit to West Germany in 1956 further cemented the relations between the two countries.

Adenauer requested Nehru to press for German reunification, to which Nehru replied that India's non-alignment policy—which was strengthened at the Bandung Conference in 1955—precluded it from interfering in such matters; nevertheless, as a friendly gesture towards Adenauer, Nehru did not accept East Germany's invitation to visit East Berlin. In the early 1950s, the Indian prime minister hoped that Germany would unite, and that—in Nehru's words—the 'puppet regime' of East Germany would fall, as would the 'unnatural state' of Pakistan, leading to a similar Indian reunification.

Nehru's opinions, which were far more charitable towards West Germany than to its eastern counterpart, stand in contrast to those who interpret the first prime minister's worldview in terms of neutrality and equidistance between the East and the West. Nehru argued that India could align closely with only one of the two Germanys, and his decision to pursue stronger trade and aid ties with West Germany reflected a pragmatic streak in him.

East Germany and India only began diplomatic relations in 1972, when the Hallstein Doctrine—according to which West Germany would view any country's recognition of East Germany to be an unfriendly act and suspend economic aid to it—was abolished. The Hallstein Doctrine was abolished in the early 1970s during Chancellor Willy Brandt's 'Neue Ostpolitik' that sought productive engagement between the two German states.

The post-Nehru years saw India and Germany drift apart. Germany offered Pakistan military aid and equipment during its war with India in 1965, which rankled the Indian foreign policy establishment. The Indira Gandhi administration's affinity with the Union of Soviet Socialist Republics (USSR)—the Indo-Soviet Treaty of Peace, Friendship and Cooperation was concluded in 1971—was not received well in Germany. Germany also viewed the Emergency declared by Prime Minister Indira Gandhi in 1975 in a negative light, campaigning against the Indian government and calling for clemency for its jailed dissidents.

German Chancellor Helmut Schmidt was far more interested in deepening ties with China than he was with India. From the mid-1960s to the mid-1980s, Indo-German relations were marked by 'benign neglect'—as described by Dirk Oncken, the West German ambassador to India—in which India's economic stagnation and Germany's reduced official development assistance towards it led to a dwindling of relations between the two countries.

In the 1980s, Indo-German ties grew with Chancellor Helmut Kohl's visits to Delhi in 1983 and 1986, and Prime Minister Rajiv Gandhi's visit to Bonn in 1988. Once again, drastic changes in the two countries and upheavals in the global order brought about cooperation between the two countries. India's drift towards the Soviet Union and state-led socialism were made unviable after the USSR's demise and the end of the Cold War. The fall of the Berlin Wall in 1989, the unification of Germany and the liberalization of India's economic regime in 1991 were pivotal moments that affected the foreign policy trajectories of both countries.

Towards Security Convergence

The upheavals of 1989–91 compelled the leaders of India and Germany to initiate a more intensive bilateral engagement, and transformed a relationship of 'benign neglect' into one where Delhi and Berlin began considering each other to be 'natural partners'—the term used in the Agenda for Indo-German Partnership for the 21st century, a document which the foreign ministers of both countries signed in May 2000. Today, the relevance of Indo-German ties has become even more pressing, with the two growing economies—Germany is already Europe's largest economy, and India is Asia's third-largest one—becoming increasingly interested in playing a larger role in global power politics and its myriad, conflicting theatres.

For the first time in their bilateral relations, India and Germany concluded a defence cooperation agreement in 2006, which led to joint defence production projects and increased technology transfers. Two years later, the two countries began joint naval exercises and training programmes. There are other areas of engagement as well. India is the largest troop contributor to UN peacekeeping missions, and Germany is one of the UN's largest financiers. Peacekeeping and stability operations provide a useful template for Germany, as it sheds past inhibitions and commits itself to a security role in the world.

India, which has long been at the forefront of international peacekeeping under the UN flag, has begun to take a more strategic view of its military possibilities beyond the subcontinent. Delhi is also shedding many of its past self-imposed constraints on defence cooperation with major powers. This has set the stage for more productive international security cooperation between Delhi and Berlin.

Fighting terrorism is among the top national security priorities in both countries—after the terrorist attacks on Mumbai in 2008, German elite forces provided training to the commandos of Indian's National Security Guard. With Europe reeling under new terror threats, the limited current engagement on counter-terrorism between the two countries has huge potential for expansion.

Both Germany and India have long believed in their own 'soft power' and the attendant capacity to shape global political outcomes. While some of that confidence will be tested amidst the return of realpolitik, Berlin and Delhi have every reason to build on their shared commitment to international law and norms. As they confront the rise of illiberal forces in their Eurasian space, Germany and India have a common interest in protecting their own domestic democratic orders and weakening the forces spreading darkness.

The prospects for security cooperation have got a new boost with Prime Minister Narendra Modi's emphasis on modernizing India's defence industrial base through partnerships with advanced countries. He has partially delicensed state monopoly in defence production and is actively courting foreign direct investment in the production of arms. At the Hannover Fair in April 2015, he asked German companies to see a new, changed India that was 'transparent, responsive, and stable'. The following month, German Defence Minister Ursula von der Leyen highlighted technology transfer between the two countries, and suggested opening strategic collaboration to cyberspace and maritime security as well.

In reimagining the possibilities for defence and security cooperation, India and Germany have some unfortunate incidents from the past to overcome. The first major defence deal between the two countries could hardly have gone more awry. The purchase of the HDW-manufactured submarines by the Indian government in 1979–81, and the payoffs it involved generated much controversy and cast a shadow over bilateral cooperation. Renewed collaboration in recent times has led to a new round of talks on the purchase of submarines in 2014, and in June 2016, the German defence contractor ThyssenKrupp Marine System signed a $38.4 million contract for the modernization of the Indian Navy's Shishumar-class submarines.

As rising powers, Delhi and Berlin see their nascent militarization efforts not as an act of belligerence, but as one of protecting their trade interests, preventing piracy on the high seas, securing the major sea lines of communication—such as the Strait of Malacca and the Strait of Hormuz, the world's key choke points for energy and goods. Their militarization efforts are also aimed at preventing the rise of transnational terrorism, which in 2016 affected both Germany and India—Islamic State of Iraq and Syria (ISIS) sympathizers conducted two attacks in Germany in July 2016, while Indian intelligence agencies are reported to have found ISIS sleeper cells in Hyderabad.

Reconnecting the Reflective Powers

The future of Indo-German relations seems bright. Both countries have put the era of 'benign neglect' behind them and have laid the foundation for economic, cultural and strategic cooperation. In the mid-1990s, the Indian co-chairman of the Indo-German Consultative Group, P.N. Dhar, had said that 'Indo-German cooperation has not really begun'. In the last twenty years, much has been done to erode this cooperation. It is now time for the countries to open new vistas of cooperation ranging from non-military threats such as climate change, and new challenges in the global commons, including the maritime, space and cyber domains.

With Brexit—or Britain's decision to leave the EU and become a 'second-rank world power' in the words of David Folkerts-Landau, the chief economist at Deutsche Bank—and the rise of the 'America First' ideology—or the isolationist foreign policy view held by a number of influential American politicians and policymakers—traditional great powers are increasingly growing disinterested in providing global leadership. India and Germany are among the rising nations that are willing to fill in the power vacuum.

After an extended period of peace and a limited international security profile outside the North Atlantic Treaty Organization (NATO), Germany, under the Berlin Republic, is seeking a more active international role. Germany now calls itself a 'reflective power'—a term coined by German Foreign Minister Frank-Walter Steinmeier. It is ready to be more assertive in global politics but is undertaking this new role with 'restraint, deliberation, and peaceful negotiation'.

Although India has not been under any constitutional or externally imposed constraint, qualities such as restraint, peaceful orientation, and commitment to liberal internationalism have long characterized the country's own prudent global policies. As its material capabilities grow and its international standing rises, Delhi is moving, ever so gingerly, towards a greater global security activism.

Amid their changing external orientation, Delhi and Berlin could join forces for level-headed foreign policy interventions in the future to contain global terrorism, patrol crucial sea-lanes and prevent piracy, prevent proliferation of weapons of mass destruction, counter revanchism and broker peace in Eurasia and the Asia-Pacific. 'Germany is ready to lead', announced a German white paper or Weißbuch published in July 2016—Germany is presently mediating in the Ukraine crisis, taking the lead in accommodating migrants in the country, coordinating EU policy, arming Kurdish fighters against ISIS and employing troops in Afghanistan and Mali.

On its part, India is undergoing a massive military modernization, projecting forces in the Asia-Pacific region to secure national interests as well as global public goods, and expanding its collaboration with other liberal powers like the US and the EU.

In an era of increasing international instability, marked by the rise of China, an assertive Russia and an ambivalent America weighed down by strategic ennui, Germany and India can no longer remain reluctant powers. Berlin's defence 'Weißbuch' affirms that Germany is now willing to contribute 'early, decisively, and substantially' to the protection of Western security. India too, feels beckoned to play a larger role in global affairs.

In the words of India's Foreign Secretary Subrahmanyam Jaishankar, Delhi 'aspires to be a leading power, rather than just a balancing power.' There is no doubt that the strategic paths of India and Germany are converging again. If the convergence of the early twentieth century was brief and unsustainable, this time around Delhi and Berlin are poised to construct an enduring and consequential security partnership that can contribute to the stability of Eurasia and the Asia-Pacific, as well as strengthen the liberal forces around the world.

Perception Building

◈

Ashok Malik
'Widening Understanding'

◈

Nicole Bastian
'Friendship Needs Opportunities'

Ashok Malik, senior media person and columnist, is a distinguished fellow at the Observer Research Foundation, one of India's leading public policy think tanks, and head of the foundation's Neighbourhood Regional Studies Initiative. His work focuses on Indian domestic politics and foreign/trade policy and their increasing interplay, both in the region and beyond.

Malik has a background in media and is a prominent columnist for a variety of publications, including *The Times of India*, the *Hindustan Times*, *The Economic Times*, *Pioneer* and ndtv.com. In 2012, Ashok authored *India: The Spirit of Enterprise* (Lustre-Roli), a study of the growth of the Indian private sector in the post-liberalization period.

Widening Understanding

Ashok Malik

Few of India's European relationships have the richness and depth of its engagement with Germany. This is even more remarkable given that the Germans were not among the European powers that colonized India. The Germans came to India as seekers, not of material wealth but of the subcontinent's wisdom. The word 'came' is used metaphorically because the greatest such 'seeker' and exponent of India's classicism and tradition, Friedrich Max Müller, didn't come at all. That German scholar lived in Oxford for many years and his study of the ancient religions, history and cultural practices of India was an awakening not just for the rest of the world but for Indians themselves. It was an impetus for the growing consciousness of Indian nationalism in the nineteenth century.

Max Müeller represented the zenith of a golden age for Indo-German intercourse. It was almost two hundred years ago, in 1818, that Sanskrit began to be taught in Germany. Ten years earlier, in 1808, Friedrich Schiegel published *On the Language and Wisdom of the Indians*, a foundational text exploring what we today call the Indo-European family of languages. Schiegel's work began the tradition of Indology, an academic discipline in which nineteenth-century Germany was the global leader.

This German keenness to understand and celebrate India, along with the rise of Germany as a unified nation and a great power in the late nineteenth and early twentieth centuries, won over the Indians of that period. During both the world wars, individual Indians turned to Germany for help in their own national liberation efforts. One example is the so-called Indo-German or Hindu–German 'conspiracy', which implicated the German consulate in San Francisco as well as a group of intrepid Indian revolutionaries, and led to a well-known legal case in the United States in 1917.

In the late 1940s, the post-war landscape posed similar challenges for both countries. Germany had to reconstruct itself while India, emerging from two hundred years of British rule and an economy recently hijacked for the Allied war effort, was faced with an immense task of industrialization and modernization. The paths the two countries chose, and the political instincts they responded to were different; nevertheless, their goodwill and mutual sympathy went a long way in cementing their ties.

In the 1950s, two of the greatest monuments to Indo-German engagement were constructed—the Rourkela Steel Plant in the Indian state of Orissa (now Odisha) and the Indian Institute of Technology in Madras (now Chennai), the premier city of southern India. These projects were underwritten by German technology, knowledge sharing and developmental assistance. They were as evocative and inspirational in the 1950s, and had as much impact on public opinion, as, say, the opening of the Mercedes-Benz factory near Pune in the first decade of the twenty-first century; actually, they had a greater impact.

Civil society and people-to-people links have been strengthened by what may be called the soft infrastructure of Indo-German relations. German businesses and chambers of commerce have invested immensely in understanding the Indian market and the Indian psyche, Indian habits, mores, tastes and the like. They have done so not out of an innocent curiosity or some adventure of learning but as a process preceding investment.

Nevertheless, this has given German business an insight into India that is lacking in investors from certain other European or Western countries. Some of the latter have made astonishingly lazy assumptions about India in the past twenty-odd years, since the economy was opened up. There have been facile comparisons with China; or quick assessments based on the English-language skills of the Indian elite. A deeper excavation of society, even as a business-preparedness exercise, has been absent. In this regard, German companies are cited as an exception.

In the realm of ideas and activism, the sextet of politically-fostered foundations—a noteworthy German concept whereby political parties are obligated to invest in beliefs and philosophies that underpin them, rather than be consumed by pure electoral tactics—is active in India. Representing Germany's major parties and helping expand public and policy discourse in India, as well as enhancing Indian and European dialogue, these foundations have had their influence on Indian academia, think tanks and the media. The pan-Indian network of the Goethe-Institute, housed in India at the Max Müeller Bhawan, provides a cultural interface for interested citizens, particularly students.

Finally, of course, Frankfurt remains an important airport for all those Indians transiting to North America or destinations in Europe. Literally millions of international travellers from India would have experienced

Frankfurt airport, especially when flying west. Even so, regrettably very few of these transit passengers actually stop in Germany and see the country outside the airport. One group that does venture into Frankfurt every year belongs to the energetic Indian publishing industry, which sends a big contingent to the Frankfurt Book Fair each year.

Germany has also had a major influence on Indian medicine, specifically homoeopathy. In fact Samuel Hahnemann's homoeopathy is more popular in India than in his native Germany. Asia's largest democracy and Europe's largest economy have punched below their weight. In nurturing a popular understanding of each other, they have delivered suboptimal results.

II

On 23 June 2016, Britain voted to leave the European Union (EU) in a referendum that sent tectonic waves across the international system. The implications of 'Brexit' are still unfolding and the challenges (more obvious) and opportunities are being identified. One of the consequences, a senior Indian diplomat in New Delhi believes, could be the 'divorcing of European perceptions of India from British perceptions of India'.

The import of that line should not be discounted. Whether it is strategic reckoning, historical memory or even a position on services and space for skilled Indian labour as part of a free trade agreement, British views and interests and downright prejudices seemed to engulf all of Europe.

This is not to suggest the EU and India don't have their own set of mutual disagreements and misunderstandings, autonomous of Britain. The British overhang, however, and the sense that Britain had the greater wisdom about India has tended to cloud assessments. In India, it has led to the EU being seen as a project and European countries—including and primarily Germany, as the behemoth of the continent—being seen disproportionately through a British prism.

As the scholars Samir Saran and Britta Petersen pointed out in a recent ORF Special Report (19 July 2016), 'The British and American media have become the de facto channels through which the world beyond the Global North receives news about Europe. And if the past is an indicator, it is unlikely that these channels (US and UK media) will offer their audience coverage that is sympathetic to the EU project. For many in these two countries, this project is seen as one where the ascendancy of two countries in global affairs, France and Germany, may have upended the order that emerged at the end of World War II in Europe.'

If Europe and the EU have suffered by reportage being limited to correspondents and a news media based in Britain and the US, Germany has suffered doubly. First, the small number of Indian and German journalists stationed in their respective countries has made both dependent on third-country sources. Second, in public positioning and dissemination of a world-view, German interlocutors have been somewhat oversensitive to their EU partners. Culturally and as a goal of public diplomacy, is it Germany that is being 'sold' or the EU? This has emerged as a crucial question. It is quite apart from the dominance of the British and American news media, which is a parallel challenge.

The piquant reality is that Indians have a greater interest in Germany than in the EU as a collective. The EU is admired for its achievements, its open borders and its status as a template for underintegrated regions such as South Asia. Yet it is in Germany, as the innovation giant and largest economy in the EU, that Indian interests and aspirations are most strongly focused. How German public diplomacy finesses this remains to be seen, but finesse it needs to do.

Anecdotal evidence reveals astonishing ignorance about Germany even among well-educated and well-travelled Indians. Scepticism that Germany is a country where English is commonly understood and spoken arises fairly often, as Indians worry about a language barrier. Perhaps this is why, despite generous scholarships and financial support programmes and excellent institutions, the number of Indians who go to Germany for higher education remains small.

In the academic year 2013–14, there were only 10,000 Indian students in Germany, though that figure had doubled in the preceding five years. In contrast, enrolment in Australia, where higher education is much more expensive, was as high as 50,000 students in the same year (admittedly that number included those going for higher degrees as well as those going for professional and vocational diploma courses).

Indian outbound tourists, growing appreciably, are unaware of the diversity of Germany. It is a fair bet that most well-off Indians, when asked, would identify Checkpoint Charlie and the Brandenburg Gate as of tourist appeal in Berlin, but would not mention the city's under-reported and unappreciated museums. Statistics would bear this out. Indian travellers going abroad constitute one of the fastest-growing outbound tourism markets in the world. In 2020, the United Nations World Tourism Organization (UNWTO) estimates 50 million Indians will go abroad for business or leisure. Germany is expected to capture merely three per cent of this market.

As a result (or maybe as a cause) Indian travellers would prefer London's museums to Berlin's, and Switzerland and the Austrian Alps to the Bavarian Alps. It is a choice exercised out of ignorance. The absence of a popular media and entertainment exchange between the two countries has framed monochromatic stereotypes, and this is a two-way problem. Tackling it also needs to be a bilateral effort.

III

With the exception of the frenzy that greets Shah Rukh Khan films in Berlin and nearby pockets of Germany—a few nightclubs are known to have 'Shah Rukh Nights' or 'Bollywood Nights'—India is still the age-old land of high culture and a middling economy to a wide section of German society; and Germany to many Indians is still the stiff, largely homogeneous and native-language-speaking society it was, frankly, decades ago.

There is a need for a public diplomacy initiative to address these imbalances, but with private sector participation. The private sector has a responsibility and a stake because whether it is Indian automobile component makers that have invested in Germany or German modular kitchen manufacturers in India, business interests are driving the relationship. It has to be said though that stand-alone brands can make only a narrow impact on a larger national image.

A reinvention of Germany as a 'cool' destination, for tourists, students and skilled workers, and of India as a modernizing economy far removed from the thick tomes in an Indology Studies library, is necessary to give the relationship a contemporary feel. Specialists realize this but there is a gap in the public imagination. One mechanism to fill it is education. In the 1950s, the Indian government incubated institutions such as the five original IITs, with IIT-Madras built, as mentioned earlier, with German support.

At the beginning of the twenty-first century, the quest for world-class educational institutions is being reincarnated in an India that is demographically younger than ever in known history. In his budget speech in February 2016, the Indian finance minister announced a corpus and a provision for a new and liberal educational regulatory architecture for twenty greenfield universities—ten in the private sector, and ten with public investment. These would, so the hope goes, emerge as academic and research institutions of global standards.

The scale and ambition is there, but as yet the framework is not. It would be opportune for German educational institutions, acting perhaps as a consortium of public and private ones, to put together a blueprint for a significant (and significantly sized) university of this type, one that goes beyond just the STEM (science, technology, engineering and mathematics) template and opens avenues for students and young citizens in a twenty-first-century economy, in keeping with the workplace, creativity and manufacturing demands of the emerging post-industrial age.

It would be fitting if the initiative for this came from Germany—after identifying appropriate Indian partners, whether among private education providers or public agencies. Even the Foreign Office in Berlin has a role to play. The construction of an iconic institution of this nature will redefine Germany in the popular consciousness in India; and as such the university project should be seen as both a business investment and a transformational moment for public diplomacy.

The hypothetical university, with academic and institutional affiliations and links in Germany, and with the ability to stimulate interest in contemporary German society, could encourage students and skilled workers to look upon Germany with greater scrutiny. As a corollary, media coverage of Germany in India (and the other way around) would be beneficial.

A second project that both society and government have a stake in is crafting pluralistic and integrated societies that can act as a corrective to radicalism, particularly religious radicalism from West Asia, which has rendered itself as a global challenge today. In this regard, India and Germany have much to share with each other and the world; and it is entirely feasible that these lessons can be scaled up.

India's integration of its minorities into a democratic and, despite occasional wrinkles, a fairly easy-going society, is a prototype for many countries, whether Muslim-majority nations in the Arab regions—attempting to marry a superstructure of modernity with conservative, traditional mores of the general population—or European nations struggling to incorporate Muslim minorities of Asian origin. Despite the Syrian refugee crisis of 2015, Germany's own experience in such matters is educative. The three million Turkish people (both citizens and non-citizens) who form a very visible ethnic minority in Germany have their roots in a migration going back to the (West) German economic boom of the 1960s and early 1970s.

These different but intersecting histories provide a base for a conversation on integration and on combating radicalism, including using faith-based instruments and institutions that are receptive to agreeable messaging. In this an India–German collaboration on an integrative model could provide an alternative to, say,' the French and British models that have yielded decidedly mixed results. It could also provide the people-to-people relationship with a rigour and strategic value that has resonance beyond facile commonalities. Diplomats usually sidestep religious issues, but a genuine people-to-people bridge could use religion purposefully while attempting a useful interrogation of the social compact in both countries.

In short, as leaders in their respective regions, India and Germany have to speak as separate entities as well as conduct, subtly and with the nuance of deeply thoughtful civilizations, a negotiation between Europe and Asia. As Europe's and Asia's troubles and problems flow into each other that much more frequently, this negotiation will become even more critical. Max Müeller would have approved.

Nicole Bastian, Foreign Editor, *Handelsblatt,* has been working for the leading business and financial daily, for fourteen years, starting as Japan and Korea correspondent in Tokyo in 2002.

Since 2007, she has been working as a banking correspondent, commentator and head of the financial news department in Frankfurt and Düsseldorf, among others.

Born in 1973 in Koblenz, Bastian studied East Asian studies majoring in economics at the University of Duisburg and Doshisha Universtity in Kyoto. After a two-year traineeship at Germany's news agency Deutsche Presse-Agentur (DPA), she worked as economic editor and reporter for DPA in Hamburg and Berlin, before she started working with *Handelsblatt*.

Friendship Needs Opportunities

Nicole Bastian

It is a Bollywood adventure in Germany produced by the Indian conglomerate Essel which launched its television subsidiary Zee Entertainment Enterprises in Munich at the end of July 2016. The channel Zee One plans to build a bridge between India and Munich with Bollywood films and series, as envisaged by the German channel head Friederike Behrens. Zee One will target the mass market in Germany with its specially dubbed films and television series. The channel has engaged Indian star actor Shah Rukh Khan for marketing purposes, to raise the interest of the German audience. With free reception and financed by advertising, Zee One hopes to be profitable within three years.

The channel has to rely on the German audience, since Germany lacks a large diaspora with only 86,000 registered Indians in contrast to the European market or the United Kingdom, where there is a large Indian audience and Bollywood films are among the most watched. So far German audiences have had limited interest in structurally unfamiliar Indian film productions.

Given the size of the Indian film sector—India produces more films per year than any other country—it is amazing to see the niche presence of Bollywood films in the competitive German television market. And this is the case despite the fact that the largest Indian film festival in Europe is held in Stuttgart annually, and various other film festivals and some Bollywood series are shown by channels like Arte or RTL II.

A special interest channel exclusively showing Indian films and television series is an opportunity to increase the interest of the German people in Indian films and in India. Friendship needs opportunities. Even Johann Wolfgang von Goethe knew this. 'Friendship can be created only practically, win endurance practically,' wrote the German poet. This practical generation needs encounters. A television channel can trigger this.

The relationship between India and Germany is positive at the level of citizens, culture and media. It is also dynamic. The exchange between both countries has become stronger as is demonstrated by a glance at the trade and investment figures, and tourist and student numbers. The relationship is, however, not passionate or extraordinary.

Germany enjoys a rather good reputation in India. Based on the Anholt-GfK Roper Nation Brands Index, Indians have selected Germany as having the fifth best image worldwide. Germany's reputation in India is marked by German machines and cars, by football players and Formula 1 drivers, by beer, bread and chocolate. This is not wrong, but not so multifaceted. Relatively young German film and design, German start-ups or the social discussion on dealing with refugees at the moment, are lesser-known aspects of the country.

The image of India in Germany is rather traditional—Ayurveda, yoga, Mahatma Gandhi and an idealized image of the country, which may date back to the enthusiasm of German romantics for a traditional India as a counter model to Europe with its secularism and belief in progress. Another image is of an India that is a developing country with considerable potential to fight poverty, hunger and environmental problems. Critical tones like that of Günter Grass in his polemics about Kolkata may be seen by the Indian educated elite as an improper, condescending approach from abroad.

A third India picture in Germany is dominated by the symbol of the upcoming economy, the soon-to-be most populated country of the world and enormous success stories in industry, IT or the pharmaceutical sector, thus creating great business opportunities.

The stronger economic exchange between India and Germany—their bilateral trade volume has more than trebled in the past ten years—is a great opportunity for deepening and extending mutual perception. Any encounter with another culture in professional work motivates a more intensive interest in it. The encounter can create new images which can replace the stereotypes.

The limited knowledge that the people of the two countries have of each other is also due to the fact that Germany and India are not a priority for each other in a multipolar world. These days Germany is more than ever occupied with Europe. In the face of three rescue packages for Greece, the Brexit vote for the exit of Britain from the European Union (EU) and a remarkable disunity of the twenty-eight EU member states on the migration question, the EU has to be rescued and reshaped.

Additionally, there is the conflict with Russia due to the Ukraine crisis. Outside Europe, the US remains Germany's most important political and economic partner and also has great influence via literature and film, press and radio. China has also become a focus point for Germans because of its economic and international political significance.

Germany's political orientation has an influence on German parliamentarians as well as German media which is focused strongly on Europe and America. The reporting about India has increased with the economic rise of India and its growing economic links with Germany. The launch of a smartphone for little more than three euros in India was followed with as much interest by the German press as the reform steps and setbacks of the government of Prime Minister Narendra Modi. Both countries are also linked by foreign policy issues like the reform of the United Nations Security Council.

There is also growing interest in German media about the multi-ethnic states of India with their growing ambitions and social challenges, which are so different from Germany. Some German papers and radio stations have their own correspondents in India, but special correspondents in India are still the exception for newspapers.

Growth markets like India are important for the *Handelsblatt* which currently covers the third-largest economy of Asia from its bureau in Bangkok. *Handelsblatt*'s South Asia correspondents based in Bangkok travel to India regularly, given the growing economic importance and dynamism of the country.

For India, too, the association with the US and Britain as well as the Arab region is stronger than that with Germany. This, again, is reflected in the reports of the Indian media about Germany. Important political and economic news from Germany is not covered in Indian newspapers which do not have correspondents in Germany the way they have in Britain. Ironically, the first Indian TV station was established with German support.

The German language is an additional access barrier, compared to English-speaking countries. Study trips or Indo-German exchange grants give journalists a certain insight, but actually living in a foreign country provides the most direct insights about issues which may not be noticed otherwise.

Friendship between two countries needs encounters. It is a good sign for the German–Indian relationship that the number of German tourists in India has increased dramatically in the past ten years to reach 239,000. The trend is clear. Looking to China, it is evident that there is potential for further increase. China has received more than 600,000 tourists from Germany per year in the past five years.

The discrepancy is greater in the other direction: India cannot compete at all with the 2.5 million tourists from China who visit Germany every year, while India recorded 278,000 private and business trips of Indians to Germany in 2014.

So far, most Indians travelling to Germany have been business people. The German Centre for Tourism (DZT) wants to establish a positive image of Germany with targeted marketing in India and strengthen the awareness of Germany as a 'travel destination in the heart of Europe'. It plans to promote Germany as a 'soft and inviting product, which corresponds to the demands and mentality of Indians'. The DZT will rely on shopping opportunities, romantic destinations and emphasize family journeys and leisure parks due to the strong family orientation in India to convince Indians to travel to Germany.

With a growing middle class arising from its ongoing economic growth, there are likely to be more Indians in a position to finance a journey to Europe. In China, the rapid increase of tourist numbers to Germany coincided with its economic development.

Learning the language is central to a lasting connection with a country. The Goethe Institut, which is still named after the German Indologist Max Müller, teaches German to about 17,000 Indians in India annually. In addition, the Indian national school chain Kendriya Vidyalaya Sangathan (KVS) teaches about 15,000 school students German in cooperation with the Goethe Institut. After a meeting between Chancellor Angela Merkel and Indian Prime Minister Narendra Modi in 2015, both governments declared in their bilateral government consultations that they will promote German as a foreign language in India and promote the teaching of modern Indian languages in Germany.

Indo-German societies, the Goethe Institut, and broadcaster Deutsche Welle have been helping to strengthen bilateral relationships at the level of citizens to create opportunities for friendship and interest. The number of Indian students in Germany has more than doubled in the last four years to reach nearly 12,000 registered students. Here, again, the comparison with China shows that a further increase is possible.

About 28,000 students from China were registered in Germany. The number of German students in China is much higher than the estimated 1,000 German students in India.

Germany and India and their societies differ in many ways—religion, economic development and even the role of individuals, women and marriage in society. However, both countries are also united in many ways. Both systems are democracies striving to have an influence in a multipolar world. Flexible alliances in security, climate or economic policy have become essential between the two countries too.

Greater economic links between Germany and India could be strengthened with political cooperation opportunities and a more intensive exchange in tourism, media and culture. The economies of both countries complement each other well. Additional stimuli could come, for example, with German support and business investment in the smart cities project in India; with progress in the negotiations for a free trade agreement between the EU and India; or with the takeover of each other's enterprises.

Discussing bilateral issues in the media, literature and films, and during the everyday lives of the people is the least discernible component of a bilateral relationship. However, there are many points of contact. Salman Rushdie or Arundhati Roy with her novel *God of Small Things*, Aravind Adiga with his social criticism or Vikas Swarup, whose novel *Q&A* was the basis for British director Danny Boyle's film *Slumdog Millionaire*, demonstrate that Indian or Anglo-Indian authors do touch the German audience with their works.

The internet makes it possible to pursue special interests in an increasingly complex and differentiated world, across continents and without time delays. This long-tail phenomenon, via social networks like Twitter or Facebook, provides an opportunity to think about topics outside the mainstream, and encourages encounters between India and Germany. Social media might also help develop platforms like festivals, newspapers or radio stations to awaken the interest of the general public, and to motivate intellectual debate and dialogue between the public in the two countries.

It is a good sign when this dialogue takes up critical topics, such as climate policy or nuclear weapons, in a growing relationship between two countries. The 'true, active, productive' friendship, as Goethe wrote, 'is that we keep up with life, that the friend approves my intentions, I approve his and that we go together no matter how different our way of thinking and living might be'.

Opportunity for the Mittelstand

◈

Mario Ohoven
'Impulses for a German–Indian Partnership 4.0'

◈

Gurjit Singh
'Opportunity 2.0 for the Mittelstand in India'

Mario Ohoven has been successful in the fields of investment banking and asset managing. Holding senior positions in a group of companies, he has been instrumental in developing tax-optimized investments for his clients. His group of companies is amongst the market leaders in its field, with a total investment of more than $4 billion.

His book *Die Magie des Power-Selling* was a bestseller for over three years, and is in its thirteenth edition and has been translated in twelve languages.

Since 1998, Ohoven has been the president of BVMW, the most powerful of the non-statutory small and medium enterprises (SME) associations. BVMW represents over 270,000 enterprises with a total of nine million employees. At the end of 2002, 2007 and 2013, he was re-elected to the top post at BVMW with an absolute majority every time.

Since 2002, he has been the European president of CEA-PME, which is the European confederation of associations of SMEs.

In 1999, Ohoven was awarded 'The Europe Prize of the European Business Institute' EWI, Switzerland. In October 2001, he was awarded the 'Oscar of the German Medium-Sized Business', and in December 2001, he received the 'Curator of Medium-Sized Entrepreneurship' prize.

His advice has been sought for the World China Economy Summit, the Malenter Symposia of the Dräger-Foundation, the University of Applied Sciences from the Deutsche Bundesbank, the German Manager-Symposium and the opening of the world's largest computer fair, CeBIT.

Impulses for a German-Indian Partnership 4.0

Mario Ohoven

India and Germany have traditionally enjoyed amicable relations. This finds expression in their close cooperation in the political, economic, cultural and scientific fields. In the context of an increasingly globalized world, it is necessary to further intensify and expand the proven partnership between the two countries in order to jointly tap future potential, for example in the field of Industry 4.0.

With this in mind, I would first of all like to give an overview of the current situation in Germany and India. Twenty-five years after it launched its economic reforms in 1991, India, which is continuing its economic catching-up process despite occasional setbacks, is on the threshold of another historic moment.

- Over the past ten years, India's gross domestic product has been growing by an average of 6.3 per cent per year.
- The proportion of the middle class has doubled from 1.7 per cent in 2001 to 3.5 per cent in 2015. At the same time the poverty rate, i.e. the number of people who have to manage on less than the equivalent of $2 per day, has decreased from 85.1 per cent to 68.7 per cent.
- Last year, India improved its ranking in the Global Competitiveness Report of the World Economic Forum by an impressive sixteen places to rank 55.
- In 2016 and 2017, experts expect India to grow at 7.5 per cent each year.

These are impressive figures. However, it is well known that where there is light, there are also shadows. There have been similar positive forecasts in the last twenty-five years but India has not been able to decide the race against China in its favour. This is because of a serious backlog in the development of its infrastructure, the sluggish approach to reform and last but not least, the slow bureaucratic machinery. This has corresponded to the common image of the elephant as a cumbersome colossus which can crush investors with its weight.

However, this biased observation does not do justice to the elephant in its entirety. Analogously, this applies to reviewing India's economic strength and India's development potentialities together since the elephant is a very intelligent creature which can run very fast once it has begun to move... By the way, I support the views of British economist Joan Robinson who wrote at the beginning of the twentieth century, 'Whatever you can rightly say about India, the opposite is also true.'

In 2016, why are the signs in India pointing to a sustainable turn for the positive? Why is India now facing a quantum leap in development which cannot be compared to its leap twenty-five years ago?

It is psychology which is responsible for at least 80 per cent of economic decisions. In other words, it is the mood in the country which is essential. Prime Minister Modi generated a new spirit of optimism when his government came to power over two years ago. The government has set itself ambitious objectives, in particular with the programme Make in India, and the objective to strengthen the manufacturing sector by facilitating the investment conditions in the country.

And in doing so, India has achieved notable successes:

- Starting from an industrial share of 15 per cent, India has gone on to achieve an industrial share of 17 per cent. The target for 2022 is 25 per cent. This would roughly correspond to the value of Germany.
- Foreign investments increased by a remarkable 16 per cent in the first half of 2015.
- New project announcements have increased for the first time in three years, by more than 20 per cent.

Important and necessary steps in the reform process were the introduction of facilitated approval procedures as well as the establishment of an authority which can immediately intervene in case of delays in the setting up of companies, and which can remove obstacles in the way.

India can take a technological leap forward if it links its existing service portfolio, especially in the IT sector, with a corresponding increase in the value-added chain of the manufacturing industry in the national economy. Small- and medium-sized enterprises (SMEs) play an outstanding role in India, a fact our association can fully confirm.

The German Association for small-and medium-sized enterprises

(BVMW) is the largest voluntarily organized representation of these enterprises in Germany. Within the scope of our SME alliance, we are speaking for more than 270,000 companies in all sectors with a total of more than nine million employees. Every year, our three hundred representatives nationwide have more than 600,000 direct on-site contacts with SMEs.

This is why we, unlike any other association, know what makes the German small firm sector 'tick', and understand where the real problems of entrepreneurs lie. Our approximately 2,000 events per year also support the local and regional small firm sector. Above our organization is the so-called 'Senate' which consists of more than two hundred outstanding entrepreneurs and 1.1 million employees, and represents a total turnover of 98 billion euros annually.

Moreover, among the voluntarily organized economic organizations, the BVMW is the only association which maintains a network of thirty foreign offices. These offices cover forty countries in the world's growth regions, especially India!

For the German SMEs, the past few years have resembled a roller-coaster ride when you consider the development of the world markets, and in particular the development of the emerging countries, most notably the BRIC states of Brazil, Russia, India and China. Lately, the negative headlines in the German media have become more frequent: 'The BRIC emerging countries are in a crisis,' the headlines claim. The media is talking about a 'faded glamour', particularly with regard to the economic boom in China, which has been the global bearer of economic hope in recent years.

This burden of hopes—and of course, I regard this in the positive sense—is now borne by India. Hence, initiatives such as 'Make in India Mittelstand' have become even more important. BVMW has massively expanded its presence and expertise in India in the past two years and we are also registering an increasingly higher interest in India from our circle of members. Indian companies are also showing greater interest in Germany's leading SME association. With the help of BVMW, Indian companies are acquiring German business partners and gaining access to the German market.

We have just received a mandate by the West Bengal state government to support their efforts in attracting more investors from Germany. An advance delegation has already visited Düsseldorf, Stuttgart and Munich, and major investor conferences have been planned in these cities in 2016.

We would like to intensify this bilateral exchange by further extending our presence in India and by looking for new possibilities of cooperation with other trade associations. For this purpose, our association has established a German–Indian network of consultants, with former executives from the German industry, in order to provide SMEs with industry-specific support in the Indian market.

At the Hannover Messe (Hannover Fair), 2015, BVMW signed an agreement with the Engineering Export Promotion Council which the Indian press described as the most significant agreement of the entire trade fair. Indian Minister of Commerce Nirmala Sitharaman and other high-level representatives of the Indian Department of Commerce, with whom the association has been maintaining a close relationship, were present when the agreement was signed.

Currently, we are planning the conclusion of a bilateral agreement with the SME Chamber of India. For this purpose, we have invited its president Chandrakant Salunkhe to Germany. Our objective is to bring SMEs from both nations together to create synergy.

Indian interest in German SMEs once again demonstrates the significance that the brand 'Mittelstand' has achieved worldwide—and deservedly so. More than 99 per cent of all companies in Germany are medium sized, employ 70 per cent of all employees and provide 80 per cent of the vocational training in the country. They are also extremely successful on an international level and are referred to as the 'hidden champions'.

The term 'hidden champions' originates from German economics professor Hermann Simon. A 'hidden champion', according to his definition, is a company:

- which is among the top three worldwide, or number one in the continent of its origin.
- which generates a turnover of less than five billion euros.
- which is known to the public.

According to these criteria, there are 2,734 'hidden champions' worldwide and as many as 1,307 companies of these are German Mittelstand!

For comparison: Germany is followed by the US with 366 companies and Japan with 220. If you take the number of 'hidden champions' per inhabitant as a basis, then the result is just as remarkable. Here, too, Germany is ranked at the top, followed by Luxembourg, Switzerland and Austria—which are basically German-speaking countries—ranked no. 2 and no. 4 respectively and the US drops to rank no. 14.

What is the secret of the 'hidden champions'? An essential element is undoubtedly their extraordinary innovative strength. A glance at the patent statistics confirms this fact: with an overall number of 130,000 patents between 2003 and 2012 as well as 1,590 patents per one million inhabitants, Germany has a significant edge over its competitors. In terms of per capita values, Japan achieves just a little more than half of this value.

With thirty-one patents per 1,000 employees, the 'hidden champions' make more than five times as many inventions as major enterprises. Furthermore, they are characterized by their proximity to customers which is five times higher than in the case of major enterprises. More importantly, 'hidden champions' exhibit relatively low labour turnover rates and low sickness absence rates. And they have strong corporate leaders who unswervingly adhere to their fundamental values and manage with flexibility.

Precisely this very management approach of sustainability and longevity, which is characteristic of the German SMEs enterprises, is more manifest in India than in any other country. After all, many believe in the idea that the duration of human existence is not a factor of individual actions!

India also possesses the important prerequisites for innovation and digitalization, in order to be in the vanguard of development in the future. Thus, the country ranks among the market leaders in the field of IT, and the global IT industry, among them the company SAP from Germany, has been relying on India for years. For SAP, India is the second largest development site in the world.

The IT industry is increasingly joined by the branch of production. The German automobile industry had ignored India for too long, but that has changed in the past five years. Mercedes and BMW are represented in India, and Volkswagen has invested in a large car factory. This led to an increase of attractiveness for the supplier industry. Needless to say, these companies are also supplying to Indian automobile companies whose market is growing dynamically.

Another sector in India with a future is the pharmaceutical industry: India has very productive pharmaceutical companies which is why the pharmaceutical industry from Germany is increasingly investing in India. Meanwhile, the chemical industry and the machine engineering industry have also discovered India's potential.

At present, India is trailing behind other countries as a production location, in the worldwide ranking, but it intends to play a more important role in this sector in the future, and I am convinced that it will be able to do so. Investments in 'Industry 4.0' are imperative to achieving this objective. This means a massive leap for some companies that are still at the stage of development of Industry 2.0, that is which have automated only partially.

In production, Industry 4.0 requires a completely new generation of robots. Therefore, many companies in India are now being given the opportunity to start with the latest state-of-the-art technology. The Indian appearance at the Hannover Messe 2015 has clearly emphasized the country's willingness to race to catch up.

The fact that India and its innovative companies are taking giant steps forward was also demonstrated at Hannover Messe 2016 where the German robot manufacturer Kuka and the Indian IT service provider Infosys have founded an Industry 4.0 joint venture. According to Infosys, the objective of the collaboration will be the development of a new software platform to provide customers with the collection, evaluation and use of process data.

Kuka is additionally working on connecting machines with an Industry 4.0 cloud platform. Apart from the automobile industry and robotics, urban development definitely constitutes another paramount example for the application of Industry 4.0 in India.

A joint project of Acatech and the Indian National Academy of Engineering has highlighted the potential in this area. Among the emerging countries, India offers particularly good opportunities for Industry 4.0; with the 100 Smart Cities programme, the Indian government is already taking concrete steps towards intelligent industrial production. New jobs are being created in this sector as well as in the service sector around the industry.

Here, Germany has been asked to come up with innovative ideas. Particularly promising would be the promotion of pilot projects of medium-sized cities in which SMEs companies from the automotive, IT or pharmaceutical industry are advised in terms of the technologies of Industry 4.0. For emerging countries that are well positioned for Industry 4.0, it would be possible to create a toolbox with instruments by means of which governments can develop their infrastructure—IT, urban development, regulatory and socio-economic prerequisites—for Industry 4.0.

If we succeed in integrating Industry 4.0 in the cities of the emerging countries, we would strengthen the growth as well as the environmental compatibility of the economy in these countries. However, what is required to achieve this objective are properly functioning logistics systems as well as a reliable supply of energy and water. It will be the well-educated people who will benefit the most from the jobs created in Industry 4.0. Investments in training and development are also likely to reach the poorer and uneducated sections of the population. Only then will Industry 4.0 contribute to the prosperity of the country and its fight against poverty.

Finally, I would like to take a look at a field in which India has vaulted to the top worldwide. I am talking about the start-up scene which has become a real shooting star in India. About $9 billion in capital investment could be gained in 2015, after $2.2 billion in the previous year. With 4,200 start-ups, India is ranked third behind the US and Britain. Notably, start-ups in India have achieved success without any government promotion programmes which will now be introduced under the new Startup India initiative.

Start-ups, which establish new ideas and business models, constitute the future of economic development, not only in Europe but all over the world. Interestingly, in the US, 22 per cent of the most innovative companies were founded after 1965, and 56 per cent were founded before 1925. In Europe, two per cent were founded after 1975 and 86 per cent were founded before 1925. What does this imply? Start-ups need better funding opportunities, for example, by means of fiscal incentives for venture capital.

In the US, approximately $20 billion of venture capital is invested per year, in Europe just about four million dollars are invested. Given this situation, it is no wonder that Silicon Valley attracts innovative founders while Europe is less attractive for start-ups. In this respect, Europe and especially Germany may learn a lot from India.

Thus, it is important that the millions of SMEs companies in both India and Germany collaborate as closely as possible in the project Industry 4.0. Because the online world doesn't have any borders, national solo efforts will no longer achieve the objective. On the European level, BVMW is active in the digital field and supports start-up businesses and the establishment of new business models in the context of workshop discussions between SMEs companies and start-ups under the aegis of the Federal Ministry of Economy (BMWi) in Berlin.

In 2016, our association has put the focus on the topic of digitalization. Thus, BVMW is involved in the national IT summit process; since March 2016, we have been holding the Kompetenzzentrum Mittelstand (Competence Center Small and Medium-Sized Enterprises) 4.0 in Berlin and Brandenburg which is sponsored by BMWi. In terms of digital literacy, there are already existing contacts with Microsoft, in particular regarding the planning of a digital education pact. With the European SME umbrella association European Entrepreneurs, we recently resolved a common issue regarding digitalization in Europe.

Let's work together and tap the enormous future potential which digitalization is already offering SMEs in both India and Germany. This way we will be able to take the cooperation between Germany and India to a new level. It is time for a German–Indian partnership 4.0.

Opportunity 2.0 for the Mittelstand in India

Gurjit Singh

Among the largest focal points of India's renewed economic engagement with Germany is Opportunity 2.0 for the Mittelstand in India. As Germany looks at Industry 4.0 and a rejuvenation of its strong Mittelstand attributes, there is a need to think of a new engagement between the Mittelstand model and the demands of Industry 4.0 and emerging opportunities in India.

The Indian small- and medium-sized enterprises (SME) sector has been the backbone of the Indian economy and the source of its dynamism for several decades. It has played a major role in our exports and also in expanding manufacturing and services, thus generating employment across India. Bringing industrial patterns to rural areas has been one of the keynotes of the development of Indian SMEs. India currently has more than 48 million SMEs which contribute more than 45 per cent of India's industrial output and 40 per cent of the country's total exports, and create 1.3 million jobs annually.

The Make in India initiative has brought new opportunities for SMEs. The Indian laws for SMEs are also being revised and will provide a greater impetus to making Indian SMEs more competitive and able to link with overseas partners, particularly in the spirit of Industry 4.0.

SMEs can nurture and support the development of new-age entrepreneurs who have the potential to create globally competitive businesses from India. The establishment of a vibrant entrepreneurial ecosystem is expected to increase the share of SME contribution to India's GDP to 15 per cent by 2020. The 'Digital India' revolution also provides a great opportunity to promote SME participation in the information, communication and telecommunication (ICT) sector, in line with the government's vision.

Indo-German economic cooperation has a long history. It stands on a solid foundation and currently, Germany is India's largest European trading partner. SMEs of both countries are driving this success story both on the trade as well as investment fronts. There is potential for collaboration and continuous exchange of knowledge not only in the traditional sectors of engineering and automotives but also in the emerging sectors of high technology manufacturing, digitalization and environmental technologies. The complementarities between the two countries and their economies provide an opportunity to unleash their potential.

The German Mittelstand are the heartbeat of Germany's successful industrial economy accounting for more than 99 per cent of German companies having a total turnover of over 2 trillion euros. These companies are typically middle-sized family-run businesses with unity of management ownership, and are focused on a single product. They contribute nearly 52 per cent of Germany's economic output, employ more than 50 million people and supply big exporters, contributing two-thirds of Germany's GDP.

These companies are the most innovative in Europe and supply their products all over the world. Many of them are considered 'hidden champions', world market leaders in their segments. There are about 2,700 companies worldwide in this category and it is incredible to note that about 1,300 of them are located in Germany.

The German Mittelstand in many ways can serve as a role model for the development of Indian SMEs despite their variation in size. The rise of the German Mittelstand into a pillar of the economy is something that India needs to closely examine and draw lessons from. German Mittelstand companies are typically long established and family owned, and are often located in rural areas. They spread employment and investment across the country.

Following Germany's reunification, the state offered tax and investment incentives to Mittelstand companies to set up businesses in the East. A decentralized banking and finance system, where large numbers of regional and local banking institutions like Sparkassen (independent and locally managed savings banks) and Volksbanken (cooperative banks) concentrate on business activities and Mittelstand clients in the regions where they are situated, has been helpful.

Further, linking business and community, Mittelstand firms are the main beneficiaries and supporters of the German apprenticeship system. About 60 per cent of young Germans train as apprentices in a range of fields, including manufacturing, IT, banking and hospitality. The 'dual training' system allows trainees to divide their time between classroom instruction at a vocational school and first-hand experience on the job at a company. Employing 83.2 per cent of trainees, the Mittelstand companies invest in skilled workers for the future. They are credited with Germany's comparatively low youth unemployment rate of less than 6 per cent.

A network of research institutes support the Mittelstand in Germany. For example, the prominent Fraunhofer-Gesellschaft (Fraunhofer Society), an independent non-governmental organization that provides high-quality, short-term, applied research that SMEs could not otherwise afford. It has been critical to the growth of Mittelstand companies in Germany.

We need to look closely at the German Mittelstand supported by a Fraunhofer model, so that our SMEs are able to further strengthen their contribution to the Indian economy. Each of these initiatives is equally relevant for India to meet the challenge of generating jobs and developing a skilled labour force, stimulating innovation in manufacturing and creating a financial, educational and business ecosystem that serves the company and the country.

These are the traditional strengths of the German model that have evolved through history. However, there have also been modern adaptations, for instance, the rise of 'micro-multinationals' where a number of Mittelstand companies, headquartered in small towns and rural Germany, are world leaders in specialized, niche products or services, with offices and subsidiaries across the globe. Examples include Kärcher's high-pressure home and office cleaning equipment, Stihl machinery and tools, PolyClip System food packaging.

These German companies, already advanced, are now studying the next leap forward. We also need to examine Germany's industrial sector and import concepts like the German-style Meister schools to produce masters of a technical trade. Both Germany and India have a strong base of locally funded SMEs with an ingrained entrepreneurial ethos, family-firm tradition and a vast network.

India and Germany have complementarities that can make them effective partners. Germany has an ageing population and stagnating domestic demand. As an export-oriented economy, Germany is always looking for newer markets. One of the complementarities is, for example, that German industry is facing a growing challenge from the inadequacy of local IT skills. While German expertise lies in engineering for state-of-the-art products, futuristic technologies require IT innovations as products are becoming increasingly integrated with the internet. Industry 4.0 adds new emphasis to this.

In such a scenario, Germany will need greater IT expertise and training in the coming years, which is exactly where India's strength lies. There is a lot of potential to convert these complementarities into possibilities, particularly given the current conducive environment for greater foreign investment with the improvement in the ease of doing business. The true potential of Indo-German relations lies in attracting SMEs that form the base of the German industrial sector.

The Potential Benefit which Indian Companies can get from Germany

The German Mittelstand needs to be harnessed quickly. India–Germany SME cooperation can be the perfect mechanism for the Indian government's Make in India effort to strengthen the manufacturing sector and make India the world's preferred manufacturing destination. Active efforts to step up our engagement with the German Mittelstand in order to attract them in large numbers to India is being undertaken by the Indian Embassy in Berlin.

Our efforts saw a quantum jump with the launch of the Make in India initiative. India's impactful participation at the Hannover Messe 2015 as the partner country with the theme of the Make in India helped the German business community, particularly the Mittelstand, develop an interest in India.

To take advantage of this renewed interest, the Indian Embassy in Berlin implemented a strategic market entry support programme 'Make in India Mittelstand' (MIIM) in September 2015, aimed at encouraging and facilitating German Mittelstand companies to enter the Indian market and help create successful business ventures. The programme is being implemented with the support of the Indian Department of Industrial Policy and Promotion (DIPP), the Investment and Technology Promotion Division of the Ministry of External Affairs, and select states of India where German companies have significant business interests.

Since its launch, the MIIM programme has undertaken significant confidence-building and capacity-building exercises to convince German SMEs to invest in India. Under the programme, companies are also being adequately equipped and briefed about different aspects of doing business in India through specialized workshops conducted by experts on topics such as company incorporation, taxation, cross-border taxation issues, location assessment for manufacturing, logistics and supply chain, sourcing and localization, financing options, pricing strategies and distribution channels, human resource management and best manufacturing practices.

The programme has offered direct support to companies on matters such as market assessment, partner search, allotment and land analysis, company registration, market assessment and strategy formulation, tax and legal topics, technology and intellectual property rights, visa matters and liaising with government authorities, etc. This support being offered by the programme has been critical to speeding up the investment decisions of German SMEs.

The German Mittelstand's overwhelming response to the MIIM initiative is encouraging. During the first nine months of the MIIM initiative, the German Mittelstand committed an investment of over Rs 3,000 crore (400 million euros) for the Make in India initiative. As of July 2016, the MIIM programme had enrolled fifty-two companies, out of which thirty-two companies had concrete investment plans. The investments are strategically spread out, with the industrial and environment sectors leading with a 56 per cent share followed by the mobility and consumer goods sectors.

These investments will result in the setting up of sixteen new manufacturing plants, six expansion projects and three pilot projects covering the states of Maharashtra, Gujarat, Karnataka and Tamil Nadu. Five companies have successfully formed joint ventures (JVs) and incorporated their wholly owned subsidiaries (WOS) in India. Five more companies are in the process of setting up their JVs/WOS in the months ahead. The MIIM programme will expand its outreach to the German Mittelstand to bring on board new companies that are keen to become part of Make in India.

The MIIM programme has emerged as the perfect complement to the Mittelstand-driven German economy. It is playing an important role in strengthening Indo-German economic partnership, particularly among the SMEs of the two countries. The MIIM programme has become the fast-track mechanism for the German Mittelstand in Germany, which German SMEs can leverage to realize their investment plans for India.

In addition, the decision to set up a fast-track system for German companies in the DIPP, which has been operational since March 2016, is also a positive step towards promoting not only Indo-German economic relations but also greater participation of German SMEs in the Make in India programme.

We have initiated diverse efforts focused on different sectors and themes to mobilize investments and technology from German SMEs into India under the MIIM programme. As part of this, the Indo-German Business Dialogue, a high-level business platform, was set up by the Indian Embassy in Berlin in partnership with German Member of Parliament (MP) Mark Hauptmann, to encourage and facilitate new investments by German companies into India.

Its first meeting was attended by German MPs, and over 250

representatives of the German industry, Chambers of Commerce, industry associations, academia and think tanks, on 8 June 2016 at the embassy, to promote the opportunities in India for German SMEs. The discussions revolved around how greater partnership can be forged between the two countries under Make in India within the three core pillars of Mittelstand, technology and skill development, the core areas of convergence. This has been done on a smaller scale in other areas of Germany like Brilon, Bremen, Hamburg, Baden-Baden, Düsseldorf, etc.

We have attempted to engage the SMEs sector-wise for promoting investments into India to identify globally advanced manufacturing trends and innovations in cutting-edge technologies for today's industry and exploring business collaborations through innovation in the Indian manufacturing sector. The embassy had organized a symposium on 'Indo-German Innovation Partnership through Industry 4.0' on 25 April 2016 during the Hannover Fair 2016. Focusing on our long-standing engagement with the traditional engineering companies of Germany exhibiting at Hannover Messe 2016, the embassy had organized a workshop during Hannover Messe 2016 on 'Make it in India Mittelstand: Succeeding through Sustainable Partnerships' to tap further potential of German engineering companies for Make in India.

India is rapidly moving on the path of urbanization. Significant measures are being taken by the India government to ensure the use of clean and green technology in all sectors to ensure green, sustainable and climate-friendly development. This has opened up a new area of partnership with Germany, which has a strong environmental industry covering water and waste technologies. To leverage this convergence, the embassy organized a business event on 'Opportunities for Indo-German Partnership in Water, Waste and Sanitation' on 30 June 2016.

The engagement has helped intensify cooperation between India and Germany in the waste and water sector through meaningful dialogue and discussion. German companies have expressed keen interest in participating and contributing to the Ganga Rejuvenation Mission, Swachh Bharat Abhiyan and the Smart Cities Mission of the Indian government. Several German companies from the waste management and waste-to-energy sectors are also keen to expand their footprint in India.

The German Engineering Federation (VDMA), which is the largest industry association in Europe and Germany's apex mechanical engineering industrial association representing over 3,100 mostly medium-sized companies in the capital goods industry, has indicated its intention to enhance engagement with India. Over six hundred VDMA members are already present in India in the manufacturing sector and their success stories need to be brought to the wider attention of German SMEs.

The VDMA and the embassy will be working together for close cooperation under the MIIM initiative to support German Mittelstand companies that are also members of the VDMA. There is a lot of potential to enhance cooperation with VDMA member companies on various national schemes such as Make in India, Skill India, etc.

In the same manner, we are planning to engage with SMEs across several other sectors through partnerships with individual sectoral industry associations like the German Electrical and Electronic Manufacturers' Association, German Association of the Automotive Industry, Association for the German High-Tech Medium-Sized Business (Spectaris) etc., and other associations such as the Federation of German Industry and the Association of German Chambers of Commerce and Industry, to broad-base German presence in India which so far has been dominated by companies from the engineering and automotive sectors.

Most of the large German companies have been in India for some time, as have many of the medium-sized ones, and their number remains at about 1,850. Most of these companies seem to be clustered in the states of Karnataka and Maharashtra. An expansion of the India–Germany economic relationship is expected to occur when a larger number of Mittelstand take it upon themselves to look at India and assess the opportunities there.

The example set by a number of such companies in India is indeed noteworthy. It was heartening to learn that at the annual general meeting of the Indo-German Chamber of Commerce held in Düsseldorf in June 2016 to mark its sixtieth anniversary, the president of the chamber, Hubert Reilard, who is also the Managing Director of EFD Induction Pvt. Ltd, Bengaluru, said, 'Those who have not yet come to India must do so quickly; those who have already invested in India must expand.' This was indeed a ringing endorsement of India, where German companies have done very well overall.

India needs Germany's Mittelstand companies to bring in capital, technology and their management expertise. Many of the companies already operating in India make niche products and are valuable members of the Indian growth story.

What are some of the significant points which must be looked at ahead? First, most German companies tend to go it alone in India. They may have branches, manufacturing units or subsidiaries, but very few have Indian partners. Some have indeed had good experiences while others are muted in their response. How can a greater trust be created between Indian and German business-to-business (B2B) contacts to achieve a larger number of JVs?

Similarly, very few German companies list on the Indian stock exchange. This is in keeping with German Mittelstand companies' key attribute, which is that most of them are closely held family enterprises. But in India, listing can provide these companies with many advantages which can be beneficial for their expansion.

Secondly, German Mittelstand companies almost always finance themselves from their internal resources with limited support from local banks. When it comes to raising finances, particularly for working capital, they normally do not adapt to local financing opportunities, be it from banks, bond markets or stock exchanges. In a way, this is good since they bring in foreign direct investment (FDI), but a greater integration of German Mittelstand companies in India with the Indian market in financial terms will be a positive move. This is again linked to the level of confidence and trust and perhaps a larger role for consulting companies.

Thirdly, some German Mittelstand companies remain concerned that the real market size in India is not perhaps as big for their type of products as perhaps for a consumer product. This often inhibits their thinking. It must be realized that large markets do not open up frequently. The opening up of China, and after the end of the Cold War, of Eastern Europe, can only be matched by the opening up of India.

Market size can be viewed incrementally rather than in a static manner. At the same time, India's regional free trade agreements (FTAs) and access to the Association of South East Asian Nations and its upcoming engagement with the Regional Comprehensive Economic Partnership (RCEP) with a larger Asian market and with Africa has not been discussed or thought about by German decision-makers. There is a lot of discussion about the Transatlantic Trade and Investment Partnership and to an extent the Transatlantic Trade Partnership, but the RCEP, which is perhaps going to be the world's biggest FTA, does not command much attention and thus perhaps, is a lost factor in decision-making.

One of the problems German companies face in India is that in large infrastructure projects or tenders, there is always a 30 per cent local content clause which inhibits them from bidding, or creating effective consortiums. This again is linked to the fact that large German companies go into India without carrying many of their friends or ancillary makers along. Each German company prefers to go it alone, and find its own market for its projects or services rather than travel overseas in a pack.

As a matter of fact, German companies prefer to operate alone even in their home country, and rarely come together like the Japanese Keiretsu. The 30 per cent local content 'challenge' is actually an opportunity for a larger German company to ask its friendly Mittelstand companies to start producing something in India which they would require for their project, and thus offer an assured market for products of their choice.

A smaller German company could then enter India assured that they would have a clear market on a near-exclusive basis. If they tie up in a JV with an Indian company, they would have an even better chance of success for other projects which are tendered, since the Indian partner would have local knowledge of the business atmosphere. This is an idea which needs development.

Conclusion

German Mittelstand companies are important strategic partners for the success of India's Make in India, Digital India and other programmes. Many have evinced interest in India and entered the market. But their numbers can easily be quadrupled. Strenuous efforts have been made by the Indian Embassy and Indian consulates in Germany through a variety of events and sensitization and information programmes. The effort to overcome the hesitancy of many Mittelstand companies is a continuing one and we remain confident that the growth story of India, and a positive view of treating challenges as opportunities, will make it much easier for Mittelstand decision-makers to see for themselves that India is truly incredible.

Overcoming Deficit in Trade Issues

◈

Jayanta Roy
'Indo-German Trade and Investment Partnership: The Road Ahead'

◈

Timo Prekop
'India and Germany as Economic Partners'

Dr Jayanta Roy, Senior Economic Adviser, Deloitte, is an internationally respected trade economist with close to forty years of post-PhD development experience worldwide, having worked as a regional lead economist in the World Bank, and economic adviser in the Commerce Ministry in India. He specializes in the area of trade policy, including World Trade Organization (WTO) policies, regional and bilateral trade agreements, special economic zones (SEZs), trade and transport facilitation, and industrial policy.

As economic adviser, he was part of the team that brought in economic reforms in 1991 and opened up the Indian economy. Dr Roy has also served as the principal adviser on trade and globalization in the Confederation of Indian Industry (CII).

He has taught at the World Bank Institute, Cornell University, the University of California at Santa Cruz, the University of Warwick, UK, and the Indian Institute of Management, Kolkata. He is a regular columnist for *Business Standard*. Dr Roy is now a senior economic adviser to Deloitte. Dr Roy holds a PhD in Economics from the University of California, Berkeley.

Indo-German Trade and Investment Partnership: The Road Ahead

Dr Jayanta Roy

Introduction

Germany and India are poised to be strong strategic partners in the coming decade. The evolving global trade landscape is dominated by global value chains (GVCs) with trade in goods and services intertwined with technology. Connection to GVCs is required to boost exports of goods and services, attract foreign direct investment (FDI), create employment and lead to inclusive growth. Germany is very well connected to GVCs through the European Union (EU) and its trade relationships with the US and Asia. Its automobile and pharmaceutical sectors provide clear evidence of that.

India, on the other hand, is yet to be well connected to the regional and global value chains. It is still plagued by high trade transaction costs with an urgent need for trade and logistic facilitation reforms. India has focused extensively on IT and IT-ES and Mode 4 of General Agreement of Trade in Services (GATS) (temporary relocation of labour) in its trade negotiations, and not paid sufficient attention to diversifying into other professional services such as accounting, engineering, architecture, design, product development, and legal and medical services that are globally delivered, combining tasks being done by professionals in various locations. India has a distinct niche in these services, and a strong capability in technology. Indian Prime Minister Narendra Modi's Make in India's initiative is a clear move in these directions.

India's regional efforts so far have largely been uncoordinated and free trade agreements (FTAs) have been established with some success only with Singapore. India has also invested a lot of negotiating energy in FTAs, mostly in goods and some services, with industrialized economies like Japan and the EU where its market access gains in goods are likely to be marginal, given that the tariffs there are already low, and agriculture and a liberalized visa regime are not likely to be agreed upon in these trade agreements.

Instead India should prepare itself for the two mega-regional partnerships—the Trans-Pacific Partnership (TPP) and the Transatlantic Trade and Investment Partnership (TTIP)—which will enable it to be connected to the world's largest GVCs. The US in the TPP, and Germany in the TTIP will be its main partners.

Our route should be to join the TPP first, and thereby connect to the TTIP. Germany will no doubt be the most important trading partner like the US to link us better with the GVCs in automobiles, pharmaceuticals, software (big data), and many other areas, including the professional services cited above.

This is the future of the India–Germany trade and investment strategic partnership. With both the 2016 US presidential contenders—Hillary Clinton and Donald Trump opposing trade deals, and with the recent most disappointing result of Brexit, TPP and TTIP will no doubt be delayed a bit. But ultimately, wisdom will prevail, and most countries will realize that integration is key to growth and income distribution through the jobs it will create. No country has yet survived with an isolation policy relying on protectionism. The strong private sector in both the US and EU will push for the full implementation of these mega-regionals.

Recent Developments in Indo-German Relations

The exchange of summit-level visits in 2015 marks another milestone in India–Germany relations. Bilateral ties comprise a comprehensive array of issues, including those of strategic significance. Trade and investment are crucial areas with bilateral trade having reached almost $17 billion. Germany is already the seventh-biggest investor in India. Indian investment is over $6 billion in Germany.

Both countries have agreed to cooperate in the energy and high technology sectors vis-à-vis the Make in India and Digital India programmes. Eighteen bilateral agreements were signed during German Chancellor Angela Merkel's visit to India in October 2015. Furthermore, an alliance on climate change, energy and technology, called the 'Indo-German Climate and Renewable Alliance' was created to build a comprehensive partnership in the field of renewable energy.

Another important milestone achieved was the setting up of a 'fast-track mechanism' for approving and assisting German investments in India. Japan is the only other country which enjoys this special facility. While almost all major German companies with global brand recognition are already in India, most foreign investors complain about endemic corruption, red tape, bureaucratic inefficiency and the inadequate infrastructure they have to face in India.

Germany's role is changing. It also has a major role to play in re-surfacing the India–EU free trade talks especially after Indian Prime Minister Narendra Modi made a special appeal to his German counterpart on this issue. Negotiations are being held to solve key issues such as tariffs on goods and services, market opening and government procurement. During the last round of negotiations held in April 2013 and January 2016, the two sides discussed finding a common landing zone on all the unresolved issues obstructing their talks, including automobiles.

India and Germany Market Overview

Germany and India are at two different stages of development. While one is a developed country, the other is an emerging market economy. In terms of nominal GDP, the German economy in 2015 had a GDP of $3,438.7 billion compared to India's which stood at $2,100 billion in the same year. Even though Germany has been hit hard by the Eurozone crisis, its GDP was about twice the size of India's in 2013. In terms of nominal GDP per capita as well Germany is about thirty times the size of India.

Trade is an important component of the GDP of India and Germany. The share of trade to GDP was 85 per cent in the case of Germany and 49 per cent for India in 2015. While Germany has a positive trade balance in its global merchandise trade, India has a negative trade balance with the rest of the world. In trade in services, India has a positive trade balance, whereas Germany has a negative trade balance.

Regarding workforce, India's large workforce is more than ten times that of Germany. In 2014, India had a workforce of 496 million compared to 42.5 million workers in Germany. India's working age population (15–59 years) is expected to reach more than 900 million by 2030. This young and growing workforce is an advantage for both the manufacturing and services sectors; it keeps the cost of production low, making India a favourable location for setting up business and manufacturing units. At the same time, skilled workers from India can contribute to the industry and services sectors in Germany.

The discussion in the preceding paragraphs shows that the Indian and German economies complement each other in several ways. The growing middle class in India provides opportunities for German companies to invest and cater to the Indian population. At the same time, India's large skilled workforce complements the technological capabilities of German companies.

German companies are also competent in providing infrastructure services, and India needs investments in infrastructure sectors such as construction and logistics. As argued earlier, India can become part of the GVCs of German companies, thereby enabling them to spread their risk. Access to the German market will help Indian companies cater to the wider EU market. Bilateral investment flows can help both countries. German companies can help the Indian economy develop its manufacturing facilities, leading to technological upgrading; diversify its research base; develop the organized services sector; and reduce unemployment. Meanwhile, Indian companies can help German companies reduce costs, improve their global competitiveness and diversify their production networks.

Economic Partnership Analysis

Germany is India's most important trading partner within the EU and the sixth most important trading partner worldwide. Bilateral trade between the two countries stood at $19.18 billion in 2015–16, according to the export–import databank of India's Ministry of Commerce. Apart from traditional sectors, knowledge-driven sectors hold good potential for collaboration. There is considerable scope for cooperation in the fields of IT, biotechnology, renewable energy, green technology, urban mobility and development, and the entertainment industry.

India's Export to Germany (2011–15)

Year	India's Export to Germany (Value in US$ '000)
2011	8,260,406
2012	7,133,757
2013	8,081,320
2014	7,745,249
2015	7,023,455

Major Indian exports to Germany include textiles, metal and metal products, electro-technology, leather and leather goods, food and beverages, machinery, pharmaceuticals, auto components, chemicals, gems and jewellery, and rubber products.

Germany's Exports to India (2011–15)

Year	Germany's Export to India (Value in US$ '000)
2011	15,211,502
2012	13,445,408
2013	12,219,924
2014	11,884,510
2015	10,891,079

Major Indian imports from Germany include machinery, electro-technology, metal and metal products, chemicals, auto components, measurement and control equipment, plastics, medical technology, pharmaceuticals, and paper and printing materials.

Total Bilateral Trade (2011–15)

Year	Total Trade (Value in US$ '000)
2011	23,543.93
2012	21,571.99
2013	20,448.22
2014	20,325.20
2015	19,182.03

Current Issues Faced by Indian and German Exporters

1. Barriers for German Companies in India

The key issues faced by German companies in India include lack of trade and logistics facilitation, lack of ease of doing business, inadequate infrastructure, dearth of information and clarity on procedures and regulations, particularly with regard to tax and foreign investments.

- **Lax law enforcement:** Even though India has an elaborate legal system in place, enforcement is weak which leads to operational uncertainty. Also, there is a general perception that the interpretation of a law depends on an individual officer residing in India, so issues are unnecessarily complex. In general, the majority of German companies have expressed low faith in the Indian legal system.

- **Corruption and bribery**: While most German companies face this barrier in India, in Germany bribery is an offence under the law, since Germany follows the anti-bribery convention. If a German company makes informal payments, it faces a legal trial in Germany.
- **Issues related to taxation**: Multiplicity of taxes in India makes the overall tax burden higher even though tax rates in India are lower than in Germany. Notably, corporate tax in India is higher than in Germany. Moreover, companies have to pay several state taxes and duties if they want to establish a pan-Indian presence. In addition, taxes are imposed spontaneously in India, such as the retrospective tax policy, which adds to operational uncertainty. German companies also face difficulties in realizing a refund of duties in India.
- **Profit repatriation**: The dividends earned by foreign owners residing in India can only be transferred once the operations are closed, and after the payment of taxes. As per the India–Germany Double Taxation Avoidance Agreement (DTTA), dividends may be taxed in both countries, with some exceptions. As a result, some Germans reinvest the dividends, but it is not their preferred option.
- **Infrastructure bottlenecks:** Infrastructure facilities which enable manufacturing are not as good in India and are located in remote places with poor road and port connectivity. This is true even of SEZs and industrial clusters. Even if companies are located in states with major ports, the roads connecting the ports are not well developed, leading to losses and pilferage during transportation. Storage and warehousing facilities in India are inadequate, and most companies have to invest in these facilities. German companies such as Deutsche Post (DHL Express) have invested in logistics services in India; however, they are unable to operate in verticals such as the processed food supply chain due to lack of supporting infrastructure in India.

2. Barriers Faced by Indian Companies in Germany

- **Language and culture:** Knowledge of the German language is a precondition to working in Germany. There are also differences in the work culture between India and Germany. The labour union regulates the salaries and grading of employees, while the worker council determines work timings.

- **Meeting standards**: Germany has strong health and safety regulations, and its health and safety standards are much higher than those in India. As a result, Indian companies have to make very high investments to meet German standards.
- **Local employment:** The staff strength of most Indian companies has to be at least 25 per cent German. It is not easy to get Germans with the required skills in software and consultancy services, because most of the good quality workforce has been hired by German companies. Indian companies have to work very hard on employee branding and human resource practices to ensure a good quality workforce. In addition, it is difficult to get an independent professional unless the individual has been appointed to provide services for specialized products such as new software.
- **Legal system**: Indian companies consider the stringent legal system in Germany a barrier. This is particularly true for small- and medium-scale enterprises.
- **Market saturation:** In some sectors, the German market is getting saturated and, therefore, there is limited scope for Indian companies to operate and expand. For instance, it is expensive to set up retail banks in Germany; and Indian banks face strong competition from German banks.
- **Work permit and visa regulations:** Indian companies often complain of problems in work permit and visa regulations in Germany, which constrains their economic relations. Indian government officials in Germany say visa norms are so stringent that even they face problems in getting their family members to Germany. Easing procedures related to visas and work permits will promote bilateral trade between the two countries. In 2010, both countries established a 'hotline' mechanism to resolve visa-related issues, but little improvement has been seen in this regard.

3. Sector-specific Barriers

An in-depth analysis of the literature available from various sources gives some useful insights about sector-specific barriers in Germany.

- **Information technology**: Data protection laws in Germany are more stringent than Indian laws and, as a result, companies cannot host any data in India. Indian companies in Germany have to make huge investments in data centres in Germany and the staff has to undergo special training to understand data-specific regulations.
- **Banking:** Unlike other countries where the capital of the parent company is treated as the capital of the branch, this is not the case in Germany. In Germany, each branch has to bring in capital, and the total capital from India for that bank is subject to a ceiling of 150 million euros. In addition, each bank can give a loan of up to 25 per cent of its total capital base. While the EU has strict banking regulations, Germany is even more stringent and follows the Basel III40 norms that have more stringent capital adequacy and liquidity requirements than what is followed in India.
- **Legal services:** German legal companies need to establish a presence in India to provide information on German laws and regulations, and also facilitate business development in both markets. However, foreign lawyers and law firms are not allowed to practise in India.

Recent Developments: Resolving Existing Barriers

- During their recent engagement, both India and Germany affirmed the fact that Make in India is an instrument along with other Government of India initiatives, that has the potential to open up investment opportunities for German companies.
- The two countries agreed that India's participation as a partner country at the Hannover Messe fair in 2015 created a positive momentum for business.
- Both sides have agreed to actively work towards scheduling the joint working groups and other mechanisms of the Indo-German Joint Commission in India in 2016, to identify new areas for practical business cooperation.
- Both sides have agreed to identify opportunities for high technology collaboration in priority areas of manufacturing under the Make in India programme, in particular defence manufacturing, through regular meetings.
- Indian Prime Minister Narendra Modi and his German counterpart stressed that India's railway modernization and expansion plans will

open up commercial opportunities for German companies in high speed rail, station redevelopment, rolling stock manufacturing, and logistics terminals, and urged the private sector to explore early participation in this sector.

- Both sides have welcomed the intense cooperation under way in the automotive sector. They have encouraged their business enterprises to enter into arrangements for co-development and co-production of commercial aviation and defence equipment in India, including transfer of know-how and technologies.
- With an aim to promote financial transparency and eliminate double taxation, both sides have decided to negotiate for amending the existing DTTA, including the Article on Exchange of Information.
- Both countries have agreed to collaborate towards developing climate-friendly, efficient and sustainable solutions for India's expanding energy needs. It should be noted that over the years Germany has offered assistance to India on many development projects, and committed 1.49 billion euros in 2015.
- With regard to visas, both sides have agreed to initiate discussions on simplifying their respective visa procedures and make them as easy and transparent as possible, especially for business persons, entrepreneurs and investors, professionals and students, journalists and members of non-governmental organizations, who contribute substantially to the development of bilateral ties.

The Road Ahead

The Indo-German strategic partnership must be aligned with the vastly evolving trade and investment landscape that is highlighted by the emergence of GVCs that have taken over from the production of goods to tasks with services and technology embedded in them. Most exports are going to go through this process, which offers both Germany and India opportunities to participate in, and link up with, these GVCs through the TPP and TTIP.

India can transform Prime Minister Modi's Make in India initiative into a big opportunity for growth and employment in this changed global trade scenario with Germany and other lead countries in GVCs, for the reasons summarized below:

- India has a very dynamic services sector and a very remarkable technology capacity, which are essential for task-oriented GVCs.

- India is still a small player in GVCs with much room to grow. Its micro, small and medium enterprises hardly participate in GVCs, unlike in Southeast Asia, China, Korea, Japan, Mexico and some East European countries.
- FDI, especially efficiency-seeking FDI linked to creating a hub in India, is at a dismally low level. Most of India's FDI is market-seeking, catering to a large domestic market.
- India is ideally placed to be a supply chain hub given its proximity to fast growing Southeast Asia and East Asia.
- Most importantly, India now has a government that has embarked upon an outstanding foreign policy which just needs to be complemented with next-generation trade and investment reforms.

However, India needs to move quickly to actual policy reforms to seize this window of opportunity. Transaction costs continue to remain high, and India's performance in major indices measuring trade facilitation and efficiency of cross-border movement of goods is still dismal. The World Bank's Doing Business Indicators ranks India 130 out of 189 in 2014, for trading across borders. India is also behind its competitors, at 35, in the Logistics Performance Index rankings.

Some of the key issues in trade facilitation that should be on the immediate agenda of the government to promote trade with Germany and other major trading partners are:

1. To rely on a system based on trust, with reliance on self-certification of importers, ex-post audits, and minimal physical inspection.
2. Introduce full automation leading to a paperless system with minimum face-to-face contacts and signatures. Unfortunately in India, the mindset is still geared towards a paper-based system with numerous face-to-face contacts. It is a pity that with its software capabilities, India has not yet moved to a fully electronic system.
3. Cargo dwell time should be reduced to levels comparable to the best performers in Southeast Asia—from weeks to hours.
4. Most importantly, there should be quarterly monitoring of cargo dwell time in major ports and airports by an Inter-Ministerial Trade Facilitation Committee (IMTFC) with the full attention of the prime minister, preferably chaired by him.
5. Accelerate the move towards a comprehensive single-window system

that integrates the customs department with allied agencies and the Directorate General of Foreign Trade, as well as with the excise department. This single window needs to run on a single operating platform. It needs to be maintained by a single service provider, and not be a message exchange system between different operating environments.

The other area of policy intervention would have to be logistics infrastructure development. The various freight corridors need to be made operational quickly. State governments need to be made stakeholders in the process of freight corridor development, not just in terms of infrastructure development, but also in terms of policy reforms. States need to become partners in the development efficient corridors that link India's hinterland to key international air and sea gates.

Trade and logistics facilitation is a dynamic national challenge. It is essential that the government considers putting together a team drawn from businesses, think tanks, technocrats and logistics practitioners in the IMTFC headed by the Prime Minister to provide continued direction to this all-important agenda. It is also essential that the concerned line ministries are made accountable for the speedy implementation of the recommendations of the IMTFC.

With manufacturing-related wages in China increasing, and other competitors like Vietnam, Thailand and Indonesia lacking the depth of Indian manufacturing and the economies of scale of India's domestic market, the time is ripe for India to make a serious bid to become a critical player in global GVCs. But to do so, it would need to ensure minimal transaction costs behind the border, at the border, and across the border.

This is the direction that will forge a strong and sustainable trade and investment partnership between India and Germany.

Timo Prekop, Executive Member, Board of OAV—German Asia-Pacific Business Association, started his professional career with Deutsche Bank AG in Hamburg in 2003. In 2005, he was appointed senior relationship manager for Deutsche Bank AG in Ho Chi Minh City and headed the Project Management Office for Private and Business Clients of Deutsche Bank AG in Hanoi from 2007 to 2009.

After his return to Germany in 2009, he worked in corporate banking for Deutsche Bank AG in Bremen/Oldenburg. Prekop became Executive Member of the Board of OAV—German Asia-Pacific Business Association in November 2010.

India and Germany as Economic Partners

Timo Prekop

The economic, political and cultural relations between India and Germany have historically grown and been enhanced over the past few years. Germany is now the most important trading partner for India within the European Union (EU) and a major source for foreign direct investment. India, in turn, is increasingly being seen as an attractive trading partner for German companies.

However, despite India's huge economic potential and the business-friendly reform agenda successive Indian governments have been following since 1991, German trade with India has remained lower than its potential. With the Make in India campaign and other national initiatives launched by the Modi government in 2014, the image of India has markedly changed and it is now a promising emerging market country.

India's economic fundamentals stand strong, and global interest in it is on a steady upswing. Still many German companies, especially small- and medium-sized enterprises (SMEs), are somewhat cautious to enter into trade with India and to invest in the subcontinent.

What is holding them back? How can bilateral trade and investments be boosted, so that both countries can fully explore the enormous potential their strategic partnership offers? How far can bilateral trade and investment be fostered through the conclusion of the free trade agreement (FTA) negotiated by the EU and India since 2007? What opportunities and challenges would be involved for German and Indian companies?

With a population of approximately 1.3 billion people combined with high economic growth rates of around 7 per cent in the past few years, India is poised to become one of the world's largest and most attractive economies. Besides population size and high economic dynamism due to favourable demographic trends, the attractiveness of India as an emerging market is due to its huge and largely English-speaking labour force, a rising consumption-oriented urban middle class, combined with a rapid pace of urbanization providing numerous business opportunities for German companies. Therefore, India has become an increasingly important trading partner and location for German investments.

Consequently, trade has picked up rapidly in the past few years. Germany has consistently been among India's top ten global trade partners. In Europe, Germany is India's largest trading partner. India was ranked twenty-fifth in Germany's global trade during 2015. Bilateral trade in 2015 was valued at $17.33 billion and increased by 8.5 per cent compared to 2014.

In 2015, Indian exports to Germany accounted for $7.56 billion, making India the sixth largest supplier country from Asia after China, Japan, Taiwan, Vietnam and South Korea. Indian imports came to $9.77 billion, resulting in a German trade surplus of $2.2 billion in 2015.

India has become the fourth largest market within Asia for German companies after China, South Korea and Japan. Major Indian exports to Germany are textiles, metal and metal products, electro-technology, leather and leather goods, food and beverages, machinery, pharmaceuticals, auto components, chemicals, gems and jewellery, and rubber products.

Major Indian imports from Germany are machinery, electro-technology, metal and metal products, chemicals, auto components, measurement and control equipment, plastics, medical technology, pharmaceuticals, paper and printing materials. There is considerable scope for cooperation in the fields of IT, biotechnology, renewable energy, green technology, infrastructure, urban mobility and development.

Germany is the seventh largest foreign direct investor in India since January 2000. German foreign direct investment (FDI) in India in 2015 was to the tune of $1.14 billion. Germany's total FDI in India from January 2000 until March 2016 amounted to $8.64 billion There are more than 1,600 Indo-German collaborations and over 600 Indo-German joint ventures in operation. At present, German investments in India are mainly in the sectors of transportation, electrical equipment, metallurgical industries, services sector (particularly insurance), chemicals, construction activity, trading and automobiles.

Most of the major German companies have already entered the Indian market. German automobile giants such as Daimler, Volkswagen, BMW and Audi have established manufacturing plants in India. Other major German companies that have significant operations in India include Siemens, ThyssenKrupp, Bosch, Bayer, BASF, SAP, Deutsche Bank, Metro, Lufthansa, Merck, and Munich Re. Besides large companies, German SMEs (Mittelstand) have started showing greater interest in doing business in India.

Indian investments in Germany have also increased remarkably in the last few years. Indian companies have invested over $7 billion in Germany and there are more than two hundred Indian companies operating in the country.

The IT, automotive, pharma and biotech sectors have received the lion's share of Indian investments. Major Indian software providers such as Infosys, Wipro and Tata Consultancy Services have operations in Germany with direct access to their German clients. Companies like Bharat Forge Limited, Ranbaxy, Piramal, Samtel, Hexaware Technologies, NIIT, Graphite India Limited, the Hinduja Group, Dr Reddy's Laboratories, Biocon, Hindustan National Glass, Mahindra and others have either acquired German companies or started their own subsidiaries.

Bilateral trade and investment volumes have shown high growth rates in the past, reflecting the vast potential for economic cooperation between the two countries. However, growth rates in trade and investments could be far higher. Until recently, the UK was an important location for Indian investors since the companies operating there had open access to the European single market. After the Brexit decision in June 2016, Germany is likely to be reassessed as an increasingly attractive investment location in Europe providing additional scope for bilateral cooperation in the above-mentioned fields.

Realizing the huge potential and synergies of a deeper economic partnership between Germany and India, a strategic partnership between the two countries was signed in the year 2000, along with a number of cooperation agreements in various fields to remove major obstacles to trade and investment. This strategic partnership is continuously being strengthened by high-level state visits from both sides.

With several institutionalized arrangements such as the Joint Commission on Industrial and Economic Cooperation, Foreign Office consultations, High Technology Partnership Group, High Defence Committee, Indo-German Energy Forum, India–Germany Committee on Science and Technology and several sectoral joint working groups, business-friendly reforms have been systematically brought forward.

Intergovernmental consultations were established between the two governments to identify and review policies, programmes and ideas in relevant areas to steadily intensify cooperation and facilitate business exchange. The third India–Germany Inter-Governmental Consultations were held in New Delhi in October 2015. One important outcome was the setting up of a fast-track system for German companies in the Department of Industrial Policy and Promotion within the Indian Ministry of Industry and Commerce, which represents a paramount step to ease market access for German companies in India.

Trade with India is still regulated by some protective trade policies and various forms of trade barriers. However, within the World Trade Organization (WTO) framework, the general tariff level in India has continuously been reduced even though tariff rates are still high—in particular in the automotive sector—besides additional duties, detailed regulations for the proof of origin of imported products, certification rules or specific product standards and other non-tariff trade restrictions. These result in long import procedures and high transaction costs for German companies in India.

FDI in India is still restricted by investment ceilings imposed by the government in some strategic and sensitive sectors. The main investment barriers, besides bureaucratic procedures, bottlenecks in infrastructure and energy supply, are limited access to land, lack of qualified manpower and a non-uniform tax system. In addition to these, companies tend to hold back their investments because of legal uncertainties concerning conflict resolution, and patent and data protection.

India has been persistently seeking to improve its business infrastructure for foreign companies, and has stepped up its efforts to open its economy for international business. India improved its rank in the World Bank's Ease of Doing Business Index by four places in 2015, and was ranked 134th out of 189 countries. The Indian government has subsequently been confronted with the dilemma of promoting economic growth and generating employment for the millions of young Indians entering the labour market each year, and to making economic growth inclusive and sustainable.

To achieve high economic growth rates, India has to depend on foreign capital, know-how and innovative production technologies. But to avoid mass destruction of jobs in the informal sector which accounts for 90 per cent of employment, the Indian government can only gradually liberalize the external sector.

The Modi government has therefore, been following a business-friendly reform agenda to facilitate trade and investments with a focus on transforming the India into a manufacturing hub for Indian and foreign companies. Mass employment in the industrial sectors is expected to be generated through the Make in India campaign and other national initiatives such as the Smart Cities, Industrial Corridors, Clean Ganga and the Renewable Energy Mission, etc.

The strong emphasis on the promotion of industrial production in twenty-five core sectors signifies numerous business opportunities for German companies reflecting their comparative advantages and strengths in delivering machinery and equipment, know-how and innovative production technologies for various industrial sectors, for example, infrastructure development, energy conservation and sustainable development.

Often perceived as inconsistent, the gradual liberalization approach mirrors the dilemma of the Indian government to attract foreign investors on the one hand and to avoid, on the other hand, negative employment effects in the non-competitive informal sector endangering the source of income of millions of Indians. It also reflects the political challenges for Indian government towards economic liberalization.

The current government does not have the necessary political majority in the Upper House of Parliament to pass nationwide investment, tax, land and labour reforms. Consequently, liberalization can only follow a gradual approach and can often be accomplished on a selective basis, such as the fast-track system granted to German companies.

One precondition to further enhance economic cooperation is to better understand India's development needs and its specific investment climate and market dynamics, as well as to translate perceived trade and investment barriers into business opportunities.

India is a very attractive but rather complex and demanding market, especially for SMEs. The advantage of German companies, however, is that India's needs and priorities, that is, that is, for renewable energy, are Germany's strengths. Thus, manifold business opportunities could be exploited through mutually beneficial cooperation which is continually being intensified by both governments through numerous cooperation agreements.

Furthermore, India can not only be seen as a potential huge market, but should also be regarded as a test-bed for market development for German producers of innovative sustainable technologies. With its progressive integration into the Asian market in the course of its 'Look East Policy', India can also serve as an important export hub for German companies.

Against this background, both governments reconfirmed, during the third Inter-Governmental Consultations in October 2015, that the intensification of trade and investments remains the core element of bilateral cooperation, especially in those areas where the investment priorities of the Indian government correspond to the strengths of German industries, that is, infrastructure development, renewable energy, water and wastewater management, vocational training, sustainable development and innovations.

With the Digital India initiative, it is envisaged that cooperation in fields such as Industry 4.0 and the Internet of Things will be strengthened. Also more state-to-state and city-to-city cooperation MoUs are envisioned. Both governments also emphasized the need for open markets to further deepen their bilateral trade relationship and attract foreign capital.

Therefore, high importance has been given to negotiations within the WTO framework. Germany and India have agreed to closely cooperate on relevant trade issues in harmony with their WTO mandate, contributing to the success of the Doha round during the tenth WTO Ministerial Conference in Nairobi, Kenya, in December 2015.

Given the high dependence on foreign capital, bilateral free trade negotiations are seen as an alternative to multilateral trade talks. Negotiations show quicker results and are less complicated. Market access can be granted on a selective basis.

To date, India has negotiated twenty-eight FTAs of which thirteen are currently in force—in Asia (Singapore, Malaysia, Korea, Japan and Association of Southeast Asian Nations [ASEAN]. The integration with Asian production, trade and investment networks is seen as being critical to India's economic future. To protect Indian industries, market access is granted on a preferential basis for a wide range of products, and limited in some critical industries through a list.

For German companies operating in India, the FTAs with Asian countries would mainly be advantageous. India's attractiveness as a potential export hub would increase for some industries due to the more open access to Asian countries from India. The competitive advantages of Indian exporters of machinery and equipment over German companies in Asian markets are likely to be limited since tariffs for machinery imports in other countries, for instance, in ASEAN countries, are already comparatively low.

The FTA between India and the EU has been negotiated since 2007. Trade volume between India and the EU increased from $46.3 billion in 2006 to $77.3 billion in 2015. After twelve official rounds of negotiations till 2013, and high growth in bilateral trade, the FTA has still not been concluded. Negotiations on the India–EU FTA should therefore be resumed as soon as possible. A compromise needs to be found between the demands of the German industries for open, unrestricted and non-discriminatory access to the Indian market, and the more gradual policies followed by the Indian government.

From the German perspective, the Modi government has adopted an extreme protectionist stand in trade negotiations by adhering to high tariffs and local content regulations, protecting sensitive home industries, and setting specific Indian business standards. The following issues thus need, to be negotiated or solved: the complete and symmetric abolition of import and export tariffs in the industrial and consumption goods sectors (especially in the automotive sector); the simplification and digitalization of import procedures in accordance with WTO standards; the simplification of rules of origin, regulations for the protection of intellectual property rights compliant with WTO rules without any separate treatment for India; more transparent rules for public tendering at the national and federal level; open market access for services and industry-related services; clear rules to avoid (new) non-tariff barriers such as national product certification security requirements.

From the Indian perspective, the FTA cannot be concluded unless the EU opens the labour market for Indian engineers and skilled workers, allows cross-border trade in services, opens market access for the most important Indian export goods such as textiles, leather, chemical and pharmaceutical products, lowers the subsidization of agricultural products, grants India data secure status and provides adequate protection for Indian investments.

The list of demands and open issues is long. So it is not surprising that negotiations on the EU–India FTA are complicated and cumbersome, and both parties need to compromise on some issues. Even though there is a mutual understanding on the economic necessities of the negotiation partner, a conclusion of the FTA is not very likely in the near future. The trade talks were not resumed as planned in September 2015 since critical issues could not be solved even though both sides were willing to further enhance the bilateral relationship.

With a better understanding of India's future economic significance and specific development needs and resultant business opportunities, bargaining positions in ongoing trade talks should be adopted where compromises can be made. Many German companies still need to realize India's growing attractiveness as an economic partner. In the years to come, Germany might become more dependent on India than vice versa, since India is also 'looking East' and is successfully developing production and investment networks with its economic partners in East Asia and Southeast Asia.

Being equal cooperation partners, the partnership between India and

Germany could translate into an 'engine of innovation' while synergizing the commonalities and accommodating the diversities of Germany and India to promote common solutions for inclusive growth and sustainable development—to mutual interest and benefit.

Corporate Social Responsibility as a Developmental Auxiliary

◈

Bernhard Steinrücke
'Commitment for Sustainable Growth'

◈

Azim Premji
'Corporate Responsibility as a Strategic Imperative'

Bernhard Steinrücke, Director General, Indo-German Chamber of Commerce

Bernhard Steinrücke was born on 29 June 1955 in Frankfurt. He studied Law and Economics in Vienna, Bonn, Geneva and Heidelberg. He obtained a Law degree from the University of Heidelberg in 1980. He took the special exam in tax law in 1982 and the bar exam at the High Court of Hamburg in 1983.

He worked with Coopers and Lybrand, Treuhand Vereinigung Chartered Accountants, Hamburg, from 1982 to 1984 and then joined Deutsche Bank as a graduate trainee. Bernhard Steinrücke was assistant to one of the managing directors of the board of Deutsche Bank. His career at Deutsche Bank is given below:

1989–91: General Manager of Deutsche Bank, Idar-Oberstein

1991–93: General Manager of Deutsche Bank, Colombo

1993–97: General Manager of Deutsche Bank, Bombay, and Joint Chief Executive Officer, India

In 1997, he left Deutsche Bank and became managing partner and speaker of the board of ABC Privatkunden-Bank, Berlin. Since July 2003, he has been Director General of the Indo-German Chamber of Commerce/AHK Indien.

Commitment for Sustainable Growth

Bernhard Steinrücke

I. Outline

Corporate social responsibility (CSR) has always been practised by German companies in India and presents one of the many important fields of mutual interest and cooperation between the Republic of India and the Federal Republic of Germany. Bearing in mind the global necessity to enhance sustainability, CSR has significant potential to further strengthen Indo-German engagement.

While there are many definitions of CSR, each definition underpins the impact that businesses have on society at large. This essay showcases the CSR activities of German companies in India against the backdrop of differing conceptual perceptions and the changing legal frameworks of CSR.

In Germany, the idea that business has duties to society is nothing new. Even before the introduction of a state-catered welfare system at the end of the nineteenth century, many German corporates were providing social benefits to their employees and local communities. A notable example is the Augsburg merchant family Fugger, which established subsidized housing for the first time in modern history.

It was also the Fuggers who built the bridge from the old continent to Asia by funding some of the Portuguese fleet expeditions to India. This was not only the beginning of European economic commitment in the Indian subcontinent, but also the trigger for an era of successful cooperation between Indian and German companies.

In Germany, there is no such thing as legally binding CSR regulations. The approach to CSR by German companies is defined by the European Union's view of CSR as a source of competitiveness, innovation and economic development, alongside its various environmental and social laws. The prevailing notion in Western Europe is to practise CSR as a component of sustainability: factoring the social and environmental impact of conducting business is important for competitiveness.

Accordingly, the German National Guidelines focus on compliance with the German and European legislation on labour, environmental and social requirements. The German government actively promotes CSR with the Aktionsplan CSR 2010, a comprehensive multi-target approach to enhance CSR in Germany and around the world.

CSR in India tends to be seen as a philanthropic activity, of which society at large is the beneficiary, and not the direct stakeholders of the companies. CSR activities in India have recently been subjected to a changing legal framework. Notably, Clause 135 of the Companies Act of 2013 encourages every company crossing one of three thresholds to spend at least 2 per cent of its average net profit in the previous three years on CSR activities. Furthermore, the top 500 listed companies are now mandated by the Securities and Exchange Board of India to report on their CSR performance through Business Responsibility Reports.

Today, there are around 1,600 registered German companies in India and the top thirty companies alone generated an annual turnover of about $16.6 billion in 2015, providing directly and indirectly more than 400,000 jobs. Not only are Indo-German economic relations thriving, German enterprises in India are also dedicated to boosting their CSR activities. The thirty enterprises mentioned above alone spent millions of dollars on CSR in financial year 2014–15.

India is a country of contradictions. On the one hand, India's GDP ranks third highest in terms of purchasing power parity ($7.3 billion) and is clearly a country with an unmatched potential. On the other hand, it is still home to the largest number of people living in poverty, and faces immense problems with illiteracy, environmental pollution and unemployment, especially in rural areas. Therefore, there are different needs for the implementation of CSR in India than in Germany.

Accordingly, the CSR programmes of German companies in India focus mainly on the following: public health, sanitation and drinking water, education, relief programmes, infrastructure and construction, aid for children, rural development and environmental protection measures. Hereafter, selected German companies and their corresponding CSR activities will be showcased.

II. General Overview of German CSR Activities in India

1. Top German Companies Listed on the German Stock Index (DAX30)

(a) Siemens Ltd

A company that undoubtedly has one of the longest associations with India is Siemens AG, the largest European engineering company, whose ties with India date back to the nineteenth century. It is one of the two German companies amongst the top 100 listed companies in India, and the only foreign corporation making it into the top 10 of the 2015 sustainability and CSR ranking of *The Economic Times*.

Project Asha (meaning hope in Hindi) is one of its notable CSR activities and showcases a sustainable approach towards integrated community development in rural areas. Its primary goal is to enhance the living conditions of people who live without basic infrastructure such as electricity, clean drinking water and basic healthcare. This is achieved through active participation of the community and the use of innovative technologies. Siemens employees in coordination with a local non-governmental organization and the community itself have set up the basic infrastructure for the village of Amle, including access to electricity and the construction of a water-filter system and an integrated irrigation system.

Siemens Ltd does not only engage in rural development, it also contributes to immediate emergency relief responses, for example, in the aftermath of the Uttarakhand floods (2013), the drought in Maharashtra (2013) and the tsunami-stricken areas (2014) along the Indian east coast. Apart from these social innovations, Siemens Ltd is also fostering its employee volunteering scheme and education initiative. In the wake of the German 'Energiewende', the transition towards renewable energy, the company has made environmental commitment another one of its CSR pillars.

In 2013, Siemens Ltd achieved sixth place in *The Economic Times* CSR ranking, due to its unique approach of asking its own employees in which areas the company should take action. Siemens Ltd spent a total of $956,000 on CSR projects in India in financial year 2014–15.

(b) Bosch Ltd

The second German enterprise appearing in the listed top 100 companies in India is Bosch Ltd, another company that has a long history of business cooperation with India. Taking into consideration that 92 per cent of the shares of the Fortune 500 company Robert Bosch are held by the non-profit Robert Bosch Foundation, it is hardly surprising that Bosch Ltd shows a strong commitment to CSR activities in India as well.

In the spirit of its founder's commitment to enrich lives and livelihood through technology and education, Bosch Ltd focuses on its expertise in these areas. One of the CSR approaches that makes the company unique is its CSR Promotion Program. Bosch Ltd holds events to promote CSR, thereby triggering bandwagon effects and fostering CSR awareness among the public. The company strongly believes that to achieve a lasting effect, vocational training should be given to empower people to act on their own. It therefore offers free short-duration skill training for various trade areas, for example, the automobile trade, IT, construction, services, rural trades, manufacturing, equipment repair, etc.

Other notable projects include supporting the Gujarat Cleft and Craniofacial Research Institute and the Maaya Foundation that conduct free corrective surgeries for about five hundred children born with facial aberrations every year.

The company spent $1.5 million on CSR activities in fiscal year 2014–15.

(c) Bayer CropScience Ltd

Bayer launched its activities in Asia with the setting up of its subsidiary Farbenfabriken Bayer and Co. Ltd in Bombay in 1896. India and Bayer share a long history of cooperation. Currently, the company is active in the fields of crop science, pharmaceuticals, and consumer and animal health.

Bayer's main CSR activities are centred around crop science which is the company's largest division in India.

Generally, the main objective of Bayer's CSR policy is to develop socially relevant innovative solutions and to improve the quality of life of those living in rural India. In particular, Bayer CropScience Ltd focuses on the areas of education, health, environment and livelihoods.

While Bayer's CSR policy has traditionally focused on rural development, the company has decided to take on innovative CSR projects in this area, and intends to make India a model for this change. The company has deduced the following areas for innovative CSR projects: rural development and education, preventive health and sanitation, as well as the empowering of women.

In its annual report, Bayer CropScience Ltd refers to the following flagship projects:

- **MSMS (Making Science Make Sense)**
  A programme that provides school students with an insight into everyday natural science phenomena, with the help of experiments. In the year 2014, the project incorporated over 12,000 students and thirty-seven schools across India. The programme was financed with a total amount of $66,242.8.
- **WASH (Water, Agriculture, Sanitation and Health)**
  This project is designed to improve public health through sanitation and conservation of pure natural resources. The three-year programme is being implemented with the help of the non-profit organization EFFORT, with a budget of $242,742.
- **Vocational Training**
  Created under the umbrella 'Learning for Life', the aim of this project is to foster (science) education globally. It has received $6,681.2 in financial support.

For financial year 2014–15, the company allocated $1,041,810 to CSR.

(d) BASF India Ltd

The relationship between BASF and India dates back to the sale of textile colours in 1890. Since then, interactions between the two have been characterized by fruitful cooperation. As stated in its slogan, 'We create chemistry for a sustainable future', the company has placed sustainability at the core of its CSR policy.

Balancing economic, environmental and social needs to find the best available solution for a more sustainable future, BASF India Ltd has adopted the following six projects for which it allocates a budget of at least 2 per cent of its average net profit:

- **Community drinking water plant**
  Working together with WATERLIFE India, BASF has financed the setting up of a community drinking water plant in Chennai, providing high quality, safe drinking water at an affordable price (₹7 for 20 litres of water).
- **Sanitation and waste management in Dahej**
  In this project, BASF provided the village Dahej with 130 household toilets, a community toilet, and a battery for a village e-rickshaw to collect household waste. Additionally, an awareness WASH programme on sanitation and waste management was also scheduled

to inform the villagers about the best practices on sanitation.

- **WASH project in schools**
  In cooperation with Samhita Social ventures, BASF has provided safe drinking water facilities and toilets for children studying in schools located in the rural areas of Mangaluru. According to BASF, more than 12,000 students across ten schools in Mangaluru have been covered by this project.
- **Quality education and nutritional facilities for urban poor**
  Providing free classes for school dropouts, and giving midday meals and healthcare services to children and their families are the core objectives of this project. It is located in the slums of Turbhe and Navi Mumbai, the project is directed at families with a daily income of less than Rs 180. About 200 children can benefit from this programme.
- **Activities under Sadbhavana**
  Among the many projects in the field of individual initiatives, the following are especially worth mentioning: BASF Kid's Lab, under which BASF has introduced 40,000 children to chemistry and natural science; Science Express (a science exhibition on trains) which has hosted 2.25 million visitors throughout India.
- **Activities to fight corruption in public life**
  Along with other anti-corruption projects, BASF has launched the 'Good Governance Icon Series' to reward individuals who have upheld the highest levels of good governance. It also organizes a seminar series on corporate governance and business ethics at educational institutions. The aim of the series is to instil good practices in students at the threshold of corporate India, by provoking thought on ethical dilemmas at work, discussing the BASF Icon stories and training them in the practical aspects of governance.

2. German in MSMEs India

(a) Lorch Schweißtechnik Ltd Micro, Small and Medium Enterprises

Not only are the large German companies committed to CSR in India, micro-, small- and medium-sized enterprises (MSMEs) are also doing their part to enhance the lives of Indians. One of the enterprises doing this with extraordinary success is Lorch Schweißtechnik GmbH, a leading manufacturer of welding equipment.

Being at the forefront of technology in its area of business, Lorch Schweißtechnik GmbH is well aware that a specific set of skills is required to participate in a developing labour market like India. As it is particularly difficult for disadvantaged young people to obtain the required knowledge, the company felt the need to act.

With the help of the develoPPP.de scheme of the German Federal Ministry for Economic Cooperation and Development it founded the Lorch-Don Bosco Welding Technology School of Excellence in 2014 in Pune. The school was set up as a model training facility to train disadvantaged young people and place them in jobs. By the end of 2016, around 420 young people would have completed their training there.

(b) Voith Paper Fabrics India Ltd

Voith Paper Fabrics India Ltd is a global engineering company specializing in cement and paper. It spent 2 per cent of its annual net profit in financial on year 2015–16 on CSR projects. The company fulfils its CSR obligations by providing donations to NGOs in various fields.

The company's flagship CSR projects in India include:

- Promoting primary and secondary education
- Empowering women, setting up homes for orphans
- Swachh Bharat (Clean-up India campaign)
- Mental healthcare
- Contributing to the Prime Minister's National Relief Fund

For financial year 2014–15, the company reported having spent a sum of $71,320.4 on CSR activities in India.

III. Future Prospects

It is evident that German companies have been very active in the field of CSR in India. Many German enterprises pursue a holistic approach covering several different projects at a time, often in cooperation with local NGOs. As this is certainly an easier task for large companies, India and Germany have joined forces again to help MSMEs to also successfully implement CSR measures.

The Indo-German Corporate Social Responsibility Initiative, supported by the Indian Institute of Corporate Affairs, German missions in India and

GIZ (German International Cooperation Agency), is helping a number of these enterprises carry out pilot schemes to run CSR programmes on their own in the future.

With its development programme, Germany's Federal Ministry for Economic Cooperation and Development is also helping to push innovative German businesses in India forward, whilst generating long-term benefits for the local population. Hence Indo-German success stories like the one of the Lorch-Don Bosco Welding Technology School of Excellence will not cease to be written. In the light of these initiatives, the commitment of German firms in the field of CSR will be strengthened even more, especially with regard to MSMEs.

It is evident that the commitment of German companies to CSR in India is not only a story of success but also of cooperation between equal partners for sustainable and long-lasting growth.

Azim Premji, Chairman, Wipro

Azim Premji is a graduate in Electrical Engineering from Stanford University, USA. He turned a $2 million company into an $8 billion IT, BPO and R&D services organization.

In 2001, he established the Azim Premji Foundation, an NGO to enhance quality and equity in the public school education system in India. In 2011, the foundation established the Azim Premji University.

Premji became the first Indian recipient of the Faraday Medal and has been conferred honorary doctorates by Michigan State University and Wesleyan University (in the US), and the Indian Institutes of Technology, Bombay, Roorkee and Kharagpur, amongst others.

Premji is a member of the Indo-UK, Indo-French CEO forums and the Indo-Japan Business Leaders' Forum. The Republic of France bestowed upon him the 'Legion of Honor' and *Forbes* India honoured him by naming him its inaugural 'Outstanding Philanthropist of the Year' in November 2012. He was conferred the Padma Vibhushan, the second highest civilian award in India, in January 2011.

In September 2013, Premji received the All India Management Association Managing India Awards' Corporate Citizen of the Year honour. In October 2013, he was honoured with the Asian Business Leaders Award by Asia House (UK) and in December 2013, *The Economic Times* presented him with its Lifetime Achievement Award.

Corporate Responsibility as a Strategic Imperative

Azim Premji

As I write this, many parts of India and the world are facing a heat wave and drought. Bengaluru, the city where I live, has been suffering from a sweltering summer, the hottest in the past 140 years. Parts of India have been so badly hit that water had to be brought in trainloads from distant places.

Perhaps we should not be surprised by all this. The writing on the wall, so to say, has been there for many years. Earlier in 2016 the annual Global Risk Report released at the World Economic Forum in Davos listed the risks due to water scarcity among the top five risks in terms of impact. In fact, water scarcity has been listed among the top risks for at least the past five years. The case is similar with risks like climate change adaptation, biodiversity loss, profound social instability and energy price shocks.

Such fundamental, long-term shifts in trends are being collectively characterized as the 'shifting normal', highlighting the fact that the nature of social and ecological issues facing us is changing so rapidly that yesterday's outliers are becoming today's normal. Let me cite some more recent examples of such shifts: 2015, already declared as the warmest year on record by the scientific community, was witness to several extreme weather events—severe drought in California, intense heat waves in India, Iran, Iraq and Europe followed by record-breaking rains in Chennai and coastal Tamil Nadu in India as well as in Texas and Oklahoma in the US.

We are also witness to the gradual but deep structural shifts on crucial socio-economic factors—for example, the record low oil prices with unpredictable consequences for the global economy, or the gradual desertification of North Africa leading to large-scale migration and social consequences in Europe. The common thread that runs through these examples is the close interlinking of economic, social, environmental and geopolitical factors.

In the face of such daunting challenges, the question of whether industry must step out of its narrow focus of business interest and engage with these issues is no longer a matter of debate. The moves to integrating the triple bottom-line framework and adopt corporate social responsibility (CSR) are testimony to this distinctive trend of the past two decades.

When we articulated our framework on good citizenship at Wipro in 2002 we were driven by the conviction that we must do the right thing and that we have an intrinsic responsibility to act and to try and make a difference. In my view, any business action on environmental and social issues must stem from inner conviction, commitment and passion. While legislation and regulatory directives have their place, they are unlikely to be effective if the actions are merely driven by compliance.

To the sceptic in these matters, let me offer two business arguments on why we need to act with a sense of conviction and urgency:

(i) Issues like changing climate, water stress or social instability pose serious risks to the viability of business. There are enough examples to support this point including those of oil companies having to pay billions of dollars as compensation for environmental damage. In summer 2016, in the Indian state of Maharashtra, which has been one of the worst hit by this year's heat wave, steel mills have had to shut operations due to severe water scarcity. Therefore, companies must act to prevent and mitigate such issues in their own interest.

(ii) Evidence also clearly indicates that acting in this way can lead to positive outcomes for business, such as improved operational efficiencies, new revenue models, enhanced reputation and brand value, and differentiation in the talent marketplace. For example, a study shows that there would be an estimated $500 billion of savings in the European Union alone if companies in the engineering and automotive sectors recycled and reused product components at the end of life. Another study indicates, on a conservative basis, that preserving biodiversity translates into a business value of $500 billion on an annual basis.

My assessment is that, by and large, industry and business have started recognizing the seriousness of these issues and are responding in different ways. Let me now present the possibilities for action and how to go about achieving them. I will articulate this largely through the example of our experience at Wipro, while frequently cross-linking it to larger industry and macro trends.

Wipro's Approach to Sustainability

Wipro's strategic engagement with social and ecological issues started about fifteen years ago, building on decades of work. The central tenet of our approach has been the emphasis on strong, meaningful work for systemic social concerns. We think that such engagement must be formed on the bedrock of long-term commitment, for that is the only way by which real change can happen. We run our social programmes on a strong foundation of ethical principles, good governance and sound management. This includes, among other things, holding ourselves up to public scrutiny through a framework of transparent, rigorous reporting.

We think that the primary responsibility of an organization is to run its business ethically and in compliance with the law in spirit as much as in letter. Our approach to social responsibility and sustainability rests on three important pillars:

a. **The Strategic:** We choose domains to engage with that are force multipliers for social change and sustainable development. Social responsibility is as much about being a sustainable organization as it is about external initiatives. Therefore, many of our areas of engagement lie at the convergence of business goals and social purpose. Our chosen domains include education, ecology, community care and diversity.

   We have well-defined programmes in these domains in the business space within our company as well in the social space outside. The nature of these programmes may differ, evidence of the boundary-less approach that companies must adopt. For example, within the company, we have a long-running programme for people with disability. We currently employ five hundred people with disabilities under this programme.

   Simultaneously, we support a significant initiative for children with disability, outside the company. Under this initiative, we have reached out to nearly 3,000 such children from underprivileged backgrounds across India, and supported multiple non-governmental organizations working in this area.

   Both these initiatives are part of our larger emphasis on diversity as an enabling principle, be it within the workplace or outside it. The other elements of our work on diversity include gender and nationality. Our decision to focus on disability is also based on two strategic factors that converge: first, the fact that disability is an area in India that is relatively less funded, and second, the social returns from investments in this space are proportionately larger than in other areas.

b. **The Systemic**: Within the chosen domains, we place a lot of emphasis on systemic issues that require deep engagement. Given the nature of social change, this implies commitment over the long term, typically for several years or decades. For example, a significant part of our work on school education centres on issues such as building teacher capacity, and improvements in pedagogy and the quality of teaching materials. These demand continuing and close engagement over several years. A quick-fix approach that focuses on short-term results never works.

c. **The Deliberative**: The third pillar of our approach is to be deliberative about the way we choose our domains of engagement. In other words, we think that it is critical to focus on just a few areas rather than many. In the social sector, where there is a long list of issues needing attention, it is easy to get carried away and want to do something in every area. But in our experience, this approach of spreading resources thin doesn't work.

Let me now articulate Wipro's responses in the two areas of focus—education and ecology—along with what the Indian industry's response in these areas has been.

Education: Our work in education is driven by the belief that education is a key enabler of change towards a better society. Our idea of good education is derived from the basic notion that it should enable the growth and development of the child in multiple dimensions, so that he or she is able to fulfil and expand his or her potential, and at the same time become an active, contributing and concerned citizen of the world.

These multiple dimensions of development are cognitive, social, emotional, physical and ethical. We have been involved in various education initiatives over the years, which try and address these dimensions across different groups in schools and colleges in the country. Wipro Applying Thought in Schools is a social initiative of Wipro's that aims to build capacities for school education reform in India.

The Wipro Academy of Software Excellence (WASE) programme is a unique four-year programme that blends rigorous academic exposure at the graduate level with practical professional learning at the workplace. We have also been running a programme for schools and colleges called Wipro-earthian, since 2011. This programme brings together two of our key concerns: school education and sustainability. Wipro Science Fellowships, a programme launched in March 2013, is focused on contributing to improving science and mathematics education in schools, and primarily serving disadvantaged communities in the US.

Let me emphasize here that there is one crucial aspect that businesses must be alert to—the power of partnering with people and organizations that may be different from them. None of the above would have been possible without our network of more than seventy partners in the education space in India, which work with millions of children in thousands of schools.

Given the importance of education for a society like India, and the issues of quality and equity that we face, it is not surprising that education is the top 'cause' that companies support as part of their CSR. While this is welcome, I would like to caution here that in seeing itself as an agent of change, business must not overreach itself. It must learn to place itself correctly in the larger scheme of things.

For example, in school education, the role of public education is critical and therefore, the primacy of the public system must be recognized. Business can best play a complementary role and be a catalyst for certain kinds of change, but it can never be the primary vehicle of delivering education. The same goes for primary healthcare which, along with primary education, is a foundational public resource.

Ecology: According to a detailed study done by the Stockholm Resilience Centre, over the past decade, the health of our planet can be conceptualized as a function of nine important parameters, just as the health of a human being can be assessed on the basis of a few indicators such as blood pressure, temperature and pulse rate.

Of the nine parameters, three—climate change, nitrogen flows and biodiversity loss—have already breached their safe boundaries or limits. Collectively, humanity's ecological footprint is already 50 per cent more than what our planetary capacity is. The consequences of this cannot be underestimated, especially with regard to our future generations. Ecological sustainability, in many ways, is therefore, the defining challenge of the twenty-first century.

Acting on ecological challenges, however, requires the coming together of several elements, some at local and regional levels and some at the global level. Combating water stress and scarcity is an example of a local concern but one with deep geopolitical undertones. Climate change, on the other hand, is a global issue that requires governments across the world to act in consonance. Last year, two significant global agreements were ratified and signed by the majority of the world's 191 countries.

The first is the 'Sustainable Development Goals', the successor to the Millennium Development Goals. The second is the Paris agreement on climate change or COP-21 which seeks to establish a binding agreement to keep our planet's average temperature rise within 2°C. While these agreements are commendable, we must be clear that real change is determined by what happens on the ground day after day—inside business organizations, schools, healthcare centres, government departments and laboratories.

Businesses must learn to recognize the changing dynamics of this space where multiple stakeholders need to come together. I am convinced that if the business sector brings to the table what it is very good at—a unique combination of innovation, execution rigour and focus on outcomes—but in a way that complements the roles of government and civil society, we can hope for truly visible progress.

At Wipro, our engagement with climate change goes back to 2007. During the last nine years, our renewable energy footprint has increased fourfold and comprises 22 per cent of our total electricity consumption today. It is only limited by the current supply situation.

Renewable energy, combined with our energy efficiency initiatives, has helped us avoid more than 250,000 metric tonnes of greenhouse gas emissions on a cumulative basis. Analysis from expert groups like the Carbon Disclosure Project indicates that organizations around the world are taking action and the carbon intensity of operations is coming down significantly every year.

The year 2015 also saw the rebound of investments in green energy touching nearly $270 billion. Lord Stern, the well-known economist and former chancellor of the exchequer in the UK, has suggested in his 'Stern Report on Climate Change' that by spending between 1 and 3 per cent of the global GDP, we should be able to reverse the effects of climate change. In my view, this is a small price to pay, and the costs of not acting far exceed that of investing for our future now.

In a similar vein, our engagement with water issues goes back more than a decade. While it started out with internal initiatives around recycling, rainwater harvesting and improvements in water efficiency, we soon realized that water was fundamentally a common resource that needed collaborative governance with other stakeholders.

Aligned with this vision, we started a programme centred on our campuses in Bengaluru and Chennai three years ago, to critically understand the larger picture of our water trail. As part of this programme, we have completed a detailed map of the groundwater aquifer spread over 33 sq km around our campus on Sarjapur Road, Bengaluru.

What we are really attempting to do here is to evolve a citizen-led model of water governance that will be informed by groundwater science, empirical data and a rich exchange of good practices. I am bringing up this example to re-emphasize that businesses can no longer operate on an efficiency-based model when it comes to a critical natural resource like water.

The fact that we have done quite well in our operational water efficiency over the last few years—we have cumulatively saved more than 700 million litres of water over four years—is not good enough if we have to understand water risks in their entirety and act on them. One has to go beyond organizational boundaries and look at the larger interconnected picture.

India and Germany: Germany has a long history of 'doing good while doing well'. It has been one of the early pioneers in social legislation, showing how humanitarian concerns must inform the rubric of industry and business. Starting with laws to abolish child labour in 1869 and establish obligatory medical insurance for workers in 1883, Germany has had a series of powerful legislations that have been calls to action for business.

What is remarkable though, is that unlike in many countries, these laws have been put into practice very effectively. This has been reinforced in recent times by Germany's leadership in renewable energy which accounts for more than 25 per cent of its electricity generation. Germany has achieved this again through skilful regulatory nudges and pushes that have managed to align the incentives of producers, distributors and consumers of electricity.

Similar to India's CSR rules in the Companies Act, 2013, the German government introduced the 'CSR in Germany Action Plan' in 2014 that enjoined companies of all sizes to engage in useful social programmes. It will be interesting for us in India to see how this plan evolves with time.

I have no doubt in my mind that India and Germany can learn a lot from each other in the arena of social responsibility. While India can learn how to design and implement regulations that work effectively on the ground, Germany can perhaps learn how India's vibrant civil society has been working together with the business and government sectors to jointly push the social agenda forward.

Similarly, I am sure that Indian companies will gain by learning how German companies in the engineering and automotive sectors are leading the charge on the circular economy that seeks to upcycle end-of-life-product waste back into the manufacturing and reuse cycles. German companies could learn how several Indian organizations are seeing social responsibility and corporate sustainability as part of the same continuum, rather than separate ones.

Working with communities everywhere: In this context, I must emphasize how important it is for a global company to engage with communities wherever it is present, and not only in its home country. Wipro has a presence in more than sixty countries around the world, and we have tried to engage with proximate communities wherever we have a significant presence.

For example, in the US, we have a large programme on science and mathematics education that aims to strengthen the capacity of teachers in schools that serve children from disadvantaged communities. We recently started a major initiative of augmenting libraries in such schools across the US. I would therefore strongly exhort companies both in Germany and India to engage in community actions in their respective centres of operations in each other's country.

Let me conclude by drawing from the thoughts of two central personalities of the twentieth century, one German and the other Indian. Albert Einstein had said that '...the significant problems we have cannot be solved at the same level of thinking with which we created them'. This has deep implications for us collectively as a society. For one, it means that it would be disastrous for the world to continue on the same trajectory that it has been on, in the past two hundred years.

We have to pause, deeply reflect and change course to a path that is more sensible, a way that will lead to a more equitable and sustainable society. In short, our entire way of thinking will need to change. But that, as we all know, is easier said than done. Such fundamental change can happen only when the majority commit themselves wholly to walking a path which is unfamiliar and difficult. That's what Gandhi meant when he exhorted people to '...be the change they want to see'. On both these counts, it is my firm belief that the business sector is well positioned to excel itself, and to do more than what is expected of it if it chooses to. It is on this optimistic note of promise that I would like to conclude.

Joint Efforts for Renewable Energy to Achieve INDCs in India

◈

Leena Srivastava and Sapan Thapar
'India and Germany: Global Frontiers Towards Energy Transition'

◈

Tobias Zech
'Working with India to Improve the Global Climate'

Dr Leena Srivastava

Sapan Thapar

Dr Leena Srivastava, Vice Chancellor, TERI University

Dr Leena Srivastava is the vice chancellor of TERI University–a uniquely inter-disciplinary higher education institution, focused on sustainable development. She is a member of various committees and boards, including the advisory board to the president of the Asian Development Bank (ADB) on climate change and sustainable development, the administrative board of the Sustainable Energy for All Initiative, Bharti Infratel, Meridian Institute, US, and the Stockholm Resilience Centre, Sweden. She is also on the editorial boards of several international journals and has a number of publications to her credit. She did her master's in Economics from the University of Hyderabad and her PhD in Energy Economics from the Indian Institute of Science, India.

Sapan Thapar, Fellow, TERI University

Sapan Thapar has over fifteen years' experience in the area of energy, including clean energy technologies. He is a certified energy manager, with a master's in Energy Management from IIT-Delhi.

He has worked at the Indian Renewable Energy Development Agency, where he developed certain innovative financial models for renewable energy project financing. He has several publications to his credit in the areas of renewable energy policy assessment, and his current area of interest is community energy business models.

India and Germany: Global Frontiers Towards Energy Transition

Dr Leena Srivastava and Sapan Thapar

Introduction

India and Germany have shared a strategic partnership for several decades, buoyed by a strong focus on people-to-people contacts and mutually beneficial economic links. The trade between the two countries touched an all-time high of 16 billion euros in 2014. Machinery and chemical and electronic products were among the major German exports to India at that time, while textiles, IT solutions, leather and agricultural products were the main items of export from India. Both the countries are progressive democracies striving towards sustainable development of the world.

Germany has over 170 GW of installed power generation capacity, dominated by coal, with a significant share from renewables—45 GW of wind, 40 GW of solar and 9 GW of biomass-based energy projects. Most of the wind projects are located in its northern areas, whereas the solar projects are largely located in its southern provinces. During 2015, renewable-based power contributed over 38 per cent of total power generated in Germany; the share of wind power was 15 per cent, biomass was 10 per cent and solar contributed another 8 per cent.

The roots of the growth of the renewable sector in Germany can be traced to the strong anti-nuclear sentiments and setting up of projects under the community model, aided by local manufacturing of wind turbine facilities. The sector has been promoted by consistent policy support from the government in the form of feed-in tariff and priority dispatch principles.

With respect to India, the total installed power capacity has crossed the 300 GW mark, with a major share attributed to coal-based plants (over 60 per cent), followed by renewables, hydro and nuclear-based plants. The renewable capacity has crossed 43 GW, with 27 GW contributed by wind and 7.5 GW by solar technologies. Of the total 1,100 billion units (BU) of power generated in financial year (2015–16), the share of renewable energy was 60 BUs (about 6 per cent). The initial impetus for promoting renewable energy technologies in India was enhancement of energy security and virtual extension of the grid using off-grid systems in remote and rural areas.

However, after being tagged as a leading greenhouse contributor (due to the dominance of coal in its power system), countering climate change has become a kind of national goal. The Indian government has committed to achieving 40 per cent power generation from non-fossil-based sources by the year 2022, and has concomitantly revised its renewable energy capacity targets—100 GW for solar and 60 GW for wind capacity, to be achieved by 2022. Similar to the case in Germany, the renewable energy sector in India has been supported by several fiscal and financial incentives.

Both India and Germany rank among the top five countries globally in terms of installed renewable energy capacity (Germany is at rank 3 and India is at rank 5) as well as the Renewable Attractiveness Index (India is at rank 3 and Germany is at rank 5). Germany is amongst the leaders in the Organization for Economic Cooperation and Development countries in terms of both installed renewable energy capacity and its grid penetration. With a deep political commitment, India is among the fastest growing emerging economies in terms of renewable energy capacity addition, and has set ambitious targets.

Opportunities for Collaboration

The level of cooperation between the two nations in the renewable energy sector has been extensive and unparalleled. Under the Indo-German Energy Program, the German Federal Ministry for Economic Cooperation and Development has been supporting energy efficiency improvements and renewable energy generation in the rural and urban areas of India.

Recently, the two countries agreed on the India–Germany Climate and Renewable Energy Alliance—a comprehensive partnership to harness technology, innovation and finance in order to make affordable, clean and renewable energy accessible to all, and to foster climate change mitigation efforts in both countries.

As strategic partners, the two countries can engage in a long-term partnership in terms of sharing of best practices and lessons learnt to accelerate the growth of the cleantech sector within their own geographies, and further collaborate with other nations aiming for sustainable development of the world. Some areas, identified in the following sections, enunciate the opportunities for collaboration that exist between the two great nations for accelerated development and deployment of renewable technologies.

From Germany to India

German utilities, experiencing a high penetration of renewable power (over 38 per cent), have considerable experience in accommodating intermittent solar and wind power in their grid. These utilities exchange power with neighbouring nations to maximize the use of renewable power, and for balancing the grid. In the case of India, states like Tamil Nadu, with a significant share of renewable energy capacity in their grid (due to the high level of wind velocity), are finding it difficult to manage the intermittent power in the absence of sufficient power transfer corridors.

The Indian government is contemplating setting up a Renewable Energy Management Centre (REMC) in each of the renewable energy-rich states to facilitate the forecasting and scheduling of green power. German utilities can provide input on the technologies and tools which can be used for effectively running the proposed REMCs as an extension of smart grid techniques.

India, with twenty-nine states, can be looked upon as similar to the European Union (EU), and the norms for exchange of power being followed across the EU nations can be adapted in India so as to facilitate power transfer among its states. This will enable the utilization of renewable energy-rich areas, minimizing the technical and financial constraints encountered by the host utilities.

Another aspect of cooperation can be in the area of biomass energy. Germany is effectively using biomass-based energy projects for both district heating as well as for grid balancing purposes. Most of the projects are set up under community business models, with the ownership vested with the local people. Being a primarily agrarian society with a large segment of its population residing in rural areas, India can learn from the sectoral best practices followed in Germany to promote community-based biomass projects.

This can help to meet the energy needs (beyond electricity) of the local people, besides promoting entrepreneurship and employment in the rural areas. Bio-based projects further facilitate grid balancing (required to regulate intermittent power), acting as energy storage systems, and can even support off-grid solar-based systems in hybrid mode.

One of the key strengths of the German renewable energy industry is the high penetration of rooftop systems, having about 75 per cent share of total installed solar photovoltaic capacity in the country. The rooftop systems in Germany have come as a result of promotional policies (net metering schemes) and innovative financial schemes. With a 40 GW rooftop target to be achieved by the year 2022, India can leverage some of the best practices followed in Germany in terms of the technical requirements of utilities and roll-out of retail lending schemes for building owners.

A notable aspect in Germany is the patronage enjoyed by the renewable energy sector across the political spectrum, making the framing of renewable energy laws less cumbersome than what is being experienced in other countries. There can be exchange visits of lawmakers across different political groups of both the countries in order to sensitize them and streamline their thoughts towards climate-friendly legislations.

Germany boasts of a large number of cooperative modelled energy projects (over 2,000 cooperatives in operation), encouraging active participation of the local community with regard to project formulation, implementation and maintenance. The citizens own about 35 per cent of renewable energy projects, with farmers owning another 11 per cent.

In the case of India, most of the renewable energy project sites are located in rural areas. With a large segment of the rural population seeking remunerative employment outside agriculture, setting up renewable projects with community participation can promote entrepreneurship in rural areas, aided by the Startup India and Skill India missions.

Though renewable energy technologies are environmentally benign, projects can have an impact on local ecology and society. Also, renewable projects in Germany are required to undertake environmental and social impact assessment studies. To enable large-scale deployment of renewable energy projects with wider acceptance of the local community, similar practices can be adopted in India.

Germany is one of the top two countries globally in terms of harnessing ocean winds, with over 3 GW of offshore wind installations, and can hand-hold India, which has a long coastline, in its quest to set up offshore wind power projects. Besides being land neutral, offshore wind resources are associated with higher levels of energy generation.

Germany has recently joined the International Zero-Emission Vehicle Alliance, which aims at making all passenger vehicles emission-free by the year 2050, and is working vigorously in this direction. With growing prosperity levels, the use of personal vehicles is bound to increase in India, leading to higher consumption of fuels (India imports over 80 per cent of its crude oil requirements) besides causing air pollution. Solar panels, aided by a smart grid, can effectively resolve these issues. Key learnings from Germany can be shared with India to develop the next-generation electric and hybrid vehicles as part of the National Electric Mobility Mission Plan.

From India to Germany

India has its share of success stories in the renewable sector which can be shared with its German counterparts. Among the most notable is the coming up of large-size solar parks, over several hundred megawatt capacity, spread over thousands of hectares of land. These are a kind of pioneering public–private partnership (PPP) models and engineering marvels which support large-scale generation of clean energy using economies of scale.

With limited availability of land as well as solar radiation, the concept of solar parks cannot be emulated in Germany. However, the PPP-based solar park model can be suitably adapted in many of the developing countries being supported by Germany (in terms of clean energy technical and financial assistance).

A related innovation is the successful use of bidding as a tool to discover solar tariffs at market prices. This has helped Indian utilities reduce their cost of solar power procurement by up to 70 per cent, thus minimizing the impact of the tariff on the end-user. With reservations being expressed by some German experts on the feed-in tariff scheme, auctions can be used there to enhance acceptability.

Another best practice which can be shared by India is promoting the renewable energy sector in a multi-regulated environment. Energy is a concurrent subject, according to the Indian Constitution, which has bestowed powers upon both the central government and state governments to frame appropriate laws in this area. In order to promote the renewable energy sector, the Central Electricity Regulatory Commission has come out with model regulations on several aspects related to renewable energy, including tariff determination. These regulations are being adapted by the state electricity regulatory commissions based on their respective requirements.

With multiple countries in its fold, the EU can be thought of as similar to the Indian federal structure, and a quicker dissemination of renewable energy regulations across EU member states can be made by using the approach followed in India. This endeavour can be spearheaded by Germany in EU member countries.

To circumvent the site-specific nature of renewable energy projects, dedicated technical agencies (National Institute of Wind Energy and National Institute of Solar Energy) have undertaken extensive mapping of the Indian land mass, and developed a wind and solar atlas to earmark prospective project sites for investors.

The Indian government has also set up a dedicated financial institution for the sector (the Indian Renewable Energy Development Agency) which has made mainstream banks and financial institutions look upon the sector as creditworthy for financing. The Indian agencies can enable the building of similar institutions in Germany and other countries to undertake resource mapping and financing of renewable projects.

Another important strength of India is in the field of decentralized energy applications. Due to the unavailability of a grid network and unreliable supply, a large number of households and establishments in India have been using improvised renewable energy-based mini-grids and systems. These include solar lanterns, irrigation pump sets, solar street lamps and family-size biogas plants. The business models as developed with regard to off-grid systems can be of immense relevance to developing countries which are being supported by the German government.

The Indian government is promoting land-neutral solar power installations to minimize land requirements. Solar projects are being promoted over canal tops, railway and metro stations, schools and colleges, medians over highways and parking areas. This can be another area of cooperation in terms of business models and technological innovations.

As part of its Skill India mission, the Indian government has also set a target to equip its large workforce (human resources) to work in the clean energy sector across the entire value chain. Specific skill areas are being mapped for each of the sub-sectors, and training-cum-certification centres are being established. Faculty as well as the learning modules can be shared with the German agencies for skill development of the relevant stakeholders.

The government is also incubating budding entrepreneurs to develop and scale up their clean technology innovations by creating an enabling ecosystem. The innovations, as generated in these incubator labs and prominent universities, can be shared between the research communities of the two countries to develop long-term holistic solutions for humanity.

Conclusion

Germany and India can collaborate in several areas to meet the emission reduction targets of the Paris Climate Accord. German utilities and the research community can share their know-how in the areas of grid integration of renewables, community energy business models, biomass technologies, retail lending schemes for rooftops besides offshore wind technology and electric vehicles. On the other hand, Indian agencies can share their domain knowledge in the area of solar parks, off-grid and land-neutral solar installations, resource assessment and skill development techniques, besides cleantech incubation centres.

Additionally, India needs to mobilize huge investible resources to be able to finance its renewable energy programme. Germany, on the other hand, is looking for options through which it can increase the returns to its people on their savings. Germany should be able to provide low-cost finance to facilitate India's transition to a low-carbon economy while providing a higher return on its savings—a win–win option for both countries.

Renewable energy can become a major area of trade between the two great nations, a symbol of North–South cooperation aiming towards the sustainable development of the global community.

Tobias Zech, Member of Parliament, Christian Social Union

Tobias Zech was born on 9 July 1981 in the German town of Trostberg in Traunstein district. Since 2010, he has been a commercial employee at the EADS headquarters, and has been a member of the Garching an der Alz municipal council since 2002. He has been chairman of the Upper Bavaria district branch of the Young Union (youth section of the CDU/CSU) since 2011 and a member of the county council of the Altötting administrative district since 2013. In 2013, he became a member of the German Bundestag.

He is also a member of the Committee on Labour and Social Affairs and the Committee on Economic Cooperation and Development of the Bundestag, and has been a member of the Parliamentary Assembly of the Council of Europe (PACE) since 2014. In 2016, he was vice chairman of the group of the European People's Party/Christian Democrats at PACE.

Working with India to Improve the Global Climate

Tobias Zech

In 2025, India is set to overtake China as the world's most populated country. How more than 1.3 billion Indians produce their energy will have an enormous impact on the global climate. This is one reason why India has a key role to play in the area of global development issues—helping to protect global goods, achieve the Millennium Development Goals (MDGs) and the Sustainable Development Goals (SDGs), as well as support international processes such as the Doha Round at the World Trade Organization (WTO) and climate negotiations. India is one of Germany's most important global development partners.

Climate change and pollution have long since made it to the country's agenda. The World Health Organization (WHO) has rated New Delhi as one of the most polluted cities in the world, and India is already the world's third biggest emitter of greenhouse gases after the US and China. According to WHO, thirteen of the twenty cities with the poorest air quality worldwide were in the Indian subcontinent in 2014. The levels of particulate matter recorded in New Delhi are, in some cases, higher than those measured in Beijing.

There are multiple ways to redress these shortcomings. Energy efficiency must be increased and energy production made cleaner and more efficient with the use of modern filter technology. And, above all, renewable energy for electricity production must be more widely used. Furthermore, India needs to focus on more environmentally friendly ways to meet its growing population's energy needs.

The Modi government has long since taken this to heart and is working intensively to come up with solutions. Prime Minister Narendra Modi and Piyush Goyal, minister of state with independent charge for power, coal, new and renewable energy, have brought about a spirit of change in the country and are working tirelessly to promote renewable energy. In mid-March 2016, India quintupled its development target in the solar sector from 20,000 MW to 100,000 MW, by 2022.

The objective is for renewable energy to contribute a total of 175,000 MW to the grid by 2022. In so doing, Modi has made good on the symbolic promise India made by founding—along with Germany, the People's Republic of China, Denmark, France, the UK, South Africa and other nations—the Renewables Club in Berlin in June 2013.

Germany is the ideal partner for these plans. In 2015, renewable energy accounted for 30 per cent of Germany's gross electricity production. By 2025, the objective is for 40 to 45 per cent of the electricity consumed in Germany to come from renewable energy sources.

Therefore, it comes as no surprise that renewable energy is one of the most important fields of Indo-German collaboration. This cooperation is on an equal footing, as Federal Development Minister Dr Gerd Müller stated at the signing of bilateral agreements on development cooperation during his official visit to India in February 2014.

One of the major projects that Germany is supporting in order to promote the development of renewable energy in India is the Green Energy Corridors project, for which low-interest loans totalling 1.15 billion euros have been pledged for a period of three years.

With this extensive loan, the German government is helping Green Energy Corridors to develop transmission lines in order to improve the connectivity of renewable energy to the national power grid. The aim is to devise environmentally friendly corridors to distribute electricity produced from renewable sources in an effective manner.

Another important aim is to increase the efficiency of energy production and transmission, as well as enhance the efficiency of electricity consumption. Germany is, among other things, supporting projects to improve the energy efficiency of residential buildings.

Another project is the Indo-German Solar Energy Partnership, which comprises an overall multi-annual commitment of 1 billion euros. The Indo-German Solar Energy Partnership was established in the course of cabinet consultations between the Merkel and Modi governments in New Delhi in October 2015. The partnership primarily supports rooftop solar systems and solar parks.

German development cooperation is also working to promote rural electrification in isolated regions and fight poverty with the programme IGEN Access, which provides financial support for the sustainable operation of solar mini-grids. Alongside climate protection, this offers new sources of income for local populations, helping to achieve a second important knock-on effect of development cooperation—poverty reduction.

Bilateral Indo-German development cooperation has long been one of the most visible driving forces behind the vital project of expanding India's renewable energy sector. Moreover, India represents, in terms of volume, the biggest commitment of the German Ministry for Economic Cooperation and Development in this area, by a considerable margin.

Renewable energy, energy efficiency and environmental and resource protection are the most important aspects of bilateral development cooperation with India. Vocational training is set to become a priority of the Indo-German partnership in the future alongside sustainable urban development.

India and Germany have shown themselves to be ideal partners in all these areas and Germany is able to draw on its wide-ranging experiences within this partnership on an equal footing. It is not for nothing that Germany has a reputation for being one of the world's most environmentally friendly countries.

In the 1970s, Germany embarked on a process of development that India still has to undergo in some areas. At that time, there was already a growing appreciation in Germany of the fact that maintaining high living standards for all the country's citizens went hand in hand with a responsible, long-term industrial policy, while key concepts such as 'environmental policy', 'clean air' and 'clean water' came to the fore. Air quality directives were followed by regulations on waste management and the recycling economy, and Germany became a pioneer in the realm of environmental policy.

The knowledge and skills that German companies, and engineers in particular, have acquired in this field should also—for the good of the entire planet—be harnessed now for the benefit of Indian projects in the context of development cooperation. Future cooperation must therefore not be restricted to financial support, but must also entail more intensive collaboration and exchanges of knowledge at all levels.

The onus here is not only on the state, of course, but also on German companies, which must seize the opportunities offered by the developing Indian market in a safe environment, in one of the world's biggest democracies. According to calculations made by the World Bank, some one million people will come on stream in South Asian employment markets in the next fifteen years, the majority of whom will be in India. Their numbers will begin to decline gradually only from 2030.

From an economic perspective, India is on the cusp of a 'demographic dividend' phase with a most favourable ratio of working-age population to non-working children on the one hand, and the elderly on the other, which is set to continue until about 2040. India can take advantage of this opportunity by investing in future technologies and allowing as many of its citizens as possible to share in this growth.

At the same time, German companies operating around the world should also grasp the opportunities that such a dynamic market offers them. With their expertise in the area of renewable energies, they will be more than welcome in India. As is so often the case, the aim will be to combine the good and the useful.

These figures make it clear once again that the objective of Indo-German cooperation must be to make a major contribution to a global structural, resource and climate protection policy, thereby helping to address key global development issues. I believe that the preconditions for this are excellent. Germany and India are two countries that are well known for their highly trained engineers and technicians. These are excellent foundations on which to tackle the challenges that we all face as a result of climate change and environmental pollution.

However, those who intend to address these problems with technology need not only engineers who develop solutions, but also technicians who attend to, install, operate and maintain such technical facilities. They must first be trained, and then constantly receive additional training. Germany can provide a training system for this that has been emulated around the world. The practical (dual) vocational training system is one of Germany's flagships—a hub of industry and knowledge.

Particularly in the area of training, Germany could show India how it might enable a large part of its population to benefit from enormous mechanical and technical knowledge and skills. Though this is one of the most rewarding fields in which Germany and India are already cooperating, I believe there is scope for them to work together more intensively in this area.

The fact that the Modi administration has realized that vocational training plays a key role in India's economic and social development is reflected by the establishment of the new Ministry of Skill Development and Entrepreneurship, in November 2014.

This initiative was very well received by Germany. After a five-year pause, the Federal Ministry for Economic Cooperation and Development relaunched its cooperation in the field of vocational training in 2015 with the Indo-German Skill Development Program (3 million euros over three years) in response to the high levels of demand shown by the ministry's Indian partners.

The project seeks to strengthen the structures and capacities of federal, national and private actors. It aims to improve the regulatory framework for cooperative vocational training and to implement and structure these measures together with the National Skill Development Corporation, the Sector Skill Council and other professional and trade associations.

The project seeks to implement exemplary, replicable models for cooperative vocational training programmes in close cooperation with the business community. The focus of these measures is currently at the central government level, as well as on selected project regions in the states of Maharashtra, Karnataka and Bihar.

Vocational training programmes in the renewable energy sector could help to address two problems that are putting the brakes on India's economy—rising levels of unemployment, underemployment and a rising proportion of precarious employment relationships on the one hand, and a glaring lack of qualified professionals on the other. The German practical (dual) vocational training system could replace this ineffective system.

Over twenty ministries are currently implementing more than seventy different Central Skill Development Schemes, ranging from short courses lasting for just a few days to three-year training courses. A lack of control and coordination has resulted in duplication and misallocation of funds. Moreover, these programmes will need to give more people access to this type of education. Only some 10 per cent of all school leavers enjoy access to vocational qualifications each year to date. Trainees often have insufficient skills for qualified employment as a result of training programmes lacking in practical input.

If efforts to expand the renewable energy sector are to be successful in India, then it will be crucial not only to construct large numbers of power plants, wind turbines and solar panels, but also to ensure their upkeep. As in Germany, expanding the renewable energy sector could become an engine for employment, and ensure that poverty, which is still a major problem in India, is reduced.

Another key focus of Indo-German development cooperation is the environment and sustainable food production. The priorities here are protecting biodiversity and sustainable rural resource management. As is the case in the projects mentioned earlier, environmental protection and economic progress are certainly not mutually exclusive, but actually go hand in hand.

The best example of this is a German development cooperation project that, from 2003 to 2010, helped farmers use their regions' natural resources in a sustainable manner in collaboration with public authorities, non-governmental organizations and rural self-help organizations. The result was four times as much grain than before the project, clean drinking water for all, increased vegetation cover and a fourfold increase in the number of jobs—along with empowered women able to earn their own living after the project.

Promoting ecologically sustainable and socially balanced urbanization offers great energy-saving potential. The 1,000 Smart Cities in India initiative, launched by the Indian government, is a most welcome development in this regard—a project that is also supported by the German federal government. The Federal Ministry for the Environment, Nature Conservation, Building and Nuclear Safety is helping three Indian cities—Bhubaneswar, Kochi and Coimbatore—implement their smart city plans.

At a conference in Berlin at the end of May 2016, which was attended by India's Minister of Urban Development Venkaiah Naidu, Federal Environment Minister Barbara Hendricks said that the federal government would support German companies looking to work intensively with Indian partners to help the country's cities implement their concepts.

Initial talks will be conducted in the region by the Deutsche Gesellschaft für Internationale Zusammenarbeit GmbH. One of the priorities is to come to grips with existing problems such as housing shortages, poor water and energy systems, and overstretched infrastructure. Germany will start by conducting feasibility studies, on the basis of which its subsequent work in India can be controlled effectively, for example by promoting long-term cooperative projects between German and Indian companies.

So what can Germany do to continue to support the numerous measures that have already been launched, and to have a positive impact on the expansion of renewable energy that is under way?

On the one hand, Germany can, insofar as it is feasible, provide start-up support and financial resources for innovative development and energy policy approaches. It must provide not only monetary support, but also expertise to a greater degree than has been the case until now. Exchange programmes between German and Indian universities, research institutes and developers must be intensified significantly and exchanges promoted at all levels. The state can improve the necessary conditions for this, for instance by launching new exchange programmes that are tailored to transfer knowledge in this field.

The federal government can promote the work of German companies in India by ensuring that the right conditions are created, for instance with bilateral or multilateral agreements.

My personal experiences in India, and during meetings with Indian parliamentarians in Germany, have made me extremely confident that Germany and India will be able to work together to make a major contribution to expanding renewable energy.

Plotting Urban Development and Smart Cities Together

◈

Pedro Miranda
'India and Germany: Smart Cities and Urban Infrastructure'

◈

Ravi Parthasarathy
'Urban Infrastructure and Smart Cities: An Opportunity for Enhanced Indo-German Cooperation'

Pedro Miranda, Global Head, Siemens, Smart Cities (2012-2016)

Pedro Miranda is the corporate vice president, head of corporate development, Siemens One, Siemens AG. He was born on 3 May 1958 in Lisbon, Portugal.

He studied Electrical and Industrial Engineering at Purdue University, West Lafayette (US), and took executive management programmes at the Krannert School of Management (US), Universidade Nova de Lisboa (Portugal) and Management Centre Europe in Brussels. In 1981, he joined the Inland Division of General Motors Corporation, in Dayton, Ohio (US), as a production engineer.

In 1983 he became Production Engineering Manager of low voltage miniature circuit breakers at Siemens SA, Portugal, ASI Group, Fa. Seixal, Portugal and IBGR Regensburg, and was promoted to Factory General Manager for low voltage installation products in 1986. In 1989, he joined Nissan Motors Corporation, Amsterdam, and Entreposto Comercial, Lisbon, as country director for after-sales service.

In 1993, he became engineering and sales manager, large infrastructure projects for industry and building technology, and was the project director for the World Exposition in Lisbon in 1998. In the same year, he became engineering and sales general manager and worked as the project director for the 2006 Asian Games, and the airport in Doha, Qatar. In 2007, he was project director for Hospital da Luz in Lisbon. In 2008, he became industry sector CEO and a member of the CEC, and a year later became corporate vice president, head of corporate development, Siemens One. He holds global responsibility for Siemens One in fifty-five countries.

"In 2012 he became Executive Head of the Global Center of Competence Cities in London, overseeing business development in 70 cities worldwide, focusing on intelligent infrastructure in the domains of Buildings, Energy and Transportation."

India and Germany: Smart Cities and Urban Infrastructure

Pedro Miranda

The Direction of Travel

India's growth has impressed international observers for a number of years. Though the story of urbanization is familiar to nations across the world, the sheer scale and speed of India's transformation is remarkable.

As Germany's history shows, cities like Frankfurt, Munich and Berlin provided the economic engines for development and growth across the nation. For India, over a third of its population lives in urban areas and contributes around two-thirds of the country's GDP. By 2030, urban areas are expected to house 40 per cent of India's population and contribute 75 per cent of its GDP.

Germany's trade with India is mirroring this change. Total trade between India and Germany was $5.5 billion in 2004 and grew to $21.6 billion in 2013. Germany is India's largest trading partner in Europe and is the eighth largest foreign direct investor. Germany's investment totalled about $5.2 billion during the period 2000–12, constituting about 3 per cent of total foreign direct investment (FDI) in India. India's own investments in Germany have also seen a sharp increase in the past few years. Symbolic of this strengthening relationship was India's role as partner nation at the 2015 Hannover Messe.

Indian Prime Minister Modi's choice, on his maiden visit to Germany, to open the fair along with German Chancellor Angela Merkel has set the tone for cooperation and partnership between the two nations. Germany has every intention of supporting the successes and opportunities in India. Siemens has been in India for nearly 150 years, employs over 19,000 people and has invested capital in twenty-three factories and nine software centres.

All our Indian partners bring in local expertise and leverage global thinking from their businesses into ours. Siemens and our partners have learned by working with thousands of cities and city agencies, that changing cities takes time. Like many other rapidly developing countries, India's cities face infrastructure bottlenecks that are undercutting their performance.

In developing cities around the world, there is an ever-present risk of urban growth that directly impacts health and quality of life. While India is going through significant changes, there are important positive feedback loops between urbanization economic productivity and agglomeration economies that hold real possibilities for development. Conversely, unhealthy or inefficient patterns of urbanization are not only damaging today, but lock in high costs for the future. This poses a real risk of stifling the rate of progress in the years to come.

In this context, emergent technologies have proved to be true game changers for India. Along with the seismic shifts we see in Indian demographics, advances in technology are rapidly evolving and changing citizens' relationships with services and utilities. One of the most impactful examples is Indian's increasing use of wireless technology. It is estimated that every second, three Indians experience the internet for the first time. By 2030, more than one billion Indians will be online.

India currently has 100–130 million mobile internet users and 60 million smartphone users. In both cases, the figure could reach 900 million by 2025. What this means, beyond the successful adoption of technology, is the opportunities for India to leap forward in the technology stakes. A key example of this is Paytm, which provides digital wallets with online accounts and transfers. Indians have opened 120 million accounts, nearly six times the number of credit card accounts in the country.

This means that a form of commerce that has defined retailing in Europe and North America is being bypassed in favour of the most cutting-edge and efficient solutions today. This 'leapfrogging' of technology is in no way limited to the online space. Intelligent infrastructure in our cities is one of the leading ways growth can be tied with improved living standards and resource efficiency. One form of infrastructure in which German technology leads the way is water, which can be used to benefit India.

Intelligent Urban Infrastructure

Mumbai's relationship with water shows how the resilience of a city's water supply is of paramount importance, and how complex social and environmental issues overlap. Drought affects millions of people in India, according to government figures. The consequences of this drought have been extensive given that about 15 per cent of India's GDP comes from agriculture and farmers account for 68 per cent of the country's 1.3 billion population.

The lack of water for irrigation has been devastating for farmers causing many of them to leave for the city where water and new jobs are more accessible. However, this migration exacerbates the pressure on Mumbai's water supply and creates a demand for better solutions. Across the world, water demand is projected to increase by 55 per cent by 2050. This means that in thirty-five years, more than 40 per cent of the world's population will live in areas of severe water stress. The challenges that India faces today are not unfamiliar to people in other parts of the world.

Renewable freshwater resources are falling around the world at a rate of over 10 per cent every ten years. The rise in sea level, changes in precipitation, and warming temperatures all threaten the water supply. As climate change induces sea levels to rise, freshwater sources will be increasingly contaminated by salt water. In many places, drought, reduction in winter rain, and warmer, drier springs have caused reservoir levels to drop. This has not only restricted the water supply, but has also resulted in a decrease in hydroelectric power generation where this is in place, often forcing the already energy-strapped area to switch to other, less sustainable types of fuel.

Too much water can also be damaging and present the city with further systemic problems. The development of buildings and more transport means higher levels of concrete and roads, exacerbating stormwater run-off and potentially causing flooding. In informal settlements, which house 32 per cent of the world's urban population, this can be especially challenging. Here, a lack of sewage systems and unstable construction can lead to collapse and deadly results during floods.

Cities around the world are effecting improvements in water and wastewater infrastructure with solutions that are often coupled with investments in pollution reduction and flood prevention. One of the hardest aspects of tackling problems with water is knowing where to begin. Water networks are complex, consisting not only of collection points, but also a whole host of other infrastructure that links supply with demand. Groundwater, lakes and rivers connect through pipes to purification, treatment and storage facilities; clean water is pumped from pumping stations to consumers; and then wastewater is collected by sewage pipes, ultimately returning the used water to wastewater treatment plants.

In cities without extensive water systems, city leaders are required to work across sectors to map current and future land uses, and seek out synergies across infrastructure projects. This can seem expensive at the outset, but as Mumbai's recent challenges show us, failing to do it can lead to a real upheaval. Technologies are empowering city leaders to update, replace and rebuild all aspects of the urban water network. From combining water treatment with energy generation to digitalizing water meters, technologies improve energy efficiency, reduce water losses and manage demand.

In Perth, Australia, one water treatment plant converts sea salt into potable water using reverse osmosis technology. The plant, which supplies 20 per cent of the city's water, is powered entirely by renewable energy from a wind farm. Furthermore, the water treatment plant itself includes components that minimize energy use, as well as enable scalability and quick repair. Highly efficient motors have replaced older, less efficient technologies, and uniform technologies and tools facilitate plant maintenance. Combining clean energy sources with energy-efficient instruments within the treatment plant ensures that Perth's water supply is smart and sustainable in the long run.

The production of biogas at wastewater treatment plants offers another method for combining energy generation and water supply cycles. The anaerobic digestion of sewage, manure, human solid waste, and green waste results in biogas which can then be sold for heating and cooking, vehicle fuel, and even fuel for power plants.

The wastewater treatment plant in Higashinada, Japan, generates 10,000 cubic metres of biogas per day, 45 per cent of which is used to power the wastewater treatment plant itself. Another 20 per cent is used to fuel vehicles, demonstrating the possibilities of using infrastructure investments to address issues in not one sector, but across three sectors. Further automation and digitalization of water treatment processes can improve energy efficiency significantly.

Through smart systems, it can even be possible to separate potable water ready for residential distribution from non-potable water which has lower energy intensity for treatment and can be delivered directly to industrial customers. Where complete infrastructure already exists, retrofitting water treatment plants with automation and digitalization technologies can mean major cost savings for municipal utilities, as treatment often accounts for 40–60 per cent of energy use.

For the developing world, outfitting new water treatment plants with these technologies ensures high quality of water and low levels of energy usage. A World Bank study reported that these types of technologies aimed at enhancing energy efficiency in treatment plants can result in substantial financial savings, with energy savings estimated at 10–30 per cent per measure with as little as one-to-five year payback periods.

Watergy, the Vizianagaram Municipal Council programme on energy and water efficiency, is one example of this type of project in India. The council conducted energy audits of the water supply system, and implemented efficiency measures that lowered the city's energy costs by 18 per cent and eliminated 600 tonnes of carbon dioxide emissions.

Efforts made to minimize and decarbonize energy usage on the supply side of the water network are complemented by technologies monitoring the water distribution itself. Controlling leakages, losses and consumption have to be top priorities for Indian municipal utilities. Mitigations for these issues include smart valves and pipes, hydraulic modelling, water metering, and demand control programmes.

The UN has reported on leakage loss rates across the world of up to 50 per cent in urban water distribution systems, with an estimated 250 to 500 million metres cubed of drinking water lost in megacities across the world each year.

This is even an issue for European cities and one that is being addressed through long-term strategic planning and through the use of digital technology. Copenhagen, the capital of Denmark, has pledged to replace its entire water main network, but the project will take the next hundred years, with just 1 per cent of the existing network replaced each year. Here smart pipes and valves offer the most accurate method for detecting leakage.

Sensors embedded throughout the materials of the distribution network allow for continuous monitoring of water flow and water pressure. The use of sensors, pinpointing where pressure reduces and where outflow fails to match inflow, provides operators with the insights they need to directly tackle faults in the system, or incidents of water theft which are otherwise too difficult to identify. This same technology can be both integrated at the outset of new developments and retrofitted to existing infrastructure. The data produced by such systems can be significant and its benefits are extensive.

In 2008 a new high-speed route between Madrid and Barcelona opened and the journey time was reduced from three hours to two and a half hours. In addition, predictive maintenance was introduced. For much of industrial history, maintenance has been reactive. A part breaks and it is subsequently fixed.

However, as industry has evolved, so has maintenance. The first evolution was the emergence of prescriptive maintenance—a part breaks every five years, therefore you replace it every four and a half years. This led to a reduction in unplanned outages (though not a complete mitigation) but increased maintenance costs, with parts being replaced earlier than necessary.

The use of data is revolutionizing maintenance in the twenty-first century, enabling predictive maintenance. Based on data captured from hundreds of sensors on critical train components, analysis is carried out to detect impending part failures. Due to the in-depth knowledge of which parts are likely to fail in the near future, Siemens has been able to ensure close to 100 per cent availability.

Even in the century-old Taj Mahal Palace Hotel in Mumbai, sensors and data can be found, maximizing the efficiency of the building and supporting its management. Siemens has been involved in recent years in the renovation of the power distribution network developing building automation to monitor and control ventilation and air-conditioning systems, and introducing the most secure fire detection and security.

Building management systems (BMS) are becoming standard in the construction of new buildings. But as the Taj Mahal Palace Hotel shows us, the existing buildings that make up the city are equally important and can make significant contributions to reduce inefficiencies and environmental impact. The retrofit of our historic buildings presents an opportunity for basic automation, and BMS can make an immediate impact on a huge scale.

All this points to a marriage between the digital and the physical that India is primed to capitalize on; it is a layer of data intelligence which is not currently being exploited at city level. Urban analytics and remote diagnostics come into play as increasingly infrastructure is being developed to incorporate sensors which can then monitor both the equipment and the wider system. Utilities can automatically report on performance and communicate with remote diagnostics, which can then trigger alarms at the earliest signs of irregular activity, highlight in advance the need for maintenance, allow for remote maintenance, and enable interventions to enhance performance and efficiency.

City Performance Tool as an Example of German Oversight Capabilities

A further example of incorporating data is the City Performance Tool (CyPT) by Siemens. This is a data-driven tool which helps urban decision-makers identify technologies that offer the maximum environmental and economic benefits for their city. The CyPT is an example of how data collection can help cities plan to meet targets and set future priorities for infrastructure investment. If we accept, as we should, that India's cities will have an increasing role to play in protecting the environment, this kind of planning will be essential. Now urban decision-makers can use the CyPT by Siemens to select bespoke technologies that offer their own cities maximum environmental and economic benefits.

Using exclusive Siemens data on more than seventy transport, building energy technologies, the CyPT delivers a detailed insight into the carbon dioxide and air quality improvements that are achievable. It also identifies new local jobs that each technology can create in the city. It covers greenhouse gas emissions from buildings and transport, as well as air pollutants such as particulate matter and nitrogen oxides. It also looks at the creation of new local jobs to install, operate and maintain city solutions.

The model calculates the environmental and economic impacts of individual technologies at different implementation levels. In transport, for example, the CyPT assesses how a technology will reduce demand, shift the mode (such as public transport instead of cars) or improve efficiency. The model is based on life-cycle assessment methodology and builds upon technology expertise and global databases of deep process knowledge.

New jobs that will be created are based on reference projects or economic studies in the transport, building and energy sectors of different regions. This versatile leading-edge simulation tool can be used in many different decision-making scenarios. It can determine the implementation rate needed for a city to meet its future environmental targets. It can also measure the impact of a city's strategic plans, and compare traditional methods with state-of-the-art technologies in terms of their benefits and value for money.

Conclusion

With the rapid pace of city growth, and increasing demands on city infrastructure and services, from water to energy, there is an unprecedented pressure on city leaders to plan for a smart and sustainable future for their cities. This increasingly complex planning environment is driving demand for more comprehensive knowledge on city performance, smart analytics and intelligent infrastructure.

With its rapid demographic change and embracing of new technology,

India boasts the world's fastest growing large economy. Combined with the planet's biggest population of millennials and the development opportunities this presents, it is evident that India is poised to be a leading light in the twenty-first century.

In June 2015, the Indian Ministry of Urban Development published its 'Smart Cities Mission & Guidelines'. The document points out that there is no single, universally accepted definition of a 'smart city'. It can mean different things to different people, from city to city and country to country. Siemens' approach defines three components of a smart city; technology, physical connectivity across core infrastructure elements, and electronic connectivity in services, governance and modelling.

As Prime Minister Narendra Modi notes: 'Cities in the past were built on riverbanks. They are now built along highways. But in the future, they will be built based on availability of optical fibre networks and next-generation infrastructure.' What I have argued for here shows that the technological opportunities are out there, and it is for India to capitalize on them.

Ravi Parthasarathy, Chairman, Infrastructure Leasing & Financial Services Limited (IL&FS)

Ravi Parthasarathy was born in 1952 and holds a Bachelor of Science degree and a Master of Business Administration degree. Since 1988, he has been the Chairman of IL&FS, which commenced operations that year, and has been in the forefront of the commercialization of infrastructure projects.

IL&FS pioneered the concept of public-private partnership in India, and has promoted, developed and financed diverse projects in surface transport, power, telecommunications, ports, special economic zones (SEZs), water supply and area development, working closely in this regard with central government agencies, state governments and local authorities, with an emphasis on environmental sustainability and local area development. In financial services, IL&FS specializes in structured finance, and private equity.

Before joining IL&FS, Parthasarathy was executive director of 20th Century Finance Corporation Limited, which grew to be the largest private sector company in the financial services sector, and a manager at Citibank NA.

Urban Infrastructure and Smart Cities: An Opportunity for Enhanced Indo-German Cooperation

Ravi Parthasarathy

CII National Mission on Smart Cities

Prime Minister Narendra Modi's government has now been in office for a little over two years. This has undoubtedly been a period that has seen frenetic activity in policymaking, with the implementation of both structural as well as tactical reforms. The latter category has been less noticed, and indeed, has generated few comments in the global media. However, significant administrative efficiencies have been realized by combining co-generic, but hitherto independent, ministries, in retrospect, a fairly obvious requirement.

The consolidation of ministries such as renewable energy and conventional energy, and coal and power, for example, have led to administrative efficiencies in resource allocation, and the creation of a grid that is today more susceptible to the receipt of baseload capacity, as well as cyclical energy production. In an impressive list of structural reforms undertaken, the recent and long-awaited enactment of the bankruptcy code is expected to have seminal impact, contributing significantly to the revitalization of the banking system. The anticipated passage of the Goods and Services Tax (GST) in the near term will enhance the creation of a more homogeneous market, and will augur well for an era of stable and secular growth.

India: A Growing Market for Global Corporates

The impact of government actions is already discernible, with foreign direct investment (FDI) across a host of sectors reaching a level of $44 billion in financial year 2016, as compared to $20 billion a few years earlier. The surge in FDI has also resulted from a clearly enunciated programme of debottlenecking so-called stalled projects, with consensus evolved amongst multiple counter-parties as to the best way forward.

During this period, global recessionary trends have continued, with growth limited, and even diminishing, in multiple markets that are important to India. Nonetheless, the government's strict adherence to fiscal discipline has ensured that the advantages of a favourable tailwind brought in by low commodity prices have not been frittered away. This is the backdrop to the opportunity that has been presented to deepen the economic relationship between India and Germany.

Towards Enhanced Indo-German Cooperation

Germany has long been regarded as a dependable partner as far as the government and the Indian corporate sector are concerned. As is well known, India was designated the partner country at the Hannover Messe in 2015, and it was this forum that was used by the government to launch its Make in India campaign. This campaign has resonated within the country, and has made an explicit effort to shake off the image of a country that is deemed to be proficient only in the services sector. India actually has a demonstrable capability for manufacturing to global standards. It also has a long history of hosting foreign manufacturing capability, and its own home-grown endeavours have been enhanced by the competitive landscape induced by international companies.

The government has taken steps to enhance the component of manufacturing in India's GDP, by opening new sectors where foreign companies can profitably establish their presence, including sectors such as defence that have hitherto been largely closed even to the Indian private sector. It would be appropriate to point out that there are currently few sectors where prior government approvals are required for initiating investment.

An increasing number of sectors are today permissible for investment under the 'automatic route', wherein only post facto reporting of the investment is required to be made by banks to the monetary authorities. There has also been a singular focus on improving the ease of doing business. These activities have effectively set the stage for India to invite its partner countries to mesh more deeply with its economic and developmental initiatives.

German companies have operated successfully in India for decades, and are well known, and widely respected. They span all sectors of manufacturing, including power, automobiles, engineering and chemicals. Over the decades, they have established a formidable reputation for quality, consistency and technological capability. They are perhaps ideally poised to benefit from the opportunities resulting from the market-oriented policies of the Modi government.

The Kreditanstalt für Wiederaufbau (or KfW as it is more commonly known) has long been an important catalyst in India's economic development. As possibly the largest developmental bank in the world, KfW has supported India's economic development for decades, with both the extension of grants for conducting feasibility studies, as well as by extending project term loans on a government to government basis, for as long as a forty-year period. The new initiatives of the government are expected to spur the activities of KfW, and enhance their effectiveness significantly. The private sector arm of KfW has also been proactive in supporting German corporates coming to India, as well as established Indo-German joint ventures.

The Smart City Programme

A number of initiatives have been launched similar to Make in India, and one of the most important and far-reaching programmes of the government is undoubtedly the 100 Smart Cities initiative. The smart city programme is fast being crystallized today at the level of numerous municipal corporations and urban local bodies (ULBs). Although relatively nascent, the initiative has sparked what is emerging to be possibly the most comprehensive and inclusive federal programme with defined outputs.

Herein lies an unprecedented opportunity for the German companies present in India, as well as the large number of high technology specialist Mittelstand companies that are widely acknowledged to be the industrial and economic backbone of Germany. Most importantly, this programme is likely to trigger ongoing and sustainable demand. While the initial programme envisions the enhancement of a hundred cities, there will literally be a thousand more Indian cities waiting in the wings to adopt similar initiatives. Therefore, there will undoubtedly be a first-mover advantage for companies involved in this initiative.

There is a need to appreciate the context in which the Smart Cities programme has been conceived. It is estimated that over the next twenty years, approximately 200 million people will be migrating from rural areas as well as Tier 3 cities to the larger cities of India in search of better economic prospects. While it is obviously not to forecast the exact number of individuals who will be migrating, and the precise time frame for this migration, it is certain that the migration will constitute perhaps one of the largest movements of humankind in history.

Indian cities are overcrowded and many lack even basic infrastructure such as potable water, sanitation and adequate power supply. It is clearly an imaginative and intelligent endeavour for the government to initiate the modernization of Indian cities in a pan-Indian federal framework, so that larger cities are able to cope with the influx of job seekers, and smaller cities acquire the capability to offer economic betterment. This is the context in which the Indian government launched its Smart Cities programme.

Cities in Germany are technologically advanced, and can easily claim the title of being 'smart'. There is a host of conventional literature on this subject, and German companies are possibly at the vanguard of technologies facilitating the creation of a smart city. There is a bewildering array of products and services that Indian cities require in order to be responsive to the requirements of citizens. While the specific needs of each urban habitat will necessarily vary based on demographics, there are perhaps four overarching requirements that will account for perhaps as much as 70 per cent of the investment required:

1. Transportation, including intra-city arterial corridors, which will lead to economic efficiencies such as savings in fuel, decongestion and a reduction in social tensions.
2. Sustainable energy, including renewables and two-way smart grids that will encourage the installation of rooftop solar energy production.
3. Water supply including, most importantly, recycling and wastewater treatment.
4. Solid waste management and its disposal in an ecologically sustainable manner.

The Confederation of Indian Industry (CII) has been at the vanguard in the debate on the nature, form and basis on which smart cities can most effectively be created. There is obviously more than one model which will work, and it may even be counterproductive to try to achieve overnight what Germany has achieved for its citizens over a span of several decades.

According to CII, going beyond products and services that will address the basic requirements of citizens, there is a need to appreciate the context in which the migration is taking place, and to fulfil the aspirations for economic betterment. There is also a need for 'liveability' to be one of the principal parameters for assessing the smartness of a particular urban habitat. Therefore, CII has advocated to the Ministry of Urban Development (MoUD) that any programme for establishing a smart city should go beyond the provision of goods and services, and also be based around three key criteria:

1. The city should facilitate employment opportunities to enable it to remain a viable host for migrants who are today largely coming from rural settings; in effect, to provide them an alternative meaningful livelihood. For example, the smart city proposal of Pune (which includes retrofitting and transforming about 900 acres along the Mula River) envisages an increase in employment through a start-up hub and commercial zones.

   Similarly, in the city of Chandigarh, 350 acres of greenfield development has been conceived as a transit-oriented development, focusing on knowledge/incubation/financial services for rejuvenation of the local economy through employment opportunities.
2. It is imperative that the productivity of citizens be increased by improving the ease with which they undertake their daily interactions with service providers, in both the government as well as the private sector. There is a need for a dependable delivery system which does not transgress on the time of an individual by treating it as a 'no cost' product.

   In the average metropolis, precious hours are wasted not only in commuting in inefficient transport systems, but also in accessing even rudimentary services that are, in fact, the right of every citizen. Minimizing wasted hours will result in an increase in productivity, which alone can provide an uptick to per capita GDP.
3. Finally, liveability can significantly be enhanced by the more effective use of public spaces. More recently, in Mumbai, a major bridge has also spawned a public park. Although it is endowed with only minimal amenities, it is a green space that can be accessed by citizens. A well-planned and meaningful augmentation of public spaces with a range of amenities can easily dovetail into urban infrastructure and improve the living standards of ordinary citizens. It can also bring about the attendant tertiary employment, stemming from the less-than-formal hospitality and entertainment sectors.

Accessing International Technologies

At the present level of development, every city in India will need a host of sub-initiatives in order to achieve the objectives of a smart city, as defined in the Indian context. There will be a large number of technologies required for this purpose, and no single corporate or government entity will have the wherewithal to implement all facets of the Smart Cities programme. Hence, there is a need for a consortium approach, with the lead member assuming the responsibility for integrating and supervising the implementation of all the subcomponents of the programme.

There is a need to go beyond technologies that Indian agencies are familiar with, and to ensure that tenders are not formulated on that basis. Since more efficient technologies are sometimes inadvertently excluded from consideration, CII has actively sought the formation of consortiums of companies with the full range of technologies required to equip a modern smart city.

CII has been gratified that Siemens AG has taken the lead in fielding a German consortium to work in close coordination with the ULBs concerned, in order to conceive and develop an integrated programme at the level of that ULB. It is even more gratifying that KfW has also joined the Siemens consortium, bringing to bear its own proven expertise in addressing the challenges of economic development in India.

The procurement and assessment of tenders needed for city-level development are invariably complex, and will remain a challenge. In view of this challenge, CII has recommended that individual cities and ULBs consider the procurement of products and services on the basis of the following:

1. A consortium approach led by a strong entity: this will effectively ensure that the physical roll-out as well as the subsequent maintenance programmes are not only well coordinated, but also integrated into the basic design of all subcomponents.
2. Life-cycle costs, including maintenance: Considering only the upfront capital cost, and disregarding maintenance obligations for an asset with a typical life of twenty-five years is usually inappropriate. The net present value of all costs, including maintenance, will prove to be the more appropriate measure.
3. Weightage of 75:25 for technical prowess and cost implications:

> There is a need for an apple-to-apple comparison between competing benefit-of-vendor credits, and the long-term sustainability and efficacy of performance guarantees that are demanded.

All individuals with knowledge of urbanization in India will readily grasp the significance of the Smart Cities programme. It is also easy for concerned individuals to be daunted by the sheer scale of the challenge, and the magnitude of technical and financial resources required for programme implementation. The creation of technical consortiums headed by corporates of the calibre of Siemens is an important part of the solution to this challenge.

Financing the Smart Cities Programme

At this stage, barely a year after the programme was first announced, numerous municipal corporations have been stimulated to look afresh at their objectives, and to define, possibly for the first time, the elements of 'smartness' that are needed to be embedded in their developmental plans. Their detailed submissions in this regard have been assessed by the MoUD, and twenty cities were selected as the initial candidates to lead programme implementation.

The government has decided to provide the requisite financial resources to enable each applicant to procure the required professional expertise needed to formulate its programme. More recently, the MoUD and CII have issued a compendium of the requirements of the first twenty cities that were selected for the programme, which breaks down an individual city's plan into 'projectized' components. This publication has been well received, and provides an excellent template that other cities can emulate.

Most importantly, it will help international companies that seek to participate in the programme to focus on specific opportunities more narrowly. In a manner of speaking, it has for the first time established a road map with a degree of clarity, of the exact steps and projects that need to be undertaken in a city seeking to be smart enabled, and with a broad estimate of attendant costs.

As an intended consequence, the issue of financing has become less daunting. The identified components can easily be segmented into three broad categories of projects:

1. Those that can be financed only by the government, e.g. dredging or cleaning up a minor waterbody. Ideally, this can be financed by

the issuance, by the ULB, of bonds in the capital market, with appropriate collateral.
2. Projects that are fully commercial in nature, e.g. telecom service providers can well be induced to pay the city for the privilege of providing specified services.
3. Projects that require some element of government support via a public–private partnership structure, a format that India is fully conversant with. Segmentation in this manner renders the task of raising resources more manageable.

A Cultural Interface

On an aspirational note, it would be beneficial if the enhanced Indo-German cooperation to facilitate the creation of smart cities also incorporated a cultural interface. The active propagation of the latter, including music that is enjoyed on a universal basis, would in fact be an important contributor to the advancement of the relationship.

It is gratifying that Hamburg proved to be, after Liverpool, virtually the launchpad for the Beatles. Similarly, the Spice Girls found their global mark with the German version of 'Wannabe', again attributed to the tumultuous reception they received in Hamburg.

More recently, the global acclaim accorded to the South Korean singer Psy's 'Gangnam style' solo which went viral, succeeded in enhancing awareness of the cultural potential of South Korea far more than that achieved by the export of high quality consumer electronic goods. There is great cultural innovation, including at the level of a host of music (including jazz) clubs, in a number of modern German cities. The use of cultural groups appealing to a wider mass of people—similar to popular Bollywood numbers—would dovetail well into the objective of increasing the liveability of cities, resulting in a more sustainable engagement at the level of the two cultures.

Conclusion

When the Smart Cities programme was first announced in India, its contours and resultant opportunities were not very clear. It is heartening that in just twelve months, the programme has stimulated not only a great deal of debate, but has also evolved to the extent where the first twenty cities have presented identifiable and projectized opportunities for international corporations to consider.

Going forward, I am sure that the Siemens consortium and other German corporates will more than meet the expectations of their Indian counterparts, and will deliver high quality products and services on a sustainable basis, while fostering employment and liveability. The momentum which already exists in the economic cooperation between India and Germany will be propelled to a new and higher plane of endeavour by this initiative.

Water Resources and Sanitation: Business from Bare Necessities

◈

Naina Lal Kidwai

'Swachh Bharat Campaign in Cooperation with Germany'

◈

Michael Beckereit

'Indo-German Partnership in the Water Sector'

Naina Lal Kidwai, Chairman, India Sanitation Coalition

Naina Lal Kidwai is the Chairman of Max Financial Services; Chairman of Harvard Business School, South Asia Board; Senior Adviser, Advent Private Equity; a Non-Executive Director on the global boards of Nestle, CIPLA Ltd and Larsen and Toubro; and past president of Federation of Indian Chambers of Commerce & Industry. She retired in December 2015 as Executive Director on the board of HSBC Asia-Pacific and Chairman of HSBC India.

An MBA from Harvard Business School, she makes regular appearances on listings by *Fortune* magazine, and listings of international women in business, and is the recipient of awards and honours in India, including the Padma Shri, for her contribution to trade and industry.

Her interest in water and the environment is reflected in her engagements with the Shakti Sustainable Energy Foundation, International Advisory Council of the United Nations Environment Program Inquiry, and the Global Commission on the Economy and Climate.

Swachh Bharat Campaign in Cooperation with Germany

Naina Lal Kidwai

The sanitation problem in India cannot be understated. While decades of sustained economic growth has made India the seventh largest economy in the world, public services such as water, sanitation, solid waste management, and drainage continue to be a challenge. According to the 2011 Census, India is home to the world's largest number of people—620 million—who defecate in the open. With an urgent need to re-energize and remodel its approach, the Indian government launched the Swachh Bharat Mission (SBM) in 2014.

Today, India has a historic opportunity to address the problem of sanitation in its entirety using the momentum generated by the SBM to realize the ambition of sustainable sanitation. However, in order to move away from the danger of being purely driven by numbers and shift the focus to the entire value chain of build–use–maintain–treat (BUMT), India can and must build partnerships with countries like Germany that have been successful in forward planning and addressing the last mile.

While some collaboration between the two nations has already been undertaken, there exists vast scope for further engagement and the sharing of expertise to connect current efforts with long-term sustainability, as well as gaining from the experience in the management and governance of national sanitation programmes.

Sanitation in the Indian context is multifaceted, layered in behavioural, social and cultural complexities. Prior to Independence, revered figures such as Mahatma Gandhi spoke about the need to improve hygiene and cleanliness in the country. Mahatma Gandhi notably stated in 1925, 'The cause of many of our diseases is the condition of our lavatories and our bad habit of disposing of excreta anywhere and everywhere.'

Since Independence and the initiation of planning frameworks, there have been various fronts of sanitation-focused government policy and programmes. India came on board as a signatory to the Mar del Plata resolution of 1977 that declared the period 1981 to 1990 as the international decade of water and sanitation, reflecting the global concern about sanitation. However, the 1981 Census showed rural sanitation coverage to be a mere 1 per cent. Therefore, until the latter half of the 1990s, progress on the sanitation front in India was abysmally slow.

Comprehensive efforts to improve the rural sanitation situation began with the Central Rural Sanitation Programme (CRSP) in 1986, a nationwide programme dedicated to rural sanitation. However, this programme focused purely on providing household sanitation facilities and relied mainly on subsidies and provision. It did not consider 'generating demand' for household toilets. It had only a limited impact on coverage, and studies indicated low usage by households.

The CRSP was reformed in 1999, to become the Total Sanitation Campaign (TSC) and subsequently, the Nirmal Bharat Abhiyan (NBA) in 2012. The NBA also included software components like information, education communication (IEC), and capacity building apart from infrastructure. It was only in 2008 that the issue of urban sanitation gained attention when the Indian government came out with a National Urban Sanitation Policy (NUSP). Access to improved sanitation in urban areas rose from 50 per cent in 1990 to 60 per cent in 2011. With regard to rural areas, significant progress was made with a jump from a coverage rate of just 7 per cent in 1990 to 31 per cent in 2011. However, as is evident, a lot still remains to be done.

With about half of India still defecating in the open and many households still unconnected to the sewage system, over 1.3 lakh tonnes of human waste is generated every day and this number is ever increasing. Only 30 per cent of this waste is being treated. Added to these jarring statistics are the problems of poor and insufficient systems of collection, transportation, treatment and improper disposal of solid waste. As research has continued to show, such deplorable sanitation conditions have an adverse effect on human health.

It is estimated that around 37.7 million Indians are affected by water-borne diseases annually, 1.5 million children are estimated to die of diarrhoea alone, and 73 million working days are lost due to waterborne diseases each year. In 2002, unsafe water and poor sanitation contributed to 7.5 per cent of total deaths and 9.4 per cent of total disability-adjusted life years in India, according to a 2008 World Health Organization (WHO) study.

Thus, despite recent progress, access to improved sanitation in India continues to lag behind the Millennium Development Goals target (goal 7) set for sanitation. With the renewed targets recently put forward under the Sustainable Development Goals (SDGs), a reworking of India's national sanitation programme has become imperative.

On 2 October 2014, a few months after taking over as prime minister of India, Narendra Modi launched the SBM. The launch of a national sanitation programme and the need to address the country's sanitation crisis was by no means revolutionary. However, never before has any other sanitation-focused government programme been able to sensationalize and popularize the issue to such a great extent, generate such fervour and capture attention at both a national and international level.

The SBM objectives are aligned with the SDGs, which urge state governments to achieve adequate and equitable sanitation and hygiene for all and end open defecation by the year 2030. The SBM strives to accelerate efforts to achieve universal sanitation coverage, improve cleanliness and eliminate open defecation in India by 2019, operating under two verticals—Swachh Bharat Mission, Urban, for cities and Swachh Bharat Mission, Gramin, for rural areas.

Further, the SDGs aim to improve water quality by reducing pollution, eliminating dumping and minimizing release of hazardous chemicals and materials, halving the proportion of untreated wastewater and substantially increasing recycling and safe reuse globally. Not only does the SBM plan to achieve India's sanitation-related goals eleven years earlier, but it also reflects the rising aspirations of the people, and the country as a whole.

The benefits of achieving the SBM objectives are manifold: clean villages, towns and cities; a reduction in waterborne diseases; reduced mortality arising from diarrhoeal diseases linked to poor hygiene; and higher economic growth. The World Bank estimates that 6.4 per cent of India's GDP is lost due to adverse economic impact and the costs of inadequate sanitation. Attaining the SBM goals is strongly linked to achieving good health, gender equality, and a cleaner environment. Already, the latest Swachhta Status Report shows an encouraging 45 per cent rural sanitation coverage in mid-2015 compared to the 31 per cent coverage in the 2011 Census.

Undoubtedly, the SBM has catalysed the conversation around sanitation, right from the streets to the boardrooms of corporate India. Not only has it yielded high political will and multi-ministry involvement, it has also spurred unprecedented discourse around the issue in the country. Today, the nation is at a critical junction in the SBM programme. The government, avid about infrastructure, recently announced it will build 5.2 million toilets by September 2016, or one every second.

However, the danger is that the renewed focus on sanitation may be driven purely by numbers. To move ahead, there is an urgent need to build even greater momentum around a broader understanding of what will make India truly 'swachh'. Simple infrastructure creation alone will not propel us towards the government's target to make India open defecation free (ODF) by 2019.

The construction of toilets must continue. While the SBM does recognize the importance of behaviour change, there is a dire need to shift the focus of the current efforts away from just building toilets to the entire value chain of BUMT in order to achieve sustainable sanitation.

Additionally, while the announcement in the 2016–17 budget of a generous $1,686.57 million for the SBM is commendable, the lower budgetary allocation of just $343.28 million to the urban leg of the programme vis-à-vis the $1,343.28 million to the rural leg continues to underplay the need for urgent attention to the issue of fecal sludge management.

Moreover, the amount allocated towards software and capacity building remains low. It is imperative that India uses this historic opportunity to address the problem of sanitation in its entirety, and use the momentum generated by the SBM to realize the ambition of sustainable sanitation, that is, to move away from merely the provision of toilets to toilets that are used and maintained, and where all human waste is safely treated and disposed of.

Germany has long served as a case in point for a nation that has managed to achieve sustainable sanitation by using forward planning to address the entire value chain of BUMT. As outlined by the German Development Cooperation (coordinated by the Federal Ministry for Economic Cooperation and Development), the country pursues the following policy objectives in the sanitation sector: 'To uphold the right to adequate living conditions through adequate sanitation infrastructure; to reduce health risks from waterborne illnesses and improve the standard of health; to protect the environment, especially through the sustainable management of water resources (ground water and surface water bodies); to promote economic and social development and the development of socially and environmentally sustainable towns and cities and their surroundings.'

This comprehensive approach has enabled Germany to think holistically, engage in forward planning and in turn, achieve successes such as the treatment of nearly 100 per cent of its collected urban sewage. Even though Germany is a water-rich country, it has repeatedly emphasized the need to ensure that all strategies and programmes set out for the sanitation sector include targets for environmental, social and economic sustainability.

At an international level, Germany is one of the largest international donors in this sector. While its initial focus fell heavily on the Middle East and Africa, the country has now shifted its focus to other emerging countries like India. Germany, which recently celebrated sixty years of diplomatic relations with India, is today one of India's most important partners for trade, investment and technology.

Germany and India have already undertaken various collaborations in the water and sanitation sector, particularly in the areas of river regeneration, compact water supply for small settlements, wastewater treatment systems for urban areas, energy-efficient irrigation, energy recovery from wastewater and public–private partnerships (PPPs). Examples of such initiatives so far include the establishment of the Indo-German Centre for Sustainability (IGCS) that focuses on cooperation between scientists of the two countries.

At the national level, Germany has initiated the Support to National Urban Sanitation Policy-II project, assisting the Indian government with various schemes that also include urban sanitation improvement, such as the National Urban Sanitation Policy, SBM and Atal Mission for Rejuvenation and Urban Transformation.

Reflecting Germany's increased interest and engagement in India's water and sanitation sector, the Sustainable Sanitation Alliance (SuSanA) recently established a formal chapter in the country with the India Sanitation Coalition. In January 2007, Deutsche Gesellschaft für Technische Zusammenarbeit (GTZ—German Technical Cooperation) and the Stockholm Environment Institute, launched SuSanA to improve awareness of sustainable sanitation.

In India, the chapter is anchored by the India Sanitation Coalition, formed with the objective of getting all stakeholders in the sanitation field onto one platform where they can share information, learn from others, partner and collaborate. The recent tie-up between the India Sanitation Coalition and SuSanA strives to create a knowledge ecosystem comprising an open source library and discussions revolving around the topic of sustainable sanitation.

This collaboration coincides with the latter half of the SBM. It is an opportune time to track and report on the SBM, and inform the ministries of drinking water and sanitation and urban development as well as state governments (state SBM coordinators, principal secretaries, district administrators, engineers and sanitation coordinators).

Through the collaboration, the following outcomes are envisaged: to create a dynamic interface extending beyond boundaries to share, discuss, contribute and promote sustainable sanitation systems; to be a centralized alliance for all the stakeholders of the sanitation sector; and to contribute to the achievement of current and future international development goals by promoting a systems approach to sanitation provision, taking into consideration all aspects of sustainability. This partnership is a perfect example of the potential for enhanced collaboration based on sharing of expertise between the two countries in the sanitation sector.

As the IGCS, SuSanA and other examples above illustrate, Indo-German collaboration in the sanitation sector is already under way. However, given the particularly re-energized environment and conducive political, legal and institutional framework created under the SBM, the opportunity and potential for further engagement is imperative. In particular, India must learn from the expertise and forward planning of the German water and sanitation sector that is centred on sustainable, resource-saving and target group-oriented approaches as well as innovation.

India needs guidance on the governance and management structures of its sanitation programmes and policy. Four possible areas of shared learning between the two countries that can be explored are: the redefining of sustainable sanitation; the need for decentralized and tailored solutions; the encouraging of closed-loop approaches; and the need for collaborative platforms.

Sustainable sanitation, as defined by the German Development Cooperation, includes: secure, affordable and dignified access to sanitation facilities; sustainable wastewater and waste management that protects people against infection and preserves the environment; and awareness of hygienic behaviour. The Indian Ministry of Drinking Water and Sanitation's recently issued guidelines define the criteria for declaring a village as 'Open Defecation Free' to include not just access to a toilet, but also usage of the toilet and safe technology.

Therefore, what is needed from all the supporters of this national programme is a shared understanding and commitment to the ministry's guidelines (water, safe disposal, operations and maintenance funds) to ensure that increased demand is met with the necessary attention to all aspects around the sanitation continuum.

The Central Pollution Control Board has estimated that over 73 per cent of all faecal sludge generated in the country is left untreated in the environment in India. It is imperative that India learn from the German experience of forward planning to include wastewater treatment and issues such as the undervaluing of operations and maintenance and sludge treatment projects in its focus on sanitation, while simultaneously building toilets.

German sanitation programmes and strategies have included a target-oriented approach, emphasizing that selected sanitation interventions must be localized, taking into account the needs and circumstances of the users. Recognizing that Germany has been able to uphold the quality and efficiency of its centralized wastewater systems owing to its water-and capital-rich profile, developing countries must explore better-suited decentralized systems.

Innovative solutions and supporting entrepreneurship are critical. This notion of promoting sustainable tailored solutions to respective localities and geographies will be imperative to the success of the SBM in India, particularly given the diversity of the country. Furthermore, in Germany the responsibility of water supply and wastewater disposal falls on the municipalities or other public corporations. India can learn about the advantages of a centralized and decentralized sanitation programme while putting the onus more on the states and municipalities. Germany can also help guide India in the creation of efficient governance structures that ensure the avoidance of the undesirable effects of decentralization, such as staggered or delayed funding.

Germany is well known for its promotion of a closed-loop approach in sanitation, that is, dealing with waste and wastewater systems. In particular, Germany's Ecological Sanitation project focuses on 'ecological sanitation systems [that] enable the recovery of nutrients from human faeces and urine to the benefit of agriculture, thus helping to preserve soil fertility, to assure food security for future generations, to minimize water pollution and to recover bioenergy'.

This waste-to-energy model represents the forward- and big-picture thinking of Germany's approach that will be critical to India's sanitation journey moving forward. Germany can provide support in sharing the knowledge and creating incentives for the use of environmentally sound, closed-loop sanitation systems. This will assist India in moving to the stage of 'sanitation plus', accruing the real benefits of ensuring universal access to safe sanitation by keeping sight of the entire sanitation value chain to ensure sustainability of this massive national effort.

Finally, in order to achieve sustainable sanitation, collaborative platforms that promote multilevel and multi-stakeholder involvement are necessary.

Germany has been particularly successful in creating PPP models in the sanitation sector wherein private companies are not permitted to provide sanitation services (including wastewater treatment) directly but instead, through contracts with municipalities. For example, Gelsenwasser AG is a multi-utility, privately owned public water company serving the North Rhine–Westphalia region contracted by multiple municipalities. This model of PPP will be a critical learning for India's growing multi-stakeholder dialogue.

In India, the government has also actively elicited the support of corporates for the programme through various channels including the setting up of an SBM Kosh as well as a Corporate Facilitation Desk. While the SBM programme has created an avenue for engagement with the corporate sector, till now, discussion around private engagement in the sector has focused on the numbers around infrastructure creation. Going forward, there is a pressing need to encourage innovation across the life cycle of a sanitation programme.

India must encourage more entrepreneurs to participate in these activities, including looking at profitable distributed models for waste management as it is done in Germany. There needs to be more attention given to financing solutions for stakeholders, innovations need to be encouraged across the value chain, actionable knowledge produced and disseminated, and stakeholders need to be supported through capacity-building initiatives. Collaborative platforms such as the India Sanitation Coalition and further learning from the German experience will help to foster such partnerships and move towards sustainable and scalable results.

In order to address the issue of fragmentation, the India Sanitation Coalition was established to serve as an aggregator of knowledge and networks with nationwide and international outreach, focusing on models for achieving sustainable sanitation in alignment with the SBM and its goals. Launched on 25 June 2015 at the Federation of Indian Chambers of Commerce & Industry, in New Delhi by Minister of Drinking Water and Sanitation Birendra Singh, and Vijaylaxmi Joshi, former secretary, Ministry of Drinking Water and Sanitation, the coalition has since been a platform to empower, act as a catalyst, galvanize stakeholders (corporates, governments, communities), while also ensuring inclusiveness.

This sort of forum will be particularly helpful for varied German stakeholders willing and able to enter the Indian sanitation space. Whether with the Indian government or other Indian players like corporates and non-governmental organizations, the coalition can play an active role in helping German stakeholders navigate the sector and facilitate Indo-German partnerships.

There is no doubt that India is moving in the right direction in its sanitation journey. It has been able to galvanize the country around the issue through programmes like SBM and platforms like the India Sanitation Coalition. It is important to recognize that India already has multiple strong players who have worked in the sector for many years, have the expertise in implementation and capacity building, and are repositories of knowledge. Besides, there are donors and corporates interested in funding. The required capital expenditure for the SBM is estimated to be $38,095.52 million for rural sanitation and $19,572.69 million for urban sanitation, reflecting a vast scope of opportunity.

What is needed with the support of partner countries like Germany is the sharing of expertise and experience in the management and governance of such vast sanitation programmes and networks. From ensuring sustainability and promoting localized tailored solutions to creating decentralized management structures, Germany can help to guide India in its mission to become open defection free by 2019. To work towards total and sustainable sanitation, it is imperative to keep the focus on BUMT and maximize collective contributions, and tap into the tremendous potential in creating entry points for these multiple stakeholders across the entire value chain. By working together, Germany can help India become a truly 'swachh' nation!

Dr Michael Beckereit, Chairman, German Water Partnership

Dr Michael Beckereit is the CEO of HAMBURG WATER, which includes Hamburg Waterworks GmbH and the Hamburg city drainage AöR. Additionally, he is, and has been since its inception in May 2009, the managing director of HAMBURG ENERGIE. After studying civil engineering, he received his doctorate at the University of Hannover and was managing director of several companies in the environmental engineering market and water management. Dr Beckereit is also a board member of DVGW, vice president of the German utilities association VKU and CEO of the German Water Partnership.

Indo-German Partnership in the Water Sector

Dr Michael Beckereit

The German Water Partnership (GWP) is a central coordination and contact office of the German water sector serving foreign partners and clients. It is a joint initiative of the German private and public sectors, combining commercial enterprises, governmental and non-governmental organizations, scientific institutions and water-related associations. The network is supported by five federal ministries. Its head office in Berlin collects and coordinates information about innovations, activities and the services of its members.

Germany has more than 150 years of experience in successful water management. Its efficiency in plant engineering, consulting and operations is complemented by unparalleled expertise in scientific research, education and training, and high levels of institutional and administrative knowledge.

GWP's fundamental aim is to make outstanding German engineering, know-how and experiences in the water sector easily available to partners and clients all over the world. GWP strives to transfer this efficiency and high standards in water treatment and management to any region in the world that needs help in solving present and future water problems, including those caused or aggravated by climate change, population growth and desertification.

Tasks and Objectives

Strategic positioning as a central contact for enquiries from abroad: GWP provides foreign customers with information and supports communication and the initiation of business with its members and partners.

Raising the profile of the German water industry and research abroad: GWP presents and explains the competencies and unique position features of the German water industry and research, at international symposiums and conferences.

Expansion of internal communication: Within its committees, at the annual conference and on its website, GWP offers a broad variety of opportunities to exchange information and experiences.

Networking and cooperation with professional associations, organizations and ministries: Continuous exchange and cooperation between GWP and professional associations, organizations and ministries strengthens the position of the German water industry and research in international markets.

Expansion of the international network in the focus countries: The regional sections within GWP are primarily responsible for building a network for members in the focus countries, to strengthen the position of the German water industry and research.

Intensifying networks of industry and research: GWP supports communication between companies and research institutes, and makes an effort to break down barriers to innovation and improve the marketing environment of the German water industry.

Competencies

Quality: From the initial project idea, development and planning to the long-term operation of facilities—our highly qualified employees cover the entire spectrum of the business and provide their expertise worldwide. The quality of products and services plays as important a role as the price-performance ratio. We stand for 'Made in Germany' in the water sector.

Sustainability: The German water industry pursues the goal of conserving global water resources through sustainable consumption and management of water. Through this effort, as well as projects subsidized by the German government, it contributes to the achievement of the UN Millennium Development Goals.

Reliability: The members of GWP are internationally renowned partners, reliable over the long term, and fulfil their contracts to the highest quality.

Flexibility: Many companies of all sizes, which offer specialized services, are responsible for Germany's competence in water matters. The members of GWP supply appropriate, practical solutions that enable them to meet the requirements of their international customers efficiently, safely and economically.

Innovation: The German water sector leads the world in the research and development of pioneering solutions, materials, technologies and products. Our members invest consistently in the development and implementation of new technologies, processes and services, as well as in ongoing education and training programmes, to ensure our employees are fit to carry on the work in the future.

Clean business: GWP and its member companies, with a commitment to fair competition as the essential foundation for a functioning global economy, confirm the 'Clean Business' initiative and pledge not to engage in corrupt practices.

Connecting People, Working Out Solutions

The activities of the network include connecting its members with partners and clients from all over the world, providing information on water issues like international cooperation offers and tenders, and organizing business trips to foreign countries, and workshops or joint representations at international water exhibitions. Experts from the water industry and research have joined forces in sixteen regional sections (country or region related) to offer a broad range of products and services.

The objectives of these regional sections are to cultivate contacts with partners and decision-makers in the focus countries, and to kick off projects and work out custom-tailored solutions in water management. The GWP regional sections deal with all enquiries from foreign customers. The regional section in India is one of GWP's biggest regional sections.

Being Part of the Partnership

Apart from various other activities, the regional section of GWP in India, in cooperation with its Indian partners, organizes the Indian GWP Days, a series of events with the headline 'German Solutions to Indian Challenges'. Here, German water experts meet Indian decision-makers to work out adapted solutions for water management in India.

At the first Indian-GWP Day that took place in Bengaluru in October 2013, more than one hundred participants from Germany and India discussed the challenges of Indian water management and looked for ways to cooperate.

With 250 people, the number of participants had already more than doubled at the second Indian-GWP Day in October 2014. This proves there is broad acceptance and success on both sides, and there is a need for future continuation. In well-proven cooperation with the SCMS Group of Educational Institutions and Kochi Municipal Corporation, GWP organized the third Indian–GWP Day in Kochi in October 2015. The interest in the annual event and the accompanying exhibition continued to be high.

At the meeting of the 'Water and Waste-working group' of Federal Ministry for the Environment, Nature Conservation, Building and Nuclear Safety (BMUB) of Germany and Ministry of Environment, Forests and Climate Change (MoEFCC), Government of India in New Delhi in April 2016, GWP chose Chennai as the conference venue for the fourth Indian-GWP Day to be held in November 2016. Its partners include the Water Pollution Control Board and the Tamil Nadu Water Investment Corps.

Water as a Driver of Economic Growth

Initiative and the economic strategy of Indian Prime Minister Narendra Modi promise to be key elements of success for the Indo-German partnership in the water sector. Prime Minister Modi has realized that India urgently needs to improve its infrastructure. Besides factories, streets and facilities such as shopping malls to improve the quality of life, he wants new cities to be built. All these investments are closely connected to the subject of water. Industrialization, urbanization and modernization lead to an increased demand for clean water.

At the moment this demand can hardly be met. Competing consumers like industry and agriculture have rapidly shrunk these resources. This is why in his first keynote address Prime Minister Modi explained that his government will give top priority to safe water supply. He knows that to achieve his economic goals, India needs improved water supply.

Specific Developments in the Sector

The connection between water and food supply is fundamental. If the steadily growing Indian population is to be fed, long-planned irrigation projects have to be launched. This requires clean rivers, stormwater management and groundwater of reliable quality and quantity. On the other hand, irrigation has to be optimized using modern methods like drip irrigation. In this context, Prime Minister Modi spoke of 'Per Drop More Crop'.

Water and energy are related in a similar way. Water is necessary for the generation of energy, at the same time water supply systems consume energy. This is why intelligent concepts are needed to supply to all three—agriculture, industry and the people. During the planning of supply systems, it is essential to consider where and for what water is needed, and how water currents can be rerouted with minimal use of energy.

The rapidly growing middle class puts further pressure on the water sector. Many well-educated young people have no sympathy for interruptions in water supply, especially in big cities. This makes it necessary to develop reliable systems. Smaller municipalities also need solutions, particularly those in arid regions with low precipitation. For financial reasons, big water projects are out of the question. This is why adapted solutions for smaller settlements or isolated properties have to be found, which are suitable for Indian conditions.

Opportunities for the German Water Sector

Indo-German collaboration is characterized by many actors on both sides. Both politics and industry strive for rapprochement and closer cooperation. However, their actions often are uncoordinated and characterized by a bewildering variety of options. The possibilities of local consulates and chambers of commerce regulating them are limited.

Regarding water management, it can be stated that due to Prime Minister Modi's prioritizing the subject, the discussion has gained new impetus on both sides. There are more and more delegations coming to India with participants from industry and politics concentrating on the subjects of water and the environment. The German water branch is made up of many small- and medium-sized businesses which seldom stand a chance to be seen or heard when facing competition from big international companies. This is why the idea of uniting under the umbrella body of the GWP offers these companies an extraordinary opportunity to play a bigger role in water management.

There are varied relations between research, consultants and industry both within GWP and between Germany and India. These relations are precious resources that can be used for collaboration, especially when it comes to adapting existing technologies and trade channels to specific Indian conditions. The experience of companies already working in India helps to learn about local characteristics. The well-developed ability to solve problems in a quick and uncomplicated way is an obvious advantage for German companies in the Indian market.

German Potential for the Indian Market

Developments in the German water sector in the last fifty years which have helped German companies acquire extensive experience in water management can be adapted to specific Indian conditions. Close cooperation between the Indian and German water sectors promises fruitful results for sustainable development.

GWP stands for an integrated approach when it comes to facing challenges for the water sector. For GWP, sustainability consists of efficient long-term solutions which take into account various aspects of the environment, the minimization of energy consumption and use of chemicals, safe working conditions for employees and a suitable integration into the surroundings. Independence in importing spare parts and chemicals is also a relevant aspect of sustainable solutions. The recovery of energy from wastewater supports economic operation of the plant and—by using fermentation—solves the problem of organic residue from industrial production.

Integrated water resources management is an effective tool to ensure safe water supply. Regarding the water balance, the reuse of water is a basic element to cover the increasing demand resulting from the growing population and higher living standards. Water can be reused in two ways: directly (for example, treated wastewater for irrigation purposes) or indirectly (for example groundwater recharge, riverbank filtration). In Germany, for example, every drop of Rhine water flowing into the sea has been used for municipal or industrial purposes more than three times on average. This recycling is only possible with an adequate water quality of the river, achieved by efficient wastewater treatment.

The monitoring of the river water quality is not only a requirement for the development of river rehabilitation but a prerequisite for river water recycling. The challenge of efficient river quality monitoring is mainly based on a good structure of the measuring points and an evaluation of the data supported by numerical river quality simulation. The technological systems for stable quality measurements, including data transfer systems, are available and have proved effective in many applications.

A wide range of technologies for the treatment of municipal or industrial wastewater have been applied successfully. In Germany, around 10,000 wastewater treatment plants are in operation. More than 1,000 plants use the sludge produced for the generation of power, to cover their own energy consumption. An energetically autonomous operation is possible when using additional organic residue from industrial production or the organic fractions of solid waste (fermentation).

Many valuables other than energy can be found in wastewater. Specific recycling technologies recover nitrogen and phosphorus for reuse. The generation of energy and recycling nutrients from wastewater are two important elements of sustainable water management. In Germany, specific technologies for these purposes have been developed and implemented successfully.

In Germany, about 350 so-called neighbourhood groups have been installed for the training of operators and to optimize water and wastewater treatment plants. Each of these groups consists of 15–20 operators from similar plants. It is fully proven that this neighbourhood organization results in reduced operation costs and better efficiency. The German water sector provides the instruments and the experience for the establishment of such neighbourhood groups.

Good Opportunities for Both India and Germany

There obviously is a large market potential in India. Many infrastructure projects are being launched due to the goals formulated by Prime Minister Modi, providing plenty of opportunities for German companies to transfer their tried-and-tested experience to the Indian water sector—not only at large-scale projects such as Ganges rejuvenation or the Delhi–Mumbai Industrial Corridor, but also the many medium- and small-scale projects.

GWP members in India have completed a number of projects in India. These include the following:

Phase I

- Project all over India—ARSOlux: The Luminous Water Test
- Project in Bengaluru—Monitoring Pressure of Drinking Water Network
- Project in Delhi—Safe Drinking Water for Hope Project in New Delhi
- Project in Delhi and all over India—Municipal Demand-side management

- Project in Hyderabad—Krishna Drinking Water Supply

Phase II

- Project in Mumbai—Rehabilitation of a sewer in Mumbai
- Project in Uttarakhand—Water Supply Scheme
- Project in Ahmedabad—Viratnagar Pumping Station
- Project in Kolkata—Water Footprint by Shree Cement Limited

To realize such large-, medium- or small-scale projects, it is essential to meet the goals set by Prime Minister Modi.

Strong Support by the Indian Ambassador in Germany

To strengthen the links between Germany and India, the Indian Embassy in Berlin has created its own programme called 'Made in India Mittelstand', which has been enthusiastically welcomed by small- and medium-sized companies in Germany that plan to export or invest in India. Additional stakeholder and business meetings organized by the embassy attest to the exceptional cooperation and partnership between the two countries.

Science, Technology, Innovation and more

◈

Reimund Neugebauer
'Research and Innovation for a Better Future'

◈

R.A. Mashelkar
'Indo-German S&T Partnership:
Yesterday, Today and Tomorrow'

Professor Reimund Neugebauer, President, Fraunhofer-Gesellschaft

Professor Reimund Neugebauer graduated from the Technische Universität Dresden in 1979 with a degree in mechanical engineering. From 1979 to 1984, he was a scientific associate and a senior scientific assistant there. He received his doctorate in 1984 and became a professor in 1989.

In 1991, he became director of the Fraunhofer Institute for Machine Tools and Forming Technology IWU. In 1993, he was appointed chair of the machine tools department at the Technische Universität Chemnitz (TU Chemnitz) and in 2000, he became managing director of TU Chemnitz's Institute of Machine Tools and Production Processes. On 1 October 2012, he took up the post of president of Fraunhofer-Gesellschaft.

He is a fellow of the International Academy for Production Engineering and a member of the National Academy of Science and Engineering. From 2010 to 2011, he was president of the German Academic Society for Production Engineering and since 2014, he has been a member of the German National Academy of Sciences. In 2016, he was appointed co-chair of the German federal government's High-Tech Forum. He is also on the executive board of the newly established 'Plattform Industrie 4.0', an alliance of representatives from politics, industry, associations, science and trade unions.

Research and Innovation for a Better Future

Professor Reimund Neugebauer

Innovation is the growth engine that transforms research ideas into products in the shortest possible time, thereby creating jobs, economic growth and prosperity for a nation. When invention becomes a part of people's lives and creates both impact and profit, it is defined as innovation. For many years now, Europe has viewed innovation as a mantra for success, securing its indelible position as a technology leader.

In industry, this has paid huge dividends for its research and development (R&D) and has led to multiplied employment and economic power for its constituencies. At Fraunhofer, we believe innovation is in our blood, and applied research forms the foundation of our organization. In partnership with companies, we transform original ideas into innovations that benefit society and strengthen both the German economy and the European economy. As an innovation driver, we lead strategic initiatives to master future challenges and thus achieve technological breakthroughs. Our motto reflects this ideology: 'In service of the future—People need a future and future needs research.'

Fraunhofer is at the forefront of smart technologies and enriches lives. Our research aims to integrate solutions across industries in a cross-functional and efficient manner that results in ground-breaking technologies and innovations, often well ahead of their time. With our industry-agnostic and application-oriented approach, all sixty-seven Fraunhofer institutes as well as the various centres worldwide are able to harness the immense capabilities from our global ecosystem and develop strategies, technologies and solutions that are fine-tuned to the various markets and client requirements.

Fraunhofer is intrinsically embedded in the research and innovation system in Germany. On the one hand, Fraunhofer is a critical link between universities that are known as centres of educational excellence and fundamental research. On the other hand, it is invaluable for innovative industries that are eager to roll out new products and processes in the shortest time and in the most resource-efficient manner. To better understand Fraunhofer's structure and how it functions, institutes in such diverse countries as the United States,

France, China, Korea, England and India are in regular discourse with us.

Fraunhofer has grown through partnerships with its stakeholders and by adopting a single-minded focus on sustainable operations. Every Fraunhofer institute is linked closely to the universities and academic centres associated with its location. This is achieved through the head of the institute, who is also a professor, and is strengthened by a vital pipeline of students who do their doctoral and postdoctoral studies at the university and their research at Fraunhofer.

Finally, Fraunhofer completes its seamless engagement through cooperation between industry and academia. This also accelerates research from the lab to the market. The fact that each institute has to generate at least 50 per cent of its budget through client-financed projects keeps Fraunhofer focused on applied research. Government funding to the tune of nearly 30 per cent of its budget makes it possible for Fraunhofer to undertake basic research and thus stay ahead of the technology curve.

Annually, Fraunhofer carries out nearly 7,500 projects and therefore, constantly pushes the research and development (R&D) envelope. In addition to working with large companies, Fraunhofer also collaborates with many small-and medium-enterprises (SMEs), which it sees as the real drivers of innovation. After the global economic crisis in 2009–10, Germany was one of the first countries to bounce back. Fraunhofer was lauded as the 'real stimulus package' for German industry as it focused on resource-efficient production and innovation to support German industry to become profitable in a very short span of time.

Innovation and the Nations

Innovation has been a game changer for Europe, helping it to leapfrog to its position among the world leaders in innovation. The recently released 'European Innovation Scoreboard 2016' has again put Germany among the leading innovators of European Union (EU) member countries, ranking it fifth, behind Switzerland, Sweden, Denmark and France. In a global comparison, the US certainly leads the way, followed by South Korea and Japan. However, with the strategic vision of Europe 2020, Europe is ready to challenge this trend.

The EU's agenda for growth and jobs for the current decade, the Europe 2020 Strategy, emphasizes smart, sustainable and inclusive growth as a way to overcome the structural weakness in Europe's economy, to improve its competitiveness and productivity, and to underpin a sustainable social market economy. The Europe 2020 Strategy sets the target of 'increasing combined public and private investment in R&D to 3 per cent of GDP' by 2020. Germany already invests 2.8 per cent of its GDP on innovation and R&D, and this is set to increase.

One of the key accelerators in this trend are the 'Leistungszentren' (centres of excellence). R&D intensity increases when geographical or industry clusters are created and supported through focused funding and coordination activities. Germany has ten such regions; in particular, the Baden-Württemberg and Bavaria regions have been a nucleus of intensified R&D or specific high technology industrial activities and knowledge-based services. Due to focused clusters and multi-stakeholder involvement, these centres of excellence result in spin-offs, attract new start-ups, and also foster value creation along the entire value chain, boosting the region's competitive advantage as well as improving the innovation potential of all the stakeholders involved.

Now for the most exciting news. According to *R&D Magazine*, the current trend of Asian economies growing faster than other world nations is coupled with the fact that their investments in R&D are often at rates several times higher than those of American and European countries. As a result, combined Asian R&D investments are growing at a faster rate than elsewhere, and their global R&D shares continue to increase at almost 1 per cent per year, while American and European R&D shares have been decreasing. Although the American and European absolute R&D investments are continuing to increase, this rise is at a slower rate than the R&D investments in other countries.

In Asia, South Korea and Japan are in the lead when it comes to intensive R&D spending. While South Korea spends above 4 per cent of its GDP on R&D, Japan is not far behind with 3.5 per cent. China is fast catching up with an amazing 1.98 per cent of GDP. China, despite an economic slowdown this past year (a mere 6.8-7 per cent GDP growth in 2015, down from 8 per cent or more in previous years) that has affected the world economy, has a well-documented programme for R&D investments (Five Year Plans) that will sustain its R&D dominance and allow it to continue to outpace other countries (including the US) for the foreseeable future. Its visionary plan for the next few years is to continue its 7 per cent annual GDP growth target.

China is expected to surpass the US in total annual R&D spending by 2026, and continue to widen the gap beyond that point in time. India, on the other hand, is also accelerating its R&D investment programme and has moved up from 0.56 per cent of GDP in 2012 to 0.88 per cent of GDP in 2015. The Indian government is placing greater emphasis on increased R&D programmes with industry and hence, this growth trend is expected to continue.

Fraunhofer Engagement with India: A Partnership to Drive Innovation

Through independent institutes, Fraunhofer has been active in India for a long time. However, the Fraunhofer brand came to India in the middle of 2008 with a concerted effort to understand the Indian market and engage with Indian industry, government and academia. Since its entry into India, Fraunhofer has steadily forged ahead with very significant partnerships with all its stakeholders and also built a credible clientele of the best large- and medium-scale industry companies. Busting the myth that Indian companies do not undertake contract research, the first million euros in contract research in India came within two and a half years of Fraunhofer's arrival in India, and has been growing at a good pace ever since.

Some highlights of Fraunhofer's Engagement in India: A Multi-stakeholder Model

Among Fraunhofer's very first partners in India was the Core Group of Automotive Research (CAR), under the able guidance of Dr R Chidambaram, principle adviser to the Prime Minister's Office, and Professor Raja Chidambaram Rama Rao, then a member of the CAR Group. This cooperation has been a ground-breaking initiative, bringing together as it does a wide variety of stakeholders from academia, industry and the public sector; four Indian institutions, namely International Advanced Research Centre for Powder Metallurgy and New Materials (ARCI), Hyderabad; Indian Institute of Science (IISc), Bengaluru; Indian Institute of Technology (IIT) Madras; and Automotive Research Association of India (ARAI), Pune; the four Fraunhofer institutes—Institute for Machine Tools and Forming Technology (IWU), Institute for Material and Beam Technology (IWS), Institute for Manufacturing Technology and Advanced Materials (IFAM) and Institute for Nondestructive Testing (IZFP); and the participation of Indian automotive original equipment manufacturers (OEMs). Together, they are working on the evaluation of four different techniques to join aluminium, steel and plastic in dissimilar combinations. This is intended to lead to the development of design guidelines for incorporating the newly generated knowledge into automotive body designs.

Government and Public Sector Cooperation: Innovation with a Human Face

A very interesting project has been implemented by the Fraunhofer Institute for Production Technology and the Tool Academy of RWTH Aachen, under contract by the development commissioner, Central Tool Room, Ministry of Micro Small and Medium Enterprises (MSME), Government of India. The objective was to evaluate the technological, HR and training competencies of the tool rooms and to develop a road map to address the issue of sustainability and research services to industry.

During a recent visit of German Chancellor Angela Merkel, Fraunhofer signed an MoU with the Indian Department of Heavy Industries (DHI) to be the 'Technology Resource Partner' for the manufacturing sector in India. The clarion call given by Prime Minister Narendra Modi, under the Make in India programme, envisages attracting increased foreign investment in manufacturing into India. The thrust of the Fraunhofer–DHI cooperation is to strengthen the innovation and R&D capability of the supply chain in India to meet the demands of the Indian market.

Fraunhofer has also signed an MoU with the Indian Ministry of New and Renewable Energy to support the renewable energy sector in India. Since Fraunhofer has immense competencies in the entire value chain of renewable energy from wind to solar to biomass, the cooperation is sure to strengthen both countries and help them make their mark on the global stage.

Industry Collaboration: Leapfrogging Technology Competencies

Fraunhofer's primary client group is industry, as it is this group that commercializes the technologies developed at Fraunhofer, and hence closes the loop. In India, Fraunhofer has received tremendous response and encouragement from industry across sectors such as production technologies, renewable energy, materials, textiles and aerospace. Today, Fraunhofer is working with more than thirty of the top fifty companies in India and has several projects under various stages of discussion and collaboration.

The cooperation with multipliers such as the Automotive Component

Manufacturers Association of India, the Society for Indian Automobile Manufacturers, or Confederation of Indian Industry is of particular significance, as it affords a great opportunity to work with equal partners who value innovation and R&D as growth engines.

Knowledge Partners: Academia

Academic and research institutes form an indelible and strong link in the Fraunhofer ecosystem as catalysts for R&D input towards commercialization. In Germany, the head of each Fraunhofer institute is also the chair of the applied research subject at the local university, creating major synergies and access to faculty and student knowledge reservoirs. In India too, Fraunhofer has aggressively engaged with its peers to support the local ecosystem and to gain valuable insights into the Indian R&D scenario.

It is cooperating with leading institutions, such as IISc, Bengaluru, and IIT Madras (Chennai). The recently signed collaboration between Fraunhofer and Brijmohan Lal Munjal University is a cooperation that will prove to be win–win for all partners. It will also support Indian industry by helping it match the progress made in developed countries in the field of advanced qualification and industry, and create institute linkages.

A 'Real' Valuable Partnership

While Germany is known for its engineering and technology expertise, India can bank on its human resources and an enormous consumer market. Together, India and Germany can define a bilateral relationship and pave the way for a long and mutually beneficial partnership.

Dr R.A. Mashelkar, Nation Research Professor, and President, Global Research Alliances

Dr R.A. Mashelkar is a national research professor and the president of Global Research Alliance. He was director general of the Council of Scientific and Industrial Research and the president of the Indian National Science Academy.

He has been elected a fellow of the Royal Society, US National Academy of Science, US National Academy of Engineering and American Academy of Arts and Sciences.

He has been a member of the Science Advisory Council to the Indian Prime Minister. He has played a key role in shaping India's science and technology institutions, policies and strategies.

Dr Mashelkar is the chairman of India's National Innovation Foundation, Reliance Innovation Council, Marico Innovation Foundation, KPIT Technologies Innovation Council, etc.

He holds honorary doctorates from thirty-five universities and has been awarded India's highest civilian honours—Padma Shri (1991), Padma Bhushan (2000) and Padma Vibhushan (2014).

Indo-German S&T Partnership: Yesterday, Today and Tomorrow

Dr R.A. Mashelkar

View from a Personal Lens

Let me begin this essay on Indo-German partnership in science, technology and innovation by presenting a view from my personal lens.

I was privileged to be a member of the Indo-German Consultative Committee (IGCC) in the early 1990s. IGCC was formed by then prime minister of India, Narasimha Rao, and then chancellor of Germany, Helmut Kohl. It met alternately in India and Germany. It dealt with several issues connected with culture, education, science and technology, trade and industry and so on. It was an informal high-powered group with eminent Germans and Indians, which included the likes of Ratan Rata and Rahul Bajaj. IGCC gave a brief report directly to the prime minister of India and chancellor of Germany. I was associated with IGCC for about a decade.

As I represented the science and technology (S&T) field, I was always asked to make a presentation pertaining to the Indo-German partnerships in this field. I distinctly recall the way the Indo-German S&T partnerships became broader, deeper and stronger with the passage of time and how the discussion on S&T got a big boost by moving from the periphery to the core in the IGCC discussion forum over the years.

I was the director general of the Council of Scientific and Industrial Research (CSIR) during the period 1995–2006, I remember that through our International Science and Technology Affairs Directorate, the most extensive partnership of CSIR was with German institutions such as DAAD, Fraunhofer, the Humboldt Foundation, etc.

During 2004–06, I was the president of the Indian National Science Academy. Again I remember having the most productive interaction and exchange with the Deutsche Forschungsgemeinschaft (DFG), which is the German Research Foundation.

Currently I am the president of the Global Research Alliance. This is an alliance of research and technology organizations from around the world, and has over 60,000 scientists. These organizations include Battelle (US), Council of Scientific & Industrial Research (CSIR, India), Commonwealth Scientific and Industrial Research Organization (CSIRO, Australia), Danish Technological Institute (DTI, Denmark), Fraunhofer (Germany), Scientific and Industrial Research Institute of Malaysia (SIRIM, Malaysia), The Netherlands Organisation for Applied Scientific Research (TNO, Netherlands) and VTT Technical Research Centre of Finland (Finland). Again Fraunhofer has been a very valued member. As I write this essay, a breakthrough technology developed by Fraunhofer is being considered for wide-scale use in India in a public–private partnership (PPP). Its implementation is likely to have a huge impact.

In short, this essay is based on an outsider's view as well as, in some way, an insider's view from a personal lens.

A Historical Perspective

The Indo-German relationship, based on common values of democracy and rule of law, has been truly enduring for several decades. Today this relationship is being enhanced in terms of aspiration, scale and scope like never before.

The course of the Indo-German bilateral relationship was set by the two visits of Prime Minister Jawaharlal Nehru to Germany in 1956 and 1960. Indo-German S&T cooperation is based on two intergovernmental agreements in 1971 and 1974, as well as numerous individual agreements between the Federal Ministry of Education and Research (BMBF) and various Indian ministries.

But it is important to remember that even before the formal institution-based partnerships started, individual partnerships of great significance and impact between two of the greatest scientists from India and Germany had already started. I'm referring to the partnership between Albert Einstein and Satyen Bose in the 1920s. They partnered with each other to write the seminal paper on Bose–Einstein condensate, which has been the basis of many Nobel prizes in the last couple of decades.

Then there was an early partnership in great institution building. The Indian Institute of Technology (IIT) Madras is one of the most respected institutes in higher technological education in India. It was exactly six decades ago (1956) that Germany offered technical assistance for establishing an institute of higher education in engineering in India. The first Indo-German agreement was signed in 1959. IIT-Madras was one of the biggest development projects at that time.

From these early interactions, Germany has become India's second most important partner in terms of S&T collaborations. India's scientific establishments have close partnerships with all the premier German R&D institutions. Indian scientists publish the second largest number of research papers in co-authorship with German counterparts. But it is not the number of research papers but their quality that matters. The quality of these publications, as measured by their impact factor, is the highest in comparison to research papers published with any other country.

The past decade has witnessed a truly impressive increase of over 400 per cent in the number of Indian students at German universities. About 83 per cent of Indian students going to Germany opt for programmes in Science, Technology, Engineering and Mathematics (STEM). So S&T collaboration is at the forefront of the Indo-German relationship.

Current Partnerships

Let's review the current and newly evolving initiatives and partnerships.

DAAD (German Academic Exchange Service) promotes the exchange of young scientific minds through sponsorships and other support systems. Each year, over 100,000 students and researchers supported by DAAD worldwide are able to gain valuable experience. A significant number of these individuals are from India. India's top twenty universities also benefit from DAAD.

In a similar vein, the Alexander von Humboldt Foundation in Germany has funded over 1,500 scientists from India since 1953. The German Rectors' Conference is involved with the Association of Indian Universities to advance the educational exchange between the two countries.

Fraunhofer is one of the world's most reputed applied research organizations. It has sixty-seven institutes and research units, an annual budget of over a billion euros and more than 24,000 employees, the majority of whom are qualified scientists and engineers. More than 70 per cent of the Fraunhofer-Gesellschaft contract research revenue is derived from industry and from publicly financed research projects.

Fraunhofer has been active in India for a long time. Fraunhofer gave special focus to India in mid-2008 with an objective to concentrate its efforts to understand the Indian market and engage with industry, government and academia. Fraunhofer's India Office in Bengaluru was inaugurated on 30 October 2012. It houses an experience theatre showcasing some of the latest technologies, and the Fraunhofer Innovation and Technology (FIT) Academy which conducts workshops, bringing together Fraunhofer's experts from various institutes and clients and partners in India. Fraunhofer partners with thirty of the fifty leading industrial enterprises in India.

Max-Planck-Gesellschaft (MPG) is one of the world's most prestigious scientific research organizations. Eighty-three Max Planck Institutes (MPIs) conduct cutting-edge basic research in natural sciences, life sciences, social sciences, and the humanities. Eighteen Nobel laureates have emerged from MPG.

Indian scientists and institutions figure prominently in MPG's international collaborations. For example, in 2014, more than eight hundred visiting scientists from India worked at MPIs. In terms of the global exchange of young scientists, India is one of MPG's major partner countries with forty-seven ongoing research collaborations with institutes in India.

There are over fifty project partnerships between MPIs and research institutions in India. New initiatives such as partner groups or Max Planck India fellowships have also been developed successfully. The Indo-German Max Planck Centre for Computer Science, and the Indo-German Max Planck Centre on Lipid Research have been set up in India to further strengthen bilateral relations.

In early 2013, Germany and India moved a step closer to each other when the Max Planck Society supported a new cooperative research programme between Mainz and Chennai to explore the health and climate impact of aerosols.

India and Germany also have specific institution-based partnerships. The following is an example.

With over 260 academic institutes in nine departments, RWTH Aachen University is a leading European institution of higher education and scientific research. RWTH Aachen University sees its educational mission as that of preparing future leaders for society, higher education and business.

RWTH activities focus on building and implementing the structures of the Indo-German Centre of Sustainability (www.igcs-chennai.org) at IIT-Madras. It serves as a platform for exchange of information for sustainable development in the areas of energy, waste and water management, land use and urban development.

The Indo-German S&T collaboration is becoming more aspirational in terms of enhancing its scale, scope and impact vis-à-vis industry. In addition to such academic institution-based relationships, more enabling collaborative platforms, where vibrant PPPs can be built, are being designed and operated.

The Indo-German Science and Technology Centre (IGSTC) is an initiative through which the German BMBF and the Indian Ministry of Science and Technology provide financial resources for joint research and development projects. The ministries founded IGSTC on 23 April 2006. It serves as a model for PPPs for scientific and industrial research. Since 2010, it has been funding bilateral research projects in the applied sciences.

IGSTC has further advanced the industrial research partnership between India and Germany by developing knowledge networks for industrial competitiveness, and establishing joint knowledge pools to address global challenges. IGSTC serves as a nerve centre to promote technology partnership.

IGSTC primarily provides support for so-called '2+2 technology projects', involving academic institutions and industrial enterprises from both the Indian and German sides. Areas such as advanced manufacturing, embedded systems, ICT for automobiles, renewable energy, food security, clean water and healthcare technologies are covered by IGSTC.

The German House for Research and Innovation (DWIH) in New Delhi, inaugurated on 27 October 2012, serves as a window to German science and research for interested students, researchers and potential partner institutions. DWIH New Delhi is one of five such centres across the globe. On 28 April 2016, DWIH New Delhi celebrated the handover of the consortium leadership from the German Research Foundation—DFG India Office—to the German Academic Exchange Service—DAAD—with a ceremonial get-together at German House in New Delhi.

Overall, the German BMBF has been doing a wonderful job of facilitating Indo-German collaboration by realizing common goals and bringing their results to fruition. The initiative 'India and Germany—Strategic Partners for Innovation' is just one example of forward thinking.

Current Standing in S&T of India and Germany

Before looking at the way forward on the new dimension of Indo-German S&T partnerships, let's take a quick look at the current state of science, technology and innovation in Germany. What is the relative standing of India and Germany in science, technology and innovation?

India and Germany have their relative strengths. In terms of investment in science, Germany spends around 2.8 per cent of its GDP on R&D whereas India spends about 0.9 per cent of its GDP on this sector. Though it has only 7 per cent of India's population, Germany produces around the same number of scientific research publications as India does. But the patent filings by Germany are four times those of India.

In terms of high-tech exports as a percentage of manufactured exports, Germany's percentage at 16 per cent is twice that of India. Research converts money into knowledge, whereas innovation converts knowledge into money. What is the global standing of India and Germany as regards innovation?

The Global Innovation Index (www.globalinnovationindex.org) provides the answer. Amongst 142 nations, Germany's rank has been 12 (2011), 15 (2012), 15 (2013), 13 (2014) and 12 (2015) on this index. The corresponding rank of India has been 62 (2011), 64 (2012), 68 (2013), 76 (2014) and 81 (2015). Thus, Germany seems to be steady in the top 10 per cent, whereas India seems to be sliding down. However, that is not the case if we view innovation in totality.

There is a saying that sometimes what gets counted does not count and what counts, does not get counted. The Global Innovation Index is a great start for measuring innovation efficiency and effectiveness, but it is only based on parameters that are directly measurable. Further, it focuses on technological innovation, not on non-technological innovation such as business models, system delivery, workflow, and the like, which can have a profound influence on a nation's performance in innovation.

For instance, India can easily find a place in the top five in the world in innovation that belongs to the category of 'affordable excellence'. An example is the Indian Mars Orbiter Mission which cost $74 million, whereas the corresponding US mission cost $671 million! Indian innovation, therefore, specializes in getting 'more from less'.

Another example is eye surgery. High quality cataract eye surgery is done by Aravind Eye Care for just $30, but in the US, it costs $3,000. And this is not due to lower costs in India, but the ingenious workflow innovation in India. Going forward, we will suggest how future Indo-German partnerships could be based on affordable excellence-led innovation.

Looking Forward

India's rapid and strong economic growth makes it one of the leading emerging economies. India is emerging as a major power not only in the

Asian region, but as a geopolitical player in the international arena.

The contours of the future landscape of S&T cooperation between India and Germany were drawn at the third Inter-Governmental Consultations of Indian Prime Minister Narendra Modi and German Federal Chancellor Angela Merkel. It was noted that 'fifteen years into the Strategic Partnership, Indo-German cooperation is founded on common democratic principles, marked by trust and mutual respect and geared towards building stability, prosperity and sustainable development through closer dialogue and cooperation in security, enhanced trade and investment, partnerships in manufacturing, skilling, clean energy, infrastructure, innovation and education'.

So what could be the path forward? Here are some emerging trends and opportunities with a potential of impact not only in India and Germany, but globally:

1. The decision to extend the tenure of the bilateral IGSTC beyond 2017 is very welcome. The funding allocation enhancement to a maximum of 4 million euros per year by each side is also welcome. However, these programmes must focus more on the national priorities of both India and Germany. As far as India is concerned, it has launched initiatives such as Make in India, Skill India, Digital India, Clean India and Smart Cities, etc. There is scope to align the S&T partnerships to such aspirational national missions.
2. Germany's key competencies in high technology, and India's growing needs, means technology-intensive manufacturing can become a key pillar of a future strategic partnership. The efforts of the High Technology Partnership Group to identify specific opportunities for high technology collaboration, including in the priority areas of manufacturing under the Make in India programme, is important.

   Strong and synergistic partnerships in seven areas have been identified. These include the digital sector encompassing electronic system design and manufacturing, photonics and optics, transport infrastructure including railways, aviation, ports and roads, renewable energy, water, engineering sectors including heavy, electrical, and mechanical engineering, machine tools, medical and life sciences, defence and space.
3. The recently launched Startup India and Standup India initiatives will provide excellent partnership opportunities for Germany. The endeavour should be to establish a vibrant Indo-German ecosystem

of innovation and techno-entrepreneurship by linking the small-and medium-sized enterprises (SME) and start-up enterprises of both countries to make a meaningful contribution to their knowledge economies.

4. There are new opportunities for German companies in the urban development sector, offered by India's initiative on 100 Smart Cities. Germany has provided 360 million euros for sustainable urban development in 2015.
5. The combined Indo-German prowess of S&T can contribute significantly to the solution of global problems (primarily climate, environment and energy) through joint programmes, while at the same time achieving the Millennium Development Goals. In such partnerships, there is a need to enhance collaboration towards the common aim of developing climate-friendly, efficient and sustainable solutions. The successful implementation of the Green Energy Corridors project, which has been expanded by 400 million euros, is a forward step in this direction.

   Improving access to clean energy in rural locations is critical. In this context, Germany's readiness to assist in meeting its renewable energy target under the umbrella of the solar partnership with 1 billion euros over the next five years is also very welcome. Both the Indo-German Energy Forum and Programme need to increasingly focus on energy supply in a socially and environmentally sound way, massively improve efficiency in energy generation, transmission and consumption and continue with sectoral reforms.
6. Both Germany and India have complementary strengths in science, technology and innovation, which through partnering can make one plus one equal to eleven, and not just two, for example, for creating products that belong to the category of 'affordable excellence'. 'Affordability' comes naturally to Indian innovators, whereas Germany is high on 'excellence'. IGSTC, for example, has initiated innovative projects on biomedical devices which belong to the 'affordable excellence' category. These include lab-on-chip for water pathogen detection and nano-materials for absorption of uremic toxins for chronic kidney disease, a successfully indigenized 'affordable excellence' product.

   It was developed in India by Mercedes-Benz for India and the surrounding markets. The original high-quality German product (excellence) was adapted to cope with India's challenging infrastructure conditions and meeting Indian requirements of a lower price (affordable). India is a unique high-tech market which seeks high quality (excellence) at a low cost (affordable), and Indo-Germany S&T partnerships will be most valuable in this space.

7. India's human talent also provides German enterprises with 'affordable excellence'. India's emergence as a global R&D hub is obvious to anyone who has witnessed the setting up of 1,000 R&D centres in India by global companies, employing over 200,000 scientists, engineers and technologists. Several German companies ranging from Bayer to BASF, Siemens to SAP, and Mercedes-Benz to Robert Bosch have set up their R&D centres in India. There is room for expansion in terms of both scale and scope in this area.
8. In the twentieth century, S.N. Bose and Albert Einstein got connected as young scientists and created breakthroughs, which form the basis of Nobel prizes today. We must create the Bose–Einstein magic in the twenty-first century by launching an 'Indo-German Bose–Einstein Young Investigators Initiative'. In this initiative, the very brightest of young Indian and German scientists in their early thirties will be identified, selected, and paired, and their breakthrough ideas will be funded. Hopefully, this will create the possibility of an Indo-German pair of scientists sharing future Nobel prizes.
9. Indo-German collaborative research and academic and institutional exchanges between universities and institutions of higher education are important. The recent Indo-German Dialogue on Excellence in Research and Education sought to bring together Indian and German decision-makers and leading experts in the education sector in order to jointly and comprehensively discuss the multifaceted and all-encompassing aspect of excellence in teaching and research. Such dialogue must continue regularly, especially as the changes are so rapid.
10. A new International Centre for Advanced Studies in Humanities and Social Sciences in India is expected to form a nucleus for ambitious research, and act as a visible forum for exchanges among outstanding scholars from both countries. German scholars and scientists should participate in India's Global Initiative of Academic Networks programme.

11. In the same way, India should participate more in the mega-science facilities set up in Germany. India has already invested in major science projects in Germany, such as the Facility for Anti-Proton and Ion Research at Darmstadt and the Deutsche Elektronen Synchrotron for experiments in advanced materials and particle physics. Mutually beneficial science and technology partnerships, which will create new knowledge and innovative technologies for addressing societal challenges, are a must.
12. The Bilateral Working Group on Agriculture, Food Processing and Consumer Protection can focus future bilateral efforts on consumer protection, food safety and plant protection issues. Fostering training and skills enhancement in the agricultural sector is important. The private sector can participate in establishing centres of excellence in agriculture. The proposed 'One World—No Hunger' initiative is an inspiring one, to which both India and Germany can contribute.
13. There are other forms of knowledge which cannot be labelled 'scientific' but are still of great economic, social, cultural and political importance. Many forms of practical and embodied, implicit and tacit knowledge are part of socially and culturally significant knowledge. Their social, cultural and political importance is often devalued.

    One such knowledge domain is India's traditional knowledge, which includes ancient wisdom arising out of Ayurveda, yoga, etc. India has built a massive traditional knowledge digital library and has shown that a combination of traditional knowledge and modern science can create novel therapeutics. In times of escalating R&D budgets for creating new therapeutics, an Indo-German partnership in seeking such alternative paths would be valuable.
14. There is a need to move the India–Germany S&T partnership into high gear by focusing on the emerging 'next' practices. Some typical examples are immune engineering, where Killer T cells are programmed to wipe out cancer, precise gene editing without leaving foreign DNA behind to create disease resistance and drought tolerance, novel conversational interfaces which combine voice recognition and neutral languages, wireless gadgets that repurpose nearby radio signals and power themselves, etc. For this, a 'Indo-German Grand Challenge Competition' could be set up, where competitive funding could be provided to the winners, who propose disruptive and game-changing ideas.

Finally

The Indo-German S&T partnership has had a great history and can look forward to a glorious future, simply because of the strong foundation of common values, mutual trust and a shared vision between these two great nations. The time is just right for both India and Germany to take a giant step forward in their aspirations to create not only a better India or a better Germany, but a better world.

Education as a Locomotive of Our Engagement

◈

Pradeep Mathur
'Education, Academic and Student Exchanges as Partnership Builders'

◈

Andreas Pinkwart
'Perspectives on the Indo-German Relationship in the Science Society of the 21st Century'

Pradeep Mathur, Director, IIT-Indore

Pradeep Mathur received a BSc (Hons) degree in Chemistry from the Polytechnic of North London and a PhD from Keele University. After two years as a postdoctoral research associate at Yale University, he joined IIT-Bombay as a faculty member in 1984. He has been a director of IIT-Indore since 2010.

Professor Mathur has been visiting professor at the University of Cambridge, University of Freiburg and a DAAD guest professor at the University of Karlsruhe.

He is a recipient of the Shanti Swarup Bhatnagar Prize, is a J.C. Bose national fellow, and a fellow of the Indian Academy of Sciences, Bengaluru. He was awarded a DSc (honoris causa) by Keele University in 2014.

Education, Academic and Student Exchanges as Partnership Builders

Professor Pradeep Mathur

Today, India and Germany find themselves at a crossroads from where one country, blessed with a large human pool of young talent, can provide the human resource foundation to meet the growing technology needs of the world. And the other country, through its intensive programme of internationalization of education, can play a prominent role in providing some of the best education, especially in the field of science and technology.

The two countries have a rich history of collaboration in India's post-Independence period. Germany, the country of Nobel laureates with a long history of excellence in research, assisted in the setting up of the Indian Institute of Technology (IIT) Madras in 1959. In fact, the connection between India and Germany goes back to the nineteenth century when the German engineering giant Siemens installed the first telegraphic connection between Kolkata and Berlin and then with London.

In the last fifty years, Germany has re-established its world-recognized stature as a leader in the areas of technology and innovation. Following the success of its education and training programmes, there has been a dramatic rise in the number of foreign students choosing Germany as one of the most preferred destinations to pursue higher studies. In fact, with more and more programmes in German institutions now being taught in English, coupled with the very high standard of these programmes, and the excellent connectivity of German cities to major Indian cities, Germany has become a favourite destination for many Indian students.

Various avenues for strengthening links between the two nations have been in place for several decades. The DAAD and the Humboldt Foundation are unique bodies and have provided opportunities to thousands of Indians to pursue postdoctoral research, and in recent times, master's degree programmes. Equally importantly, numerous senior scientists have benefited from their visits to German institutions. Unlike any other country, Germany has traditionally been open to expand its links with India.

Its initial link with IIT-Madras continues till today with active participation in several exchange programmes. At any given time, numerous German scientists and professors can be seen working in the IIT-Madras campus. Recently, the connect between IIT-Madras and Germany has led to the creation of the Indo-German Centre for Sustainability (IGCS) at the IIT-Madras campus. The centre provides an opportunity to German and Indian researchers to conduct joint research on the very relevant and timely subjects of water management, land use, waste management and energy.

Indian science has been propelled into the international spotlight in the last few decades, much of it due to the greater internationalization of its research programmes, involving a larger number of Indians than ever before. While, no doubt, the impact of India's interaction with other Western countries has been noticeable, its interaction with Germany has been quite remarkable. A consequence of this greater academic and research-oriented interaction between the two countries has been an increase in the participation of German industry in India. Over 1,600 German companies, through their active engagement in India, have seized upon the potential that a huge Indian market offers for Germany.

As more and more Indian students graduate from German universities and institutions, the scope for Indo-German collaboration in various spheres is increasing. Through an ever-increasing number of joint research projects between Indian and German groups, long-term partnerships are being established for cutting-edge research in various areas of science and technology. This provides opportunities for Indian and German research students, scientists and professors to form long-lasting professional relationships to conduct work which can push forward the frontiers of knowledge.

Training of manpower from such collaborative ventures is of the utmost significance for Indian scientists to independently and professionally conduct front-line and innovative research and development. There is positive movement in support of bilateral innovation partnerships by the creation of the Indo-German Science and Technology Centre (IGSTC) near the national capital of India.

Through its support, the centre promotes work on innovative Indo-German projects in which the top research institutions work with small- and medium-sized enterprises from both countries. Additionally, it supports the ongoing process of networking between German and Indian scientists through workshops and symposiums. I have mentioned the IGSTC here because it is a unique institution to give a fillip to the joint development of innovation projects in the two countries, and has clearly come about as a result of the expanded education and training links that have developed in recent years.

The Indo-German Chamber of Commerce has been instrumental in bringing together Indian and German businesses. Now is the right time for academia and research centres, especially those working in the areas of technological relevance, manufacturing and cutting-edge science and engineering, to use the good offices of this very important link to connect with German and Indian industry.

German universities have traditionally had strong links with industry. The engineering programmes of the TU9 universities have a strong industry foundation to support their undergraduate and research programmes. About fifteen years ago, their venture into the internationalization of some of the undergraduate degree programmes, by offering English-taught degree courses, was supported heavily by German industry. The idea was clear: offering study programmes taught in English makes it easier for students to transfer the acquired knowledge to other countries.

Furthermore, English-taught education was recognized to be attractive for foreign students as it ensures international career opportunities. Indian students, with a strong English-language background, have benefited immensely from this move. The four-year International Bachelor's degree course in Mechanical Engineering at Karlsruhe has been one such highly successful programme for selected students from around the world. It exposes the students to training and working in German industry, both at the manufacturing and research levels. Indian institutions, regrettably, lack the much desired connection with industry, local or international.

Graduates from some of the best Indian institutions often carry the tag of being 'bench-shy', even though they carry with them some of the strongest theoretical training provided anywhere in the world. Some institutes, notably the IITs, have encouraged their students to follow the path of entrepreneurship and indeed, many successful start-ups are proof of the vast potential of this approach. Outside of the IITs, there are few institutes in India that can provide training on new business models and innovations.

India and Germany can combine to offer joint entrepreneurship degree courses which deal with studying the tools to take up a business idea/concept of mutual interest to the two countries, offer the resources to turn it into reality and make that idea a viable product or service. Jointly, the partners of such programmes will be able to focus on hitherto unexplored business models, and develop and manage innovations. Such a venture can have the effect of generating entrepreneurs whose innovations will have plenty of takers in both countries, and ensure an easier path to the international markets.

Undoubtedly, India has made enormous economic progress in various sectors since it gained independence. Food production is at a comfortable level, its IT industry has grown and continues to flourish, and life expectancy has increased from barely thirty-two at the time of India's independence in 1947 to sixty-five years today. India has built approximately 1.25 million miles of new roads, and steel production has increased fifty times over the output in 1947. The list of India's successes and achievements is long, but there is a distressing twist to the tail.

India has a long way to go in many areas. Millions of people are living below the poverty line, there is a lack of access to drinking water, proper sanitation facilities and basic medicines, and there are an increasing number of malnourished children and social evils in the country. These are some of the unnerving and dismaying facts that have evaded attention for far too long and need to be addressed on a war footing. For a country which can boast of providing some of the most talented and skilled workers—from professors to doctors, IT professionals and engineers—to many countries around the globe, it is totally unacceptable that over 350 million people are officially classified as illiterate.

Though there has been a steady increase in the literacy rate, overall the performance of India in this sector cannot be described as anything but poor. There are large regional disparities. Kerala has consistently topped with more than 90 per cent literate population, whereas half the population of the states of Bihar, Rajasthan and Uttar Pradesh is classified as illiterate. Female literacy is disturbingly low and is a major cause of infant mortality, more births per woman, and malnourished children.

Whether the responsibility is given to the states or to the Centre, the fact remains that elementary education in India has been a failure, and is an area that can use Germany's help. Following the failure of the states to address the literacy problem, there have been central interventions at various stages of the post-Independence period, which have led to initiatives such as partial implementation of the Kothari Commission Report (1964), National Policy on Education (1986), etc. These have met with limited success.

In 2000, the Sarva Shiksha Abhiyan (SSA) and in 2001, the midday meal scheme were introduced. While these schemes have contributed to a greater number of children enrolling in schools, the pace of progress has been so slow that it is estimated that complete literacy cannot be accomplished before 2030. Moreover, reports from various studies indicate that there has been a drop in learning levels, which are very poor in many parts of the country, leading to an overall drop in the quality of education in the country.

It appears that lack of access and quality, along with retention, are some of the problems plaguing the primary education system in India. Much can be learned from the primary education system in Germany, and India has much to gain by engaging in joint programmes solely aimed at primary education. This is easier said than done though, as currently there is little in common between the two countries with regard to their teacher training programmes.

Teacher training programmes are often adapted for different regions, based on the prevailing needs. However, certain fundamental skills of a good teacher must be taught in every teacher training course, regardless of whether the task falls under the jurisdiction of the state or the Centre.

In Germany, there has been much debate on whether the respective regions or the central government should be responsible for the implementation of teacher training, as well as primary education issues, in general. However, in the midst of this debate, there is no doubt about what are the basic tenets of a good teacher. This bifurcation of the administrative and technical aspects of teacher training and other programmes, needs to be emulated by India.

The extensive network of researchers and academicians facilitated by DAAD, the AvH Foundation and others needs to be replicated at the primary education level to facilitate the mobility of teacher trainers and trainees between the institutions of the two countries. A major limitation in the Indian teaching methods, perceived by experts, is the lack of visible importance attached to the role of teachers in imparting skills, and as supporters of independent learning. Such an exchange would go a long way in addressing this issue.

Also, an important task that a school should fulfil is that of preparing students for the professional world. Teachers, therefore, have to be trained to provide students with the necessary skills and guidance for this world. To meet this requirement, teacher trainees should become familiarized with professional organizations, by spending some time in them during their training period.

An Indian teacher could learn a lot from a visit to a professional German organization, and likewise a German industry professional would benefit from interacting with Indian trainees in the Indian environment, given that German organizations today need to be familiar with the cultures and backgrounds of their increasingly multinational employees.

While the number of international students on a university campus can be a good indicator of the high quality of education being offered in German institutions and universities, it is in fact the cooperation amongst top German and Indian institutions of education and research that will be the key to both achieving and maintaining excellence.

Scientific and technological progress in both countries is likely to grow with mutual cooperation and the exchange of ideas between leading experts from the two countries. Pioneering approaches, such as partnerships between universities and business or industry, and the launch of collaborative networks is the need of the hour. Through a number of recent initiatives backed by the two governments, German and Indian funding organizations, research institutions and universities are providing vital support for collaborative work in the fields of research, education and industry.

The recently held round of the Indo-German Dialogue on Excellence in Research and Education is a very positive move in propelling bilateral cooperation to greater heights by bringing together Indian and German decision-makers and top experts in the education sector, to exchange ideas and identify areas of mutual interest and effort.

What was different in this round of talks was the genuine effort to identify focused points of collaboration between identified institutions and in some instances, actual research group to research group connects, as seen for the rapidly growing partnerships between researchers at IIT Indore and several groups from the TU9 universities.

This model, of allowing person-to-person collaborations to flourish, leading to a wider network, involving, in many cases, interdisciplinary projects, can and should be followed by others. It is a healthy change from the signing of numerous memoranda of understanding and then waiting for indefinite periods for some success to be observed from these 'formal' connections.

It is cooperation in the fields of education, science and research that will contribute to strong and bilateral trade ties, and make the Indo-German relationship prosper. Educating people and creating knowledge forms the core of what universities do. Industry–academia cooperation between the two countries is vital for understanding the challenges of a competitive environment, and is required to translate the knowledge thus created into products or services for the benefit of the world at large.

These are exciting times for both countries and great potential exists for their educationists and researchers to work together to take their cooperation in various areas to new levels. An exchange of ideas through greater mobility of students, teachers and researchers will form a vital and significant part of the India–Germany cooperation.

Professor Andreas Pinkwart, Dean, Handelshochschule Leipzig

Professor Andreas Pinkwart was born in 1960 in Seelscheid, North Rhine-Westphalia, Germany. After a banking apprenticeship, he studied macroeconomics and business administration at the University of Münster and the University of Bonn from where he obtained his doctoral degree in 1991, with a thesis supervised by Professor Horst Albach.

Subsequently, he ran the office of the Free Democratic Party's leader of the parliamentary group in the German Bundestag from 1991 to 1994. In 1994, he became professor of economics and business administration in Düsseldorf, from where he later moved to the University of Siegen to accept a chair for business administration.

While on a sabbatical from 2002 to 2011, he was a member of the German Bundestag (2002–05) and minister for innovation, science, research and technology as well as deputy prime minister of the state of North Rhine-Westphalia (2005–10).

Since 2011, Professor Pinkwart has been the dean at HHL Leipzig Graduate School of Management and holds the Stiftungsfonds Deutsche Bank chair for innovation management and entrepreneurship.

Perspectives on the Indo-German Relationship in the Science Society of the 21st Century

Professor Andreas Pinkwart

1. Every Cloud Has a Silver Lining: From Development Cooperation to a Strategic Innovation Partnership

The cooperation between India and Germany is based on common democratic and economic values which are translated into a representative, federalist democracy and social market economy. Moreover, both countries advocate a multipolar world order in which the United Nations plays a central role. It is, therefore, hardly surprising that both democracies were still young when they laid the contractual groundwork for their fruitful exchange in the fields of education and science.

Several projects which have been realized in the meantime, demonstrate the mutual appreciation for the research achievements of their scientific elite. Nevertheless, given the deep poverty of about one-third of the Indian population and the still large educational gradient in India, Indo-German cooperation in the field of education during the second half of the twentieth century mainly covered development cooperation projects.

This became clear in the analysis of development cooperation between India and the German Development Institute (Deutsches Institut für Entwicklungspolitik) in the context of the research project on experience and perspectives of cooperation with so-called anchor countries commissioned by the Federal Ministry for Economic Cooperation and Development (BMZ) in 2005.

Besides an inventory control of German development cooperation and adjacent fields of politics, the analysis also contains some general statements regarding the convergence and differences of interests between Germany and India with regard to global structural political topics as well as concrete proposed action regarding new topics, the use of synergies, and improved inter-development of individual development cooperation tools.

Until the early 2000s, Germany did not attribute much importance to India as a global political and economic player, and in fact seriously neglected the country compared to China. By that time, the German image of India was mainly characterized by India's poverty, social tensions and governance issues. However, India hardly made any efforts to intensify the relationship. As a consequence, their economic, scientific and technological relations were rather weak until ten years ago.

It was only within the framework of the new challenges caused by the information revolution that the Germans view of India changed—and probably also the other way around in the context of the tightening of entry conditions for Indian scientists coming to the United States and Great Britain.

Germany and India still have to ask themselves whether they have sufficiently recognized the enormous potential of their partnership that is oriented towards the use of complementary competitive advantages and anchored them in their educational, scientific and economic politics. (For example, a memorandum of understanding for promoting German as a foreign language in India and for promoting lessons of modern Indian languages in Germany was signed within the framework of the intergovernmental consultations in October 2015. Now, both sides plan to offer German as an elective subject in India starting from the 2016–17 term, and to introduce Hindi at German schools with the support of the German Standing Conference of the Ministers of Education and Cultural Affairs.)

2. Overview of Previous Initiatives of Cooperation in Education and Research

2.1 Professional Education

Indo-German cooperation on education has always been intense in the field of professional education. A lot needs to be done in this area in India, and India considers Germany to be an important partner for the reform of the Indian professional education system. For example, the partners can jointly identify suitable German professional education export offers and adjust them to the Indian market. Another important component is cooperation with the private sector which will be further expanded, among others by the International Marketing on Vocational Training (iMOVE) branch in New Delhi.

It is estimated that only about 3 per cent of the Indian workforce is qualified. Until now, training was rather theoretical and in many cases not aligned to the needs of the labour market. Despite the large population and an extremely high share of young people—500 million people are younger than twenty-five years—the lack of qualified employees has become a considerable impairment to sustaining high economic growth in India.

It is estimated that about fifteen million additional qualified employees are needed every year, and according to recent estimates, there will be a lack of more than 50 million qualified employees in India until 2020. This shortage is reflected in the quality of many products as well as the relatively low efficiency of numerous industries, particularly Indian companies operating globally.

For the Indian government, professional education therefore takes priority. In the field of professional education, professional exchange and cooperation between German and Indian representatives has been intensified for some time now. In this, the iMOVE initiative plays an important role. In the past few years, the initiative has established a comprehensive network of providers, Indian partner organizations and Indian companies. Furthermore, iMOVE has been operating an office in New Delhi, India, since the fall of 2012. Another plan is to further expand the general professional education in secondary schools with the aim of strengthening the capabilities for building up existing as well as further education capacities.

In order to provide as many children and adolescents as possible access to education, regular educational institutions of secondary level have been flanked by so-called 'open schools'. These are being funded by the 'National Open School' association, and include classes of general education and vocational classes and/or programmes. In the meantime, more than 1,000 centres have been established, and they are all officially accredited.

In December 2014, the Ministry of Labour and Employment presented a modified Apprentices Act which provides for a clear increase of flexibility of the provisions in favour of the requirements and capacities of private companies. The objective was to remunerate apprentices based on the minimum wage, with the support of scholarship programmes.

The models for interaction between operational training and theoretical lessons were made flexible, so that not only the mainly state-run Industrial Training Institutes (ITIs) but also other education providers could qualify as vocational schools. Moreover, the Ministry of Labour and Employment is working on a demand-oriented design and modernization of apprenticeship content and the underlying public–private structures. Expert commissions have been created for this purpose.

Within this framework, the Indian side has been closely cooperating with the Federal Ministry for Education and Research (BMBF) and other German agencies to align content and structures to the 'dual principles' of German professional education and thus ensure a higher degree of closeness to companies and higher orientation towards their needs.

For the advanced vocational training of skilled workers, a special programme with modular classes and terms of one to six weeks is available. The classes are offered by ITIs and Advanced Training Institutes. In parallel to the introduction of craftspersons training, craft instructor training for craftspersons-to-be has been started.

The training of industrial supervisors which is concentrated in two institutes is based on an initiative of the federal state of Baden-Wuerttemberg that supported the establishment of the first institute by providing human resources and materials. The institute offers regular diploma and post-diploma courses (technology, business administration, quality control, problem solving) as well as customized short-term courses.

2.2 Scientific Education

In an era of knowledge-based society and the rapidly progressing second phase of the information revolution, an exchange of students and young scientists is of particular importance in the context of international educational cooperation.

However, the number of students from India who come to Germany is still low—despite the quite impressive triplication of numbers between 2007 and 2015. This becomes particularly clear when these figures are compared to those from China, but the specific challenges India faces in the scientific area also play a role. India still suffers from a lack of college professors. The ratio of vacant positions is currently estimated to be almost 50 per cent.

The reasons are manifold. One is that there is still a lack of adequate colleges for India's best students. Moreover, studying at a university abroad is often rated higher than studying at an Indian institution. While many scientists do not go back to India—or not yet—since appropriate payment and good working conditions are indispensable in a globalized education landscape in order to retain and/or gain back brilliant minds, staffing professorships with foreigners has only been possible in exceptional cases until now.

Given the increasing academization in India, the increase in the number of students has led to a considerable shift in the quality of teaching. This is because of the lack of teachers. According to the BMBF, up to 75 per cent of qualified engineers are insufficiently qualified for working in companies.

Even though the German statistics on internationalization in India still reflect the restraints of the past with regard to the relative cooperation level achieved, the growth rates of the past few years give rise to hope that the intensity of cooperation in education and science can dynamically converge to the level that Germany has achieved with China or other emerging countries. For example, in the 2014–15 winter term, about 11,860 students from India were registered at German universities, corresponding to an increase of almost 24 per cent compared to the previous year.

Moreover, India now represents the fifth largest group of international students in Germany. The number of German students at Indian tertiary institutions is estimated to be not more than 1,000, which places India at rank 15 of host countries for German students. In comparison, in the 2014–15 winter term, 5,400 German students studied in China.

These figures are even lower if one compares them to the country size, which highlights the size of the strategic gap in India and Germany's cooperation not only in the educational and scientific fields. This also becomes clear from the comparison to China at the global level. While India was able to increase its share of international students from 3.8 to 5.2 per cent in the decade 2001 to 2011, China doubled its share from 8 to 16.8 per cent in the same period. In absolute figures, the number of Chinese students studying abroad increased almost sixfold, from 131,138 to 722,915, while the number of Indian students abroad only tripled from 62,018 to 222,912 in the same period.

Looking at scientific staff below the professor level, the situation looks better. In view of the huge pent-up demand in India and the looming chances for growth, however, the figure of 1,000 Indian junior scientific staff in Germany, which is impressive at first glance from the German perspective, soon loses its lustre. The evaluation of the progress that has been achieved between Germany and India in the last decade probably shows a comparably ambivalent result.

On the one hand, the mere number of activities both partners implemented in the past few years with high levels of commitment is impressive. On the other hand, the volumes achieved so far show that many opportunities were left unexploited in consideration of India's new ambitious growth targets and German transformation objectives towards a digital economy.

2.3 Bilateral Cooperation in Science and Research

Germany is India's second most important research partner, behind the United States. Joint promotion of research projects has become one of the main pillars of Indo-German collaboration. The focal areas of this collaboration are materials science, biotechnology, health research, sustainability research, production technology and civil security research. Ideally, the projects that are supported should be application related and result in new innovations which can serve both Germany and India.

Further support is provided by the specialist programmes of the BMBF as well as by the Indo-European INNO INDIGO network in which the BMBF is involved. Added to this are numerous activities of major German research organizations which are being organized in direct cooperation with their Indian partners.

The third pillar of research cooperation is in so-called mobility projects which support workshops, conferences, expert delegations, etc. These projects provide support to the planning of joint research projects.

Germany maintains a bilateral centre for promoting research with India called the Indo-German Science and Technology Centre (IGSTC). Located in Gurgaon, Haryana, it has been financed with 2 million euros per year by Germany and India, in equal parts, since 2008. The centre supports application-oriented, innovative Indo-German projects with the involvement of excellent research institutions as well as small-sized and medium-enterprises (SMEs) from both countries. It also supports the networking of German and Indian scientists by organizing workshops and symposiums. IGSTC is a unique initiative in the joint development of innovation potential.

Another example of successful Indo-German cooperation is the Indo-German Centre for Sustainability (IGCS) located at the Indian Institute of Technology-Madras in Chennai. Here, German and Indian scientists carry out research together in the topics of water management, use of land, waste management and energy.

In October 2012, the German House for Research and Innovation (DWIH) in New Delhi was inaugurated to facilitate interaction between Indian and German scientists and students, and at the same time increase the visibility of Germany as a location for science and research. The decision of the German Federal Foreign Office to establish this centre, one of six German Houses/Centres for Research and Innovation (DWIH/DWZ) worldwide, in New Delhi, demonstrates the importance of India as a partner in science and research. With its fifteen consortium members, the DWIH in New Delhi is the largest of the six DWIH/DWZ worldwide.

India is also involved in several major research institutions in Germany. The Indian contribution to the Facility for Antiproton and Ion Research in Darmstadt, Germany, amounts to approximately 30 million euros. India has also made significant investments in the rights of use for the DESY particle accelerator in Hamburg.

The branch of the German Academic Exchange Service (DAAD) in New Delhi promotes bilateral cooperation among universities and research, and offers scholarship programmes as well as student counselling. This covers all the regular promotion programmes and numerous India-specific, sometimes co-financed, special programmes. The cooperation between the Max Planck Society and India shows a highly dynamic development that is based on an agreement with the Indian Department of Science and Technology (DST).

In 2014, more than eight hundred Indian scientists participated in research stays at Max Planck Institutions. In the scholarship programmes and awards to foreign researchers provided by the Alexander von Humboldt-Foundation (AvH), India takes one of the top places behind the United States, Russia and China.

The German Research Community (DFG) has been maintaining a representation in New Delhi since 2006. Within the framework of research cooperation between the DFG and the Indian National Science Academy, five hundred scientists from India have come to Germany. The Fraunhofer Institute has been maintaining a permanent representation in Bengaluru since November 2012.

3. Development Phases of Indo-German Education and Research Cooperation

Indo-German education and research cooperation has been through several phases with varying prioritizations and intensities. Despite a long tradition of the promotion of professional education within the framework of Indo-German development and research cooperation, Indo-German education was comparatively overshadowed for a long time—particularly when compared to other emerging economies like China. This began to change, however, by the middle of the last decade, first at the analysis stage and then, starting from 2008, also at the dynamic implementation stage.

The progress achieved since then has been acknowledged by all parliamentary groups in the German Bundestag. The following initiatives were highlighted in a request submitted by several parliamentary groups:

- Conclusion of an in-depth memorandum of understanding (MoU) on vocational education cooperation between the German government and the Indian government in 2015.
- Annual meeting of the Joint Working Group under the direction of the BMBF together with the Indian Ministry of Skill Development and Entrepreneurship on the management of Indo-German vocational education cooperation;
- Establishment of a location at the Chamber of Foreign Trade in Pune, India, by 2018, in order to introduce practice-oriented local training courses following the German dual model;
- Training of Indian supervisors in Germany organized by the iMOVE programme with expenses borne by the Indian government;
- Continued support of vocational education by the BMZ beyond 2014, for supporting the Indian government's plan to reform vocational education, and continue the over fifty-year-old tradition of development-oriented education cooperation between the two countries;
- By implementing vocational courses in Indian schools, Germany supports the qualification of German and specialist teachers via the Goethe Institute, paid with funds provided by the Federal Foreign Office;
- Increase of funds provided by the BMBF budget every year for cooperation with India, from 1.4 million euros per year in 2008 to approximately 8.5 million euros in 2015;
- Education and research play an important role in the Indo-German intergovernmental consultations which are held every two years;
- Every two years, the scientific technological cooperation (WTZ) is to be negotiated under the direction of the state secretaries of the BMBF and the Indian DST, with the participation of relevant scientific organizations;
- The continuation of the programme 'A New Passage to India' which was initiated by the BMBF in 2008, with the German Academic

Exchange Service, which has positively influenced the development of academic exchange with India;

- The announcement of a new university partnership programme titled Indo-German Partnerships in Higher Education in 2015, in which both partners plan to invest 3.5 million euros respectively in the course of four years;
- The establishment of an academic exchange project titled German at 1,000 Schools to promote German as a foreign language at schools of the Indian schools association, Kendriya Vidyalaya Sangathan, to be organized by the Goethe Institute;
- Financing of the programme to support cooperation with selected Indian schools in the context of the partner school initiative PASCH;
- The establishment of the Indian M.S. Merian—R. Tagore Centre to strengthen cooperation with India in the areas of human and social sciences;
- Foundation of the advisory board for coordination of cooperation with the Indian Council of Historical Research to strengthen cooperation in the areas of human and social sciences;
- Maintaining close cooperation between German institutions and the Indian Institutes of Technology (IITs);
- Supporting the exchange of scientists between the TU9 and IIT-Mandi, in the Indian state of Himachal Pradesh, in the context of special cooperation between the BMBF and the Indian human resource development Ministry which has been in place since 2014;
- Establishment of the IGSTC and extension of the term until 2022 which had been agreed upon in October 2015, and doubling of financial means (as of 2017) from 2 million euros to 4 million euros by each of the partners;

Whether these measures, which are important and useful in the context of the imminent second wave of the information revolution, and of the ambitious development objectives and requirements of India, are sufficient will be discussed in the following section.

From the German federal government's perspective as well as from the point of view of the majority of the German Bundestag, these steps are sufficient for the years to come. At least this is the conclusion reached when looking at the additional suggestions that were recently listed by the parliamentary majority in a resolution application:

- Provision of sufficient equipment for the rooms of the German School, New Delhi.
- Continuation and expansion of Indo-German centres such as the Indo-German Centre for Sustainability at IIT-Madras as well as of the successful WISE (Working Internships in Science and Engineering) programme for Indian undergraduate students.
- Strengthening of vocational education cooperation with India under the direction of the BMBF and within the framework of the development-oriented cooperation by the BMZ.
- Further education activities, in particular in the fields of energy efficiency and expansion of renewable energy, are to be pushed forward.
- Intensification of cooperation with regard to professional training beyond the existing four sectors and the iMOVE model, by means of exchange offers for German apprentices in India.
- Inclusion of apprenticeship elements in the relevant announcement for major investment funds financed by development banks.
- Improved offers for job-related training and further education are to be expedited, and the agreement between the BMZ and the Asian Development Bank is to be taken up.
- Support of deeper embedding of dual apprenticeship in India, in order to contribute to the development of qualified skilled labour, besides graduates of technical courses.
- Continuation of the initiative 'A New Passage to India'.
- Intensification of exchange among students and scientists, in particular in the fields of mathematics and information technology, in close cooperation with the DFG, AvH and the DAAD.
- Further expansion of the Indo-German M.S. Merian—R. Tagore International Centre for Advanced Studies in the Humanities and Social Sciences that was founded in the summer of 2015 as an Indo-German joint project for ambitious human and social scientific research; securing the sustainable financing of the DWIH in New Delhi.
- Support of synergies between partners from the fields of science and researching economy within the framework of the DWIH—from now on under the consortium management of the DAAD.

4. Think Bigger: Matching Complementary Strengths and New Opportunities

On the basis of the research and innovation strategy of the German government, this opens up new opportunities for greater Indo-German education and research cooperation. For example, the expansion of cooperation with countries with dynamic research in growth markets is considered to be one of the objectives of the 'High-Tech Strategy for Germany'. According to this strategy, the German federal government supports cooperation with countries that expand their competencies in the areas of research and development and thus become interesting partners for Germany as a high-tech location.

The intensified cooperation with India might contribute to the achievement of the following three out of four objectives of the 'Strategy of the German Government for the Internationalization of Science and Research':

- Strengthen research cooperation with the best in the world,
- Develop innovation potential at an international level,
- Assume responsibility at the international level and master global challenges.

As Prime Minister Modi pointed out during his visit to Germany in 2015, these goals, especially the last one, are shared by the Indian government. As he put it: 'We see Germany as a natural partner in achieving our vision of India's economic transformation. German strengths and India's priorities are aligned…our focus tends to be on economic ties. But, I believe that in a world of seamless challenges and opportunities, India and Germany can also be strong partners in advancing a more humane, peaceful, just and sustainable future for the world.'

The themed partnership and the strong media appearance of the heads of government of both countries at the Hannover trade fair in 2015 on the concept of Fabrik 4.0 (Factory 4.0) that is very important for Germany, marked a decisive milestone in their strategic partnership.

A prerequisite, however, is that the Make in India programme, which aims at the catching-up process of business, industry and trade, is successfully implemented at full speed in the months and years to come. And that foreign investment in companies and educational institutions is facilitated by means of a consistent fight against corruption, more investment security and a powerful bureaucracy. Moreover, it is recommended that both parties seize the opportunities provided by newer concepts for supporting innovation, such as reverse innovation and frugal innovation, in a targeted manner.

Even if Brexit was both surprising and regrettable from a German and European perspective, it might bring about additional impetus for the intensification of Indo-German cooperation in education and research. Overnight, Germany has become the European Union country with the highest number of English-speaking inhabitants. This provides new opportunities for the exchange of students and junior scientists, which should be seized valiantly.

Some examples, such as the HHL Leipzig Graduate School of Management and its manifold cooperation relationships with leading Indian business schools, show how the first steps in cooperation can develop into a close-meshed network of cooperation in research, teaching and transfer.

Professor Shailendra Kumar Rai, the Indian Council for Cultural Relations (ICCR) chair at HHL that is financed by the Indian government and HHL, is the fourth Indian university teacher to accede to a one-year research and teaching stay at HHL. His three predecessors are still in close contact with the faculty, jointly mentor doctoral students, publish articles in journals and anthologies and participate in the university's International Advisory Board. In turn, several scientists from HHL have visited the partner universities in India. One holder of an HHL chair will spend his next research semester in India. There is a regular exchange of students between HHL and Indian universities.

At present, Indian students represent the largest group exchange students at HHL. In turn, more and more HHL students are spending their terms abroad in India. This mutual exchange has resulted in the foundation of several Indo-German start-ups.

In February 2016, HHL organized the first Indo-German Business Day with more than hundred Indian companies in Germany, in cooperation with Professor Sushil Khanna of the ICCR chair and the Indian Embassy in Berlin. For further intensification of their cooperation in the area of education and innovation, Professor Rai and the author suggest the following activities:

1. Designing a short-term joint programme focusing on policies where German and Indian policymakers can spend one week in India and one week in Germany. This will be aligned with Prime Minister Modi's commitment to improve the ease of doing business in India.

2. Initiating a short-term programme for middle- and senior-level German and Indian executives as part of the Make in India manufacturing initiative of the Indian government. The possibilities for Indo-German partnership in areas such as trade in advanced technology, intelligence, renewable energy as well as defence manufacturing are enormous.
3. Organizing conferences on start-ups with the aim to provide a platform for bringing together German and Indian stakeholders, stimulating dialogue on key challenges currently faced by the Indian innovation ecosystem, and providing potential solutions to address them. Prime Minister Modi launched the Startup India initiative last year with the aim to foster entrepreneurship and promote innovation by creating an ecosystem that is conducive to the growth of start-ups. Germany can help India become a nation of job creators instead of a nation of job seekers.

Germany is known for nurturing a successful culture of innovation, which has been a long and important journey for the country. The initiatives mentioned above will support India in becoming an attractive hub of innovation, design and start-ups in Asia. Thus, this is an appropriate time to cement our relationship as India is the world's fastest growing economy and Germany is the powerhouse economy in an economically struggling Europe, and both countries have much to gain from close ties with each other.

Skill Development: Linking HRD and Business

◈

Mark Hauptmann
'Skills Development in India: The German Perspective'

◈

S. Ramadorai
'Building Momentum in Skills Development through Collaboration'

Mark Hauptmann Member of Parliament, Christian Democratic Union (CDU).

Mark Hauptmann was elected a member of the German Bundestag in his home constituency in the free state of Thuringia in September 2013. He is a member of the Committee on Economic and Energy Affairs and a substitute member of the Foreign Affairs Committee. Since 2014, he has been a member of the city council in Suhl. Before joining the Bundestag, he worked in Brussels, Beijing, and the German city of Erfurt, and was head of the office of MP Christian Hirte.

Hauptmann earned a master's degree in Political Science, Inter-Cultural Business Communication and Economic and Social History. Joining the Junge Union in 1999, he became a member of CDU in 2003. From 2012 to 2014, he was a member of the federal board of the Junge Union Germany and chairman of the International Commission on European, Foreign and Security Affairs. In addition, he holds membership in the CDU's Federal Committee on Matters of Foreign, Security, Development, and Human Rights Policy.

After being awarded a scholarship by the Konrad-Adenauer Foundation, he has maintained close ties with the foundation's stipend programme. He regularly hosts seminars either as the main speaker or organizer, in order to give young awardees the opportunity to gain first-hand insights into policymaking. Recently, he became ambassador for the Town & Country Foundation, generating publicity and raising funds for projects that offer new perspectives to underprivileged children.

Skills Development in India: The German Perspective

Mark Hauptmann

In October 2015, on the occasion of the third Indo-German Government Consultations, Indian Prime Minister Narendra Modi and German Chancellor Angela Merkel signed a memorandum of understanding, declaring their will to enhance their countries' strategic bilateral partnership. Among other things, they agreed to step up cooperation in the field of vocational education and training (VET), the latter having been identified as being key to future success and prosperity.

Seeking Synergies

Both Germany and India have a lot to gain from working together in this particular area. India has enormous human resources it can bank on. With a population of more than 1.3 billion, the average age of Indians will be just twenty-nine years in 2020. By then, about 65 per cent of the Indian population will be in the working age group, providing the Indian economy with both huge opportunities and huge challenges.

If there is a way to reap this 'demographic dividend', it is through skill development. Therefore, the government of Prime Minister Modi has rolled out an ambitious plan to educate and skill 500 million Indians by 2022. Due to a lack of educational training facilities, the Indian government is keen to learn from the famous German VET system.

Shrinking cohort numbers due to demographic decline have led to a completely different contextual challenge in Germany. Even though Germany has a world-class education system, companies are desperately looking for young people to train and educate. This search is not restricted to Germany, yet. Since German companies are dependent on qualified personnel in their export markets, it is imperative for them to get into the educating and training business as well. They know that, even in an age of instantaneous communication, you cannot sell, set up, and run machinery if you're not around.

India with its fast growing economy and its demographic edge, on the one hand, and Germany with its numerous export-oriented companies and VET know-how, on the other hand, are perfect partners. There is a lot of synergy and complementarity between Germany's skills in the VET sector and India's enormous pool of young talent. This fact is further underlined by one general trend: digitalization.

Digitalization is transforming and even destroying traditional business models all over the world. Indeed, it provides great opportunities but it is immensely disruptive and demands constant adjustments. Hence, in the fast-paced business environment of today, continuous skill development is imperative.

Equally, digitalization is causing millions of low-qualified jobs to disappear. Robots are increasingly taking over repetitive tasks and are threatening the livelihood of millions of people. Again, the only solution to this is skill development. People need to be skilledup to create the workforce necessary in a digital era.

Keeping this in mind, it is fair to say that skill development is one of the most important issues of our time.

Bridging the Skills Gap

Skill development is not a recent phenomenon in India. In 1956, the National Council for Vocational Training (NCVT), an advisory body, was set up to advise the government on overall policy, prescribe standards and curriculum, and award National Trade Test Certificates. Industry associations such as Federation of Indian Chambers of Commerce and Industry (FICCI) and Confederation of Indian Industry (CII) have been active members of the NCVT since its inception. However, it wasn't until the 2000s, after years of rapid growth and a serious shortage of skilled staff, that the government and companies took a more active stand on skill development.

For the first time in the history of India, the Eleventh Five Year Plan (2007 to 2012) included a chapter on skill development. As a direct result of this, the National Skill Development Corporation (NSDC) was set up with the objective of increasing the skill training capacity in the country, and creating a market ecosystem for skill development.

In 2015, the Indian government under Prime Minister Modi approved India's first integrated National Policy for Skill Development and Entrepreneurship. In the same year, it also launched the National Skill

Development Mission, thereby acknowledging the need for a consistent skills strategy.

At the moment, the Indian government is promoting its Skill India initiative which has been created to empower the youth of the country with skill sets necessary to increase their employability and productivity. Skill India offers vocational education and training courses across a number of sectors that are aligned to the standards recognized by both the industry and the government under the National Skill Qualification Framework. The courses are designed to help individuals focus on practical delivery of work and allow them to enhance their technical expertise.

Indo-German Cooperation

Despite the great success of these initiatives, the Indian government has been wise in building on German expertise in the past. There are several examples of this.

In order to promote business relations between German VET providers and international public and private organizations, International Marketing on Vocational Training (iMOVE) was established by the German Ministry of Education and Research in 2001. This initiative comprises numerous education programmes that have been developed in cooperation with German companies and education providers.

Bosch, for instance, has established a vocational centre in Bengaluru. The engineering company recruits around sixty youngsters for a three- to four-year full-term apprenticeship each year, and provides hands-on training experience under the guidance of industry experts.

International sanitary fittings brand Grohe is another great example of a German company that engages in skill development in India. After its success in Mumbai, Grohe has decided to launch a 'Grohe Dual Tech' in New Delhi, providing training to young people from economically challenged backgrounds in the region.

Both programmes cater to the needs of both the industry and the Indian population. On the one hand, these programmes help bridge existing skills gaps, while on the other hand, they help increase young people's employability.

In 2008, the Indo-German Joint Working Group (JWG) on Vocational Education and Training was created. This working group is chaired by the Indian Ministry of Skill Development and Entrepreneurship and the German

Ministry of Education and Research in close collaboration with the Ministry of Economic Cooperation and Development.

The Indian members of the JWG include representatives from the two major industry associations, i.e. FICCI and CII; the members from the German side include representatives of the German chambers of skilled crafts as well as Indo-German Chamber of Commerce (AHK), the Federal Institute for Vocational Education and Training (BIBB), and iMOVE. The bilateral working group meets on an annual basis in India and Germany alternately. As a direct result of this working group, the Indo-German Skills Forum, a bilateral cooperation group along with iMOVE has been created. This forum facilitates private sector interaction to promote bilateral trade dialogue.

Additionally, in 2010, BIBB and iMOVE signed a cooperation agreement with FICCI. This document is the basis for regular exchanges in numerous areas associated with VET, such as the provision of training for instruction personnel and the development of occupational standards.

Finally, an agreement between iMOVE and India's NSDC was signed during the government consultations held in New Delhi in 2011. This agreement set the scene for German providers of VET and Indian public education facilities as well as private companies. The opening of iMOVE's New Delhi office marked an important milestone in this bilateral cooperation. Since 2012, iMOVE has been acting as a hub for strategic alliances between the Indian and German partners.

Areas for Further Cooperation

During the 2015 Indo-German government consultations, the following topics were identified as special areas of cooperation:

1. Training of master trainers to build up capacities in training institutes as well as within micro-, small- and medium-sized enterprises.
2. Consulting on the further development of training, assessment and certification standards.
3. Incorporating dual principles of vocational training into the apprenticeship training modules.
4. Supporting workplace-based skill development at cluster level and policy level.
5. Developing competency-based curriculum in identified sectors.

Among these four points, the following three points are, in my opinion, in need of enhanced cooperation.

I. Vocational Education and Training Capacities

In view of the surge in initiatives from both the government and industry in India, the country has already made great progress. Given the ambitious medium- and long-term targets for skill development that the Indian government has set itself, more needs to be done.

The existing annual training capacity in the country is only 4.5 million. In light of the fact that twelve million people enter the Indian labour market each year, this training capacity needs to be massively increased.

A major reason for the lack of training capacity is that, without government funding, the private sector has remained largely hesitant when it comes to contributing significantly to skill development. According to World Bank data, barely 36 per cent of Indian companies were providing enterprise-based training in 2014. These 36 per cent are predominantly larger firms that can afford to invest in the infrastructure and human resources required to provide such training. Small- and medium-sized enterprises are mostly not providing any skilling programmes.

A major contributing factor might also have been that, so far, the public–private partnership that NSDC was originally intended to be has remained almost entirely government funded. There might have been an increase of NSDC-financed private vocational training providers (VTPs). Yet these VTPs offer, at best, courses that last a maximum of four months, which is hardly sufficient to equip fresh youngsters with skills that can help them increase their employability.

This is a severe problem. Close cooperation between industry and the educational system is the only way to guarantee that people receive the skills necessary. Demand-driven practical training and individual responsibility is imperative. Therefore, there is still a need for a further increase in capacities and private sector involvement.

The German government and German companies could help by providing their expertise in setting up the structures necessary. With the Indo-German Working Group and iMove's office in India, there are already institutions which can help provide best practice models. Also, they could help create the incentive structures for private companies to invest in the skilling of young people.

II. Competency and Assessment Standards

To ensure competency-based training in India, Sector Skills Councils (SSCs) are currently in charge of preparing National Occupation Standards (NOSS). However, these standards do not constitute a consistent education and training curriculum.

Again, employers should get involved in the preparation of such a curriculum. They are the only ones to know which competencies they need their employees to have. In this vein, the private sector should also get engaged in the assessment of trainees and apprentices. This applies particularly to large companies, both foreign and domestic, which are selling their goods and services abroad. They know the kind of standards that are necessary to successfully source the human resources indispensable for competing in the international market.

German companies and trade associations with a strong foothold in India could be a perfect partner for this challenge. Firms like Bosch and Grohe could provide their expertise to train apprentices in the requisite competency and assessment standards. Together with trade associations in India, they could facilitate the creation of a nationwide set of criteria.

III. Inclusiveness

Inclusiveness has not been mentioned in the memorandum of understanding of the Indian and German governments. Nevertheless, this point is of great importance to India.

According to a report published by Oxfam, India ranks the second lowest in the Group of 20 (G-20) economies, when it comes to women's integration in the workforce. India is also one of the few countries where the percentage of women working has witnessed a decline in the last ten years—it decreased from 33.7 per cent in 1991 to 27 per cent in 2012, according to UN gender statistics. Of course, this comes at a massive cost. According to the consulting firm Booz & Co., the country's GDP could increase by more than a quarter if male and female employment rates were matched.

Thus, providing skill development opportunities for women is crucial. Germany, faced with a similar situation in the early 2000s, introduced Girls' Days, an open-day event aimed at teenage girls to acquaint them with jobs that are traditionally considered 'male dominated'.

Even fifteen years later, results show that the event is a success and the vocational choices of girls are being influenced in a positive way. For companies, Girls' Days have evolved as an important instrument of their recruitment policy.

This initiative could thus serve as a role model for a similar initiative in India. The German Ministry for Education and Research and the Ministry for Family Affairs, which are in charge of organizing Girls' Days, could certainly provide their expertise and share their experience with the Indian government.

Conclusion

In the end, however, solutions have to be found that match the particular needs of the Indian population and the Indian economy. It would not work to implement the German VET system in its original form in India. After all, India is a subcontinent with a great number of blossoming urban centres, as well as some very remote areas without any industry or facilities to run a full-fledged dual-mode VET system.

Therefore, it has to be seen what kind of models can be used successfully in India. However, it is indispensable for Germany and Indian to work closely together on this. As far as the German government is concerned, it has a vested interest in ensuring that the skills culture grows deep roots in India, the existence of relevant skills being a sine qua non for growth and prosperity in both India and Germany.

Dr S. Ramadorai, Chairman, National Skill Development Agency

Dr S. Ramadorai has been in public service since February 2011. Currently, he is the chairman of the National Skill Development Agency (NSDA) in India with the rank of a cabinet minister. He is also chairman of the National Skill Development Corporation.

He took over as the CEO of Tata Consultancy Services (TCS) in 1996 and retired from there in 2009. He was then appointed as the vice chairman and held office until he retired in October 2014.

Dr Ramadorai is currently the chairman of Air Asia (India), Tata Advanced Systems Limited, Tata Technologies Limited and Tata STRIVE. In March 2016, he retired as the chairman of the Bombay Stock Exchange. He continues to be an independent director on the boards of Hindustan Unilever Limited, Asian Paints Limited and Piramal Enterprises Limited.

In recognition of his commitment and dedication to the IT industry, he was awarded the Padma Bhushan (India's third highest civilian honour) in January 2006. In April 2009, he was awarded the CBE by Queen Elizabeth II for his contribution to Indo-British economic relations. In 2016, he was awarded *The Economic Times* Lifetime Achievement Award for his significant contribution to Tata Consultancy Services.

Building Momentum in Skills Development through Collaboration

Dr S. Ramadorai

In this essay, I shall share some of the learnings from Indo-German collaboration in skills development, further thoughts on achieving greater momentum and finally, the role that the micro, small and medium enterprise (MSME) sector in India can play in emulating some of the best practices in skills development from Germany.

Apprenticeship and Skills

Like Germany, India has historically placed great emphasis on the acquisition of skills through apprenticeship with a master teacher. Truly, this is at the very heart of the celebrated *guru–shishya* culture of India. This mode of learning and acquiring skills still continues, perhaps, in a contemporaneous manner, in classical music and dance.

However, for the development of modern industrial skills, we have created a system of ITIs, polytechnics and engineering colleges. Our Apprenticeship Act, conceptualized in 1961, formulated a strict 'inspection-based mechanism' to ensure compliance. However, as time passed, this 'inspection-centric' approach discouraged companies from hiring apprentices. Compliance rather than the spirit of developing skills acquired greater focus. I am pleased to say that a newly amended Apprenticeship Act came into force in India in December 2014.

The amended Apprenticeship Act has, indeed, enthused companies to update and adopt best practices. For example, a leading German industrial conglomerate, Siemens, has helped Indian companies understand the advantages of the German dual Vocational Education Training (VET) Programme.

At a state-of-the-art vocational training centre in Mumbai, for example, Siemens and its industrial partners carefully identify the right set of trainees from among class 10 students. Further emphasis is placed on counselling the students for a career in skills. After a rigorous selection process, the students are exposed to a carefully designed three-year programme leading to placement. The alumni of this programme have gone on to become key leaders in their respective industries.

Skills development follows the German model. Learning at the well-appointed facility is supplemented from the very first year by practical training in a partner company. As the students progress, the amount of time they spend learning in the industry increases, going up to 80 per cent in the final year. Thus, there is a close alignment and synergy between theory and practice brought about by the constant exchange of insights between the lecture hall and the workshop.

Furthermore, the students learn by working in teams and deliver outcomes like they would if they were working in the industry. Teams of trainees work on practical projects, just as they would on the job. They follow the same processes and standards followed in the industry in all their projects. So, from the very beginning, the students get a broad exposure to the culture of work and responsibility in the industry.

They are taught systems thinking in a practical sort of way. For example, if students at the Siemens skills centre choose to make a coffee dispensing machine as a first-year project, they will have to learn and implement all the procedures followed in a factory for the manufacture of a coffee dispensing machine in the real world.

In this model, the partner companies play a key role as they are equally responsible for ensuring that students get the standard quantity and quality of training set in the training descriptions for each trade. By the time they complete the skill training, the students would have also acquired the required technical knowledge, with hands-on experience. Companies benefit from this as they get employees who can be productive team members from the very first day of employment.

A standardized curriculum developed by the German government in collaboration with educational institutes, the private sector, employee unions and chambers of industry and commerce is not uncommon. Similarly, at the Mumbai facility, an updated curriculum has been adapted for the particular needs of Indian industry. The entire learning is supported by a state-of-the-art digital learning platform as well.

The assessment of the students in this programme is continuous, digitized, and multidimensional. It covers multiple aspects of a student's ability to work in a twenty-first-century manufacturing set-up. The certificates that these students get on the successful completion of the programme are also recognized by the industry everywhere.

Not only is the certification widely recognized, but through the National Skills Qualification Framework, students can transfer credits from the skills programme for higher education in the engineering and allied fields. This ensures professional growth and mobility, and creates an incentive for lifelong learning. This also enables students to enter the vocational stream at a young age and acquire practical skills, while seeing an increase in their earning capacity and steady progress in the industry.

During my visits to Germany, I have seen that the employability of students who have undergone the dual-track VET is very high. This is one of the reasons why this kind of training is very popular with young Germans, and 60 per cent of German high school students go through some kind of apprenticeship programme, which leads to a formal certificate in the chosen skill and often a permanent job at the company where the person trained.

I have met several people who have started as apprentices and gone on to become CEOs of their own companies, or other established companies. Then there are individuals who have chosen to pursue PhDs in various aspects of engineering, after their apprenticeship. There are many such admirable aspects of the German dual model that Siemens has brought into their programme in Mumbai.

The success of the Siemens vocational skills programme has encouraged other companies to adopt the dual mode of skill training. Many German companies in India are now trying to replicate this dual-track programme. For example, Bosch has started the Bosch Vocational Centre (BVC) in Bengaluru. Since it was founded in 1961, BVC has trained over 2,500 apprentices in nine trades.

Another example is the German industry body, TUV Rheinland, which operates a world-class vocational skills training centre in Jodhpur. Among other things, they have one of the best workshops for solar skills and welding skills. It is indeed noteworthy that Germany is among the leaders in solar energy and other renewable energy-related technologies and skills.

Mittelstand Companies and the Role of MSMEs in India

Mittelstand companies have contributed immensely to the German economy, helping to keep it thriving despite a global recession. With an annual turnover of up to 500 million euros, the 3.67 million small- and medium-sized enterprises (SMEs) form the backbone of the German economy and represent almost 99.95 per cent of all German companies. In fact, 87 per cent of these companies have an annual turnover of less than 1 million euros.

Mittelstand companies are mainly family-owned units employing more than 68 per cent of the nation's workforce. Equally important is the fact that they provide training to 89 per cent of all German trainees. The government also ensures that educational institutes are linked to industries, and students pursuing post-secondary education are required to execute a project in these units in order to complete their course. This has enabled manufacturing units to get a trained workforce while receiving feedback from universities and vocational training centres.

Furthermore, through a consistent commitment to excellence, innovation and efficiency, Mittelstand companies typically feature among the top three companies in the world market for their particular products.

Another key factor in the success of the Mittelstand companies is their ability to create a comprehensive and functional ecosystem. For example, the Fraunhofer Gesellschaft (Fraunhofer Society) is an independent non-governmental organization which provides high quality applied research to help SMEs continually upgrade their processes and products and stay ahead of the competition.

These are a network of institutes operating across Germany which conduct short-term projects that help focus on immediate results for SMEs. Through such institutes, Germany is able to offer its SMEs skills, equipment, services and insights which these companies could not acquire on their own. This has in turn helped Germany to strengthen its SME industry.

The contribution of MSMEs in India is absolutely critical to our growth. Our MSMEs have sustained an annual growth rate of over 10 per cent for the past few years. According to the estimates of the Ministry of MSME, the sector generates around 100 million jobs through over 46 million units situated throughout the geographical expanse of the country.

With a 38 per cent contribution to the nation's GDP and a 40 per cent and 45 per cent share of the overall exports and manufacturing output, respectively, the MSME sector is the biggest contributor to social and economic development in India.

MSMEs lead to inclusive growth because they play an important role in employment creation, resource utilization and income generation. Indian MSMEs are increasingly organizing themselves in clusters, thus improving their access to business associations and technical assistance providers.

There is certainly a great opportunity for Indian organizations to partner with their German counterparts. For example, the Indo-German Joint Working Group (JWG) on VET was set up in 2008 largely to complement the implementation of India's National Skill Development Initiative. The bilateral working group on VET meets on an annual basis alternately in India and Germany. The JWG has built continuous and trustful dialogue on skill development between Indian and German partners. Furthermore, both countries' delegations have developed a good understanding of the partner country's system.

This solid foundation allows a range of measures, partnerships and activities to foster the modernization of VET in India. The objectives of the bilateral working group on VET are upgradation and establishment of vocational training institutions, training of trainers, creating public–private partnership (PPP) on the pattern of the German dual system in companies in India, labour market administration, research and development in the field of vocational training and development of competency standards.

As part of this partnership, companies like Festo, Volkswagen, BMW, Bosch, Daimler Chrysler, Adidas, Bajaj Allianz and TuV, etc. have been delivering world-class vocational training programmes in partnership with their Indian counterparts.

In its current state, the working group is chaired by the Indian Ministry of Skill Development and Entrepreneurship and the German Ministry of Education and Research (BMBF) in close collaboration with the German Ministry of Economic Cooperation and Development (BMZ). The working group has to date deliberated on possible collaboration between institutions and agencies on both sides on key issues related to VET, including incorporating the dual principles of vocational training into the apprenticeship training modules, supporting workplace-based skill development at the cluster level and policy level for MSMEs, and exploring possibilities for setting up a national institute for skill development.

There have also been some key consultations on the further development of training, assessment and certification standards. Sector skill councils have collaborated with German experts for creating a process for validation of qualification packs/national occupation standards. German partners have also assisted the Indian team with industry-relevant curriculum and exposure to learners for the WorldSkills competition.

The Indo-German Chamber of Commerce (IGCC) is trying to implement a unique skill development programme by forming clusters of enterprises to initiate dual (combined workplace based and school based) vocational training courses as well as developing core processes and PPP—structures for quality assurance, examination and certification.

During the third India–Germany intergovernmental consultations held in October 2015, a joint statement was issued which welcomed closer cooperation in vocational training and skills development between the two countries, by supporting policy reforms and further strengthening cooperation in various skilling initiatives in India. This approach continues.

More Areas of Collaboration with Germany

While a lot of work is happening in skill development through the JWGs and partnerships with companies and institutes, there are many more areas where collaboration would be mutually beneficial for India and Germany:

- Like the Fraunhofer institutes in Germany, we can have institutes in India which can collaborate with the Fraunhofer institutes. This will also help Fraunhofer scientists learn about new technology developments taking place in India. The first step in this regard has already been taken with the settingup of a Fraunhofer representative office in India.
- Formalizing the dual-track education system through apprentices will not only help to give apprenticeship a boost, but will also help to increase the employability of students.
- While there is now a mandatory SME representation in the sector skill councils, understanding more about Germany's Mittelstand in terms of employing apprentices would not only give the SME industry the 'right skilled worker' but also contribute towards increasing apprentices in the country.
- To fulfil its skill development target, India needs to increase its institutional capacity. German vocational training partners can certainly collaborate with Indian counterparts or directly establish new centres of excellence. These would not just impart skills but would also focus on creating master trainers and master assessors.
- Certifying and assessing vocational skills is becoming increasingly important and I would look at Germany to help in designing the certification programmes which would also give international recognition to our certifications.
- We are likely to see a number of smart cities being created under

the Indian government's Smart Cities programme. This is a golden opportunity for MSMEs across India. However, MSMEs will need to have employees with the right skills to participate in the creation of smart cities in India.

This is where Germany can help. By connecting the Mittelstand companies of Germany to their counterparts in India, there can not only be collaboration at a technical level but also an exchange of skilling practices and processes.

- Thus Mittelstand companies will get more access to international markets like India and have the opportunity to scale up. At the same time, in India, we will be able to share some of the best Mittelstand practices and processes with our SMEs, enabling them to grow and employ skilled labour.
- Similarly, in India, there is a lot of innovation to create 'affordable simulators' which can help teach skills like driving, welding, weaving, to name a few. We would be pleased to share such simulators with Germany to assist in vocational training there.

With the advent of the fourth industrial revolution or Industry 4.0 which itself has its roots in Germany, the world is now advancing towards next-generation skills. The focus is now on creating 'smart manufacturing technologies' by integrating cyber physical systems into factory processes. As India enters the fourth industrial revolution, and continues to strengthen its partnership with Germany, I believe that Germany will be looked upon to mentor and guide India towards a completely new kind of skill development.

Innovation and Start-ups Will Lead Us into the Future

◈

Nisha Dutt
'Rise of Impact-focused Entrepreneurship in India'

◈

Stephan Vopel and Murali Nair
'Innovation in India and Opportunities for Indo-German Collaboration'

Nisha Dutt, CEO, Intellecap Advisory Services Private Limited

Nisha Dutt leads the technology-led innovations at Intellecap and has started new initiatives like 'Creditree' for women entrepreneurs, 'StartupWave' for innovators and 'Innovation Labs' for commercializing world-class innovations. She serves on the board of directors of Intellecap and several other listed companies in India.

She holds an MBA from the University of Ohio and an MS in Industrial Engineering, Supply Chain Management, from Oklahoma State University (US). An avid flyer and a globetrotter, she loves collecting native art.

Rise of Impact-focused Entrepreneurship in India

Nisha Dutt

Poverty is evolving from a problem of extreme starvation and deprivation to a problem of inequity in accessing wealth creation opportunities. Humanity's achievements in the past few years are akin to science fiction having come to life. The world's cheapest interplanetary satellite has been launched, and the first human organ—a liver—has been printed. However, this particular junction in our history is not just remarkable for these achievements. Our biggest collective achievement is in taking two billion people out of extreme poverty in the past twenty-five years.

Much of this change has happened in emerging markets such as India, Brazil and China. India has gone through tremendous socio-economic changes in the last two decades. Fuelled by improvements in healthcare and medicine, life expectancy in India today is three times what it was a century ago. In 1994, 45 per cent of India's population lived below the national poverty line, and by 2012, this figure had fallen to 22 per cent.

The liberalization and opening up of markets in the 1990s ushered in opportunity and wealth, followed closely by the IT revolution of the 2000s which localized wealth creation in the country. A new India emerged, standing out amongst other emerging markets and winning more flattering titles like 'fastest growing start-up ecosystem of the world'.

But, not all is well. Despite rapid growth, there remain loopholes in the socio-economic development, along with an inequitable distribution of wealth. Absolute poverty which brings images of starvation and death might have receded from many parts of the country, but it has been replaced by the poverty of *access, ability, and knowledge*. More than 334 million people lack *access* to safe water either because the public utility system fails in delivery or private sector markets are broken.

The *ability* to earn a fair wage is declining as jobs for the unskilled and semi-skilled are steadily automated. *Knowledge* about best practices in areas such as financial savings is abysmal—nearly three-quarters of Indians do not understand essential financial concepts for managing their incomes and assets optimally. Combined together, poverty of access, ability and knowledge has given rise to a deeply inequitable and unsustainable society in India.

We are living in a dichotomous India, which is simultaneously home to the world's sixth largest concentration of dollar billionaires and one-third of the world's poorest people. For more than thirty years, only two groups of actors have tried to bridge this inequity—government and philanthropic organizations. And while much of the progress made in the improvement of the basic quality of life is attributable to them, they have fallen short in changing the face of poverty in India.

While the Indian government is the largest spender on social services for the poor, shelling out about $100 billion on services in 2012–13, this expenditure is not enough to better the conditions of the country's poor, and is proportionally much less than the spending of other comparable countries.

It is one thing to address malnutrition through a vast public health programme, and quite another to create world-class healthcare systems in rural areas. Taxes and charity can foot the bill for the former, but the resources we have at our disposal today are not sufficient for the latter. Charity has a role but is insufficient in creating systemic change because it lacks signalling power and sustainability—without accountability, its ripple effect would be muted, and that's where a new model is needed.

Inequity is now a global pandemic with poverty growing at high rates across the so-called 'developed world'. The changing face of inequity is by no means a phenomenon unique to India or even to developing countries. If international movements against social inequality such as 'Occupy' show us anything, it is that inequity is equally prevalent in the world's developed countries, and could spawn a class struggle. In fact while low-income communities in developing countries have generally seen an upward trend in their quality of life over the past few decades, this cannot be said for developed markets.

As a case in point, consider Germany, which until the late 1990s was hailed as an equitable society with a robust system of wealth distribution and social security. In fact Germany's rapid economic progress in the past decade is stunning—as several parts of Europe struggled with a debt crisis in 2015, Germany created a record current account surplus. But this picture is rapidly starting to change. According to the Organization for Economic Cooperation and Development (OECD), since 2000, 'income equality and poverty in Germany have grown faster than any other OECD country'.

East Germany's incomes, industries and wealth creation capacities are rapidly falling behind West Germany's, with the result that more than 15 per cent of Germans live in low-income conditions today, up from approximately 2 per cent in the early 1970s. Until recently the federal government's wealth redistribution programmes were sufficient to bridge the income gap. It is now becoming untenable for public funding and welfare structures alone to do so.

Conscientious Entrepreneurship: A Sustainable and Scalable Approach Towards Addressing Inequity

So what does the future hold? Are nation-states, the crowning triumph of human civilization, doomed to fail? I believe not. I think the next few decades will see the rise and dominance of an alternate, more just and more equitable socio-economic structure across both developed and developing countries. It will be driven by a new class of thinking that I call 'Conscientious Entrepreneurship'—which uses the power of markets to address the poverty of access, ability and knowledge.

Unlike philanthropy or public sector programmes which rely on a continuous supply of external capital, conscientious entrepreneurship is driven by the combined purchasing power and economic productivity that low-income and underserved people who comprise 56 per cent of the world's population represent. It taps into this purchasing power and economic productivity to bring products and services that can improve the quality of life of those who need it the most.

Conscientious entrepreneurship is a philosophy that is starting to permeate across organizations and individuals irrespective of legal nature, size and mission. Conscientious entrepreneurs comprise CEOs of socially and environmentally impactful multinational corporations, promoters of small enterprises serving low-income communities, farmer cooperatives, individuals participating in peer-to-peer and circular economies, and many others.

At the core of this movement is a belief that commerce between organizations and individuals can do good while creating financial value; those two end goals do not have to be mutually exclusive. As this movement has spread, it has earned many labels—such as social entrepreneurship, inclusive business, impact investing, etc.

The essential soul of conscientious entrepreneurship, however, is in carefully and thoughtfully designing systems, businesses and marketplaces that are inclusive and create positive impact. It is an alternative to capitalism of the Wall Street variety because it does not outsource social responsibility to a nameless 'other' like the government or a charity. Instead, it is a system that facilitates and rewards those taking ownership for solving the particularly complex problems of inequity—such as housing and employment.

I have personally had the opportunity to witness and participate in conscientious entrepreneurship across South Asia, Southeast Asia and East Africa over the past decade. The organization I lead, Intellecap Advisory Services, strives towards growing conscientious entrepreneurship by providing the right insights and advice, financial capital, and access to global and local networks.

We have helped 100 plus clients develop and scale 400 plus such approaches across 25 plus countries. We have also channelized more than $200 million in equity capital to such enterprises, and created a global community of 30,000 plus professionals who are growing this movement across the world.

Conscientious entrepreneurship is on the rise in India and Germany, and in both countries small- and medium-sized enterprises (SMEs) or Mittelstand firms (German medium-sized company, predominantly family run) are powering this movement. The path that each country has taken towards this movement is different. In India, the rise of conscientious entrepreneurship has its roots in the Gandhian philosophy of self-sufficiency and preservation of human dignity. India's very first cooperatives focused on food security and economic empowerment (Amul and SEWA) arose from this philosophy.

The microfinance industry came into being in the 1990s, and rapidly gathered steam. Encouraged by the success of these models in sustainably serving low-income communities while empowering them, SMEs entered the market. These SMEs provided access to affordable yet high quality services in sectors such as education, agriculture, water, sanitation and healthcare.

Today more than $1.6 billion of high-risk equity capital has been invested in SMEs to help them grow—demonstrating market belief in their potential. Business incubators, advisory firms, and funds have established themselves with a focus on promoting conscientious entrepreneurship.

In Germany, on the other hand, conscientious entrepreneurship has its roots in two phenomena—the Mittelstand, and a large and thriving welfare sector. The envy of not just Europe, but also much of the rest of the world, Mittelstand firms power the formidable German economic engine. They comprise 99.6 per cent of all firms in Germany, employ three in five people, and account for more than half of the economic output of Germany.

More importantly, they reconcile the twin objectives of 'doing well' and 'doing good'. Strongly rooted in their local communities, the families that drive Mittelstand firms often incorporate the long-term and broader welfare of their employees, customers and stakeholders into their planning.

However, Agenda 2010 and more specifically Hartz IV, enacted to tackle unemployment by creating an economy around part-time and freelancing jobs, has impacted even the Mittelstand firms' willingness to accrue higher costs on employee benefits and community care, when cheap temporary labour is so readily available. And that is where the power of Germany's welfare sector comes in.

The German Development Cooperation and private sector charities such as Caritas and Ashoka have long held important roles in global philanthropy. They are now seeing the need to bring these lessons home to address the inequities in their own backyard, thus creating a new model of conscientious entrepreneurship in Germany. Organizations such as BonVenture, the Social Venture Fund, and Tengelmen Social Ventures are incubating and investing in this next generation of Mittelstand firms.

Key Shifts Driving Conscientious Entrepreneurship

The world has undergone paradigm shifts in terms of how people are informed, how they connect, how they transact, and what they aspire towards. Technology and the growing liberalization of markets have played a strong role in this. They also underlie five interesting shifts that have caused conscientious entrepreneurship to take root and scale, and expand its influence on the private sector, civil society and governments.

We are no longer solving problems that impact low-income and underserved communities alone; resource scarcity is growing and will affect everyone. If reliable scientific organizations such as the US-based NASA and the India-based Public Health Institute are to be believed, California and population-dense parts of the Indian state of Karnataka will run out of water in a few years. Landmark power grid failures of the northeast region of the US and Canada in 2003, and northern India in 2012, brought day-to-day activity to a standstill across rich and low-income neighbourhoods and business districts alike. The truth of the matter is that resource scarcity is a reality that our generation will have to learn to live with. It is not going to impact only the disadvantaged.

However, resource scarcity has also had a positive impact. It has unleashed a new wave of innovation around renewable energy, city resilience, and affordable housing that is taking 'world-class' solutions to mass markets. Conscientious entrepreneurs today have the tools and insights from some of the world's best minds to solve deeply entrenched social problems.

This is a game changer because until the mid-2000s, the narrative around serving low-income communities was focused on 'jugaad'—an Indian practice of using locally available resources to address immediate problems. This practice treats low-tech and less structured approaches as 'meritorious' and often confuses it with innovation. Increasingly, it is being widely recognized that this way of working is a disservice that hampers growth and real innovation, and must be replaced by best-in-class, precise and engineered business solutions.

The problem with 'jugaad' is it doesn't scale, and this becomes more apparent as the complexity of resource scarcity grows. Consider water scarcity as a case in point. In 2015, the Indian state of Maharashtra suffered from a massive drought due to failure of seasonal rains. The government's response was to send cargo trains full of water to affected areas; these trains now run on a regular schedule. This is an example of 'jugaad' in practice.

The water may suffice for communities living in the immediate neighbourhood of train tracks but how many such trains can be sent? What happens to areas that are not accessible by train? On the flip side—Israel's conscientious and structured approach to this challenge has been creating city-level desalination plants which incorporate disruptive innovations that make desalination affordable. The best of minds and capital have come together to solve a problem because it is universal in nature.

Intellectual and Financial Capital Increasingly Becoming Democratized

Information asymmetry kept intellectual and financial capital concentrated amongst a few influential individuals and organizations until the 1990s. With the rise of the internet, however, information is now ubiquitous. It can guide decision-making, match needs with opportunities, and enable cheap and accurate transactions. This has changed the way individuals, organizations and societies respond to the challenges of inequity.

Conscientious entrepreneurs are using open data and platforms such as change.org to inform the public about inequity and mobilize support.

Facebook and Twitter have turned more than a billion people into citizen journalists who report, comment on and drive action on issues that impact them. Quora and Github enable real-time collaboration and discussions amongst experts around the world.

Conscientious entrepreneurs once had no option but to struggle to get venture capital or development finance organizations to sign cheques for them. Crowd-funding platforms such as Kickstarter and Ketto now let them raise a few dollars from hundreds of individuals who not only contribute financial capital but also bring in feedback and advice, and often become first users of products and services.

This means that capital can be allocated to projects in proportion to their value creation potential. For a society, this relates to how capital is allocated and channeled to new ideas and projects to improve the overall wealth and wealth creation potential of the nation, and not exclusively to businesses that offer maximum returns. The unidirectional 'one-to-many' flow of intellectual and financial capital is now 'many-to-many'—a complex, self-sustaining, learning and evolving ecosystem.

World-class Talent is Choosing Conscientious Entrepreneurial Approaches

A decade of man-made and avoidable crises such as the US financial crisis of 2008, armed conflicts across the Middle East and South Asia, and the refugee crisis of 2015 has forced a rewiring of our moral compasses. There is more interest now than at any time in the recent past in contributing in a positive manner not just to our families or workplaces but also to our communities and societies.

Between 2004 and 2016, Google searches for 'what is the purpose of life' have quadrupled. This has in turn led to the emergence of several movements focused on better living—from lifestyle-related movements such as circular and shared economies to work-related movements such as volunteering.

These work-related movements fed the early rise of conscientious entrepreneurship. Some of India's foremost high impact ventures have been started by expatriates returning home, and individuals opting out of mainstream careers. Currently, most of the senior management in the impact sector, about 46 per cent, is usually from the mainstream. These professionals have opted to reflect on how they can bring more meaning to their work.

Today, university programmes such as Santa Clara University's Global Social Benefit Institute and the University of Pennsylvania's Humanitarian Engineering and Social Entrepreneurship, along with experiential learning initiatives such as Acumen Fund and Villgro fellowships teach the art of conscientious entrepreneurship. A fresh crop of bright young individuals specifically trained in this area enter the field every year. Perhaps the most disruptive, and to me, the most encouraging sign is that unexpected alliances are being formed between farmers, scientists, coders and financial experts to find best-in-class solutions to seemingly intractable problems.

The Individual is Informed, Connected, Identifiable and Empowered

Mobile and internet penetration the world over has led to the rise of the connected individual—and this is by no means a phenomenon restricted to mid- and high-income populations. In fact, these segments were tapped out quite early by the telecom and mobile phone industry. Instead the past decade has seen a shift in this industry's spread towards low-income and underserved markets—ensuring that eight in ten Indians today have access to a mobile phone. This has been a great leveller in terms of how individuals are informed, identified and empowered.

It has facilitated conscientious entrepreneurship by de-anonymizing individuals—and allowing systems to be designed to serve high customized needs. Consider this—India recently replaced an ageing and inefficient social security system with a direct benefits transfer programme that uses a new national identification system (Aadhaar), with no-frills bank accounts (Jan Dhan), and mobile phones to directly transfer cash to individuals who qualify for social security programmes.

Power to Effect Change is No Longer in the Hands of a Few

The rise of connected individuals is also impacting the very nature of conscientious entrepreneurship. Tackling large and complex challenges such as resource scarcity was once the exclusive domain of governments, development finance institutions and multinational corporations. This is no longer true. In early 2016, Mark Zuckerberg, Stephen Hawking, and a group of individuals committed to a long-term, open-ended and high-risk project to send probes into deep space to find planets that can support life.

Their hypothesis is that as the earth runs out of resources, our approach to solving the problem of resource scarcity should also include out-of-the-box solutions such as finding alternative homes for humanity. This is the sort of decision that governments that are answerable to taxpayers and organizations that are answerable to boards and shareholders cannot make very easily.

Another example from India is the newly launched India Stack initiative, which has made available a set of open APIs (application programming interface) developed by volunteers and managed by public organizations to drive innovation and entrepreneurship in financial inclusion. In simple terms, the initiative wants to transform the way government delivers services to citizens by using the creative energies and expertise of the private sector. India Stack is what conscientious entrepreneurship looks like, versus the rise of a few giants.

The Way Forward: Securing an Inclusive Future for All

Conscientious entrepreneurship is here to stay; there are powerful market forces acting to ensure this. Globally, more than $60 billion in assets under management is earmarked for funding such ventures. Private wealth giants such as UBS and Goldman Sachs have started dedicated arms to help high net worth individuals build assets that do good and do well.

Even Y-Combinator, perhaps the world's most famous venture incubator, has started walking down the road of conscientious entrepreneurship by inviting experts to join it in solving problems such as universal basic income and building better cities. Meanwhile, Unilever has been publicly reporting its impact on society and environment, and holding itself accountable for meeting ambitious targets for years.

All these acts of conscientious entrepreneurship are having a powerful impact on the private and public sector, civil society, and individuals like you and me. Billions of low-income people around the world may be disadvantaged but they are no longer silent. They are demanding, paying for, and improving the way conscientious entrepreneurship serves them.

The question is not so much about what we can do to ensure the rise of this movement, but more about what we can do to ensure its accelerated rise. Perhaps most importantly, we need 'metadata' from as many conscientious entrepreneurship efforts as possible to understand 'what is working and why'—so that as a collective, we can put our weight behind the right models and scale them.

Finally, there is value in establishing and strengthening collaboration between countries of the Global North and the Global South as they tackle growing inequity. The traditional view of such collaboration has always been unidirectional—with expertise, technology and money flowing from the Global North to the Global South.

But the situation is changing. For instance, conscientious entrepreneurship in India and Kenya has seen more experimentation and innovation in using health-tech and fin-tech to create positive impact for low-income communities, than most developed countries. There is value in reverse engineering this knowledge to create context-appropriate solutions in the US and Europe. India and Germany stand to benefit from such collaboration, and can use it for their bilateral development cooperation.

India and Germany have been partnering on various initiatives for over six decades. The partnership has also evolved over time. For instance, when the Indo-German development cooperation started sixty years ago, the focus of our cooperation was on industrial development and the transfer of technological know-how. Later, poverty reduction, basic needs and rural development became important dimensions of our development policy.

India can learn from Germany's thriving small enterprises (German Mittelsand [GM]. Germany boasts the world's most 'hidden champions' or SMEs that are global market leaders in their respective niches, with about 1,300 GMs, far more than No. 2 US at 366. Germany's GM firms are adept at exploiting product niches in global markets, especially in electrical and industrial products.

The dynamic innovation of GM firms makes this possible: 54 per cent of GM firms created a product or process innovation between 2008 and 2010 while the average for the European Union was only 34 per cent. Every year about 90 per cent of patent applications in Germany come from the GM.

Germany, on the other hand, can partner with India to leverage India's young employment pool and scale the operations of its small businesses (the median age in Germany is 46.5 years compared to 27.3 years in India). It can also research and analyse the requirements of developing markets to co-create solutions and innovations. India can also help German enterprises partner with Indian start-ups to help them scale and expand faster.

Early signs of such collaboration are already visible. For instance, two years ago, an Indo-German public–private partnership called Strategic Alliance was launched with the German Development Cooperation, Intellecap, and Bosch as founding partners. Together we are working towards unlocking support from large multinational corporations towards start-ups in high impact sectors such as renewable energy and healthcare. Most recently, the Alliance worked with SAP to curate a series of knowledge exchange meetings between German and Indian ventures in the renewable energy sector.

Aviation pioneer Amelia Earhart famously noted, 'Everyone has oceans to fly, if they have the heart to do it. Is it reckless? Maybe. But what do dreams know of boundaries?' I identify with the spirit of her words when I consider that fifty years from now, we will look back at this era and see the shift from extractive, unstable and inequitable to sustainable, resilient and inclusive societies. Conscientious entrepreneurship will lead that shift in our lifetime. I cannot wait to see what that future looks like.

Stephan Vopel

Murali Nair

Stephan Vopel, Director, Programme Germany and Asia, Bertelsmann Foundation

Stephan Vopel is responsible for all the Asia-related activities of the Bertelsmann Foundation, as well as projects dealing with questions of social cohesion, religion and values.

He is a graduate of the Hebrew University of Jerusalem (BA), and of the University of Bielefeld (MA). He has worked as executive director for several publishing houses. He frequently contributes articles on issues related to social development, Israel and German–Israeli relations.

Murali Nair, Project Manager, Bertelsmann Foundation

Murali Nair is responsible for the India-related activities at Bertelsmann. He has an engineering degree and an MBA and has spent six years in the automobile industry with Indian, Japanese and German OEMs. He was a marketing manager in South Asia and Africa before volunteering for an NGO active in the field of social entrepreneurship.

Nair moved to Germany in 2010 to carry out research in public policy and responsible business at Zeppelin University. At the foundation, he brings out publications on the latest developments in the Indian economy and society which have an impact on Germany.

Innovation in India and Opportunities for Indo-German Collaboration

Stephan Vopel and Murali Nair

This article is based on a study on innovation in India that is being prepared by Roland Berger in cooperation with Bertelsmann Stiftung. The focus is not only on product innovation, which is usually the case, but also on process and business model innovation at an organizational and sectoral level. The study involves two hundred CEOs, policymakers and academicians engaged through personal interviews as well as brainstorming sessions in five workshops held across India. The final study report was released in September 2016.

Since the opening up of its economy in 1991, India has transitioned from being just a source of low-cost labour and a large domestic market to being a hub of innovation for global and Indian multinational corporations. Though it is not part of the global supply chain in manufacturing, India is definitely a part of the global research and development (R&D) network in sectors like information technology (IT), automotives, pharmaceuticals, etc. Indian multinationals are increasingly acquiring high-tech companies around the world for greater access to technology and markets.

Innovation Led by Multinational Corporations

The most visible aspect of innovation in India is the establishment of technology development centres by global software giants. High technology work in India started off as a labour cost arbitrage in the IT and business process outsourcing (BPO) sector, mostly concentrated in Bengaluru. Starting with doing basic work for their headquarters, the Indian centres in the late 1990s worked their way up the value chain by focusing on industry verticals and building domain expertise.

Indians holding senior positions in Silicon Valley helped accelerate this process. International IT heavyweights like IBM and Google realized the competitive advantage of having a base in India and opened their software development centres in the country. Over the years, global multinational corporations have invested in more than 1,000 captive R&D centres in India, making it a key player in product development for the domestic as well as the global market.

The typical path of an multinational corporation (MNC) in India is described in the following model:

Figure 16.1: Maturity model for global captive centres

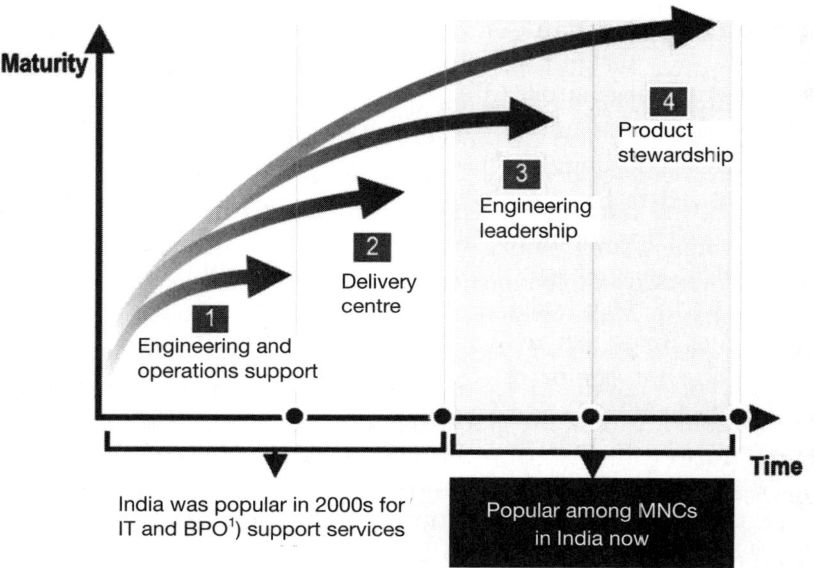

Sources: Battelle Report on Global R&D Forecast 2014; NASSCOM R&D Outsourcing Report 2010

For MNCs in India, the first phase involved basic engineering and operations support with pure labour cost arbitrage. The tasks were simple and routine and involved supporting a team at the headquarters. This progressed to the second phase where the team in India had responsibility for service delivery and was able to define and manage the global delivery process. In the more recent engineering leadership phase, the team in India takes ownership of end-to-end solutions by collaborating directly with customers, and by pursuing structured innovation programmes.

The final phase that some MNCs have achieved in India is called product stewardship. In this phase, the team leads global functions or business units by driving global technology management in terms of design, development and delivery, by collaborating directly with customers on strategic initiatives and by becoming a technology and innovation hub for the parent organization. For example, SAP Labs India has the global ownership of Internet of Things—Industry 4.0 initiatives, meaning that the Bengaluru office will drive the global development of this technology for the entire SAP organization.

Innovation Led by Indian Companies

With a government-controlled market, Indian companies did not have a lot of incentive to innovate until the 1990s. After the liberalization of the Indian economy in 1991, domestic companies faced international competition and were forced to be as good as, or even better than, their counterparts from abroad. These domestic companies responded to the international competition in various ways, from licensing technologies from abroad to taking over technology leaders in advanced economies.

Our study finds that though the innovation strategies of large Indian companies involve significant R&D spends and dedicated research teams, they differ from the classical Western model in their inbuilt frugal nature of innovation. Since India is a country with scarce capital, resources and purchasing power, the product or service being developed has to pass the frugality test to survive. Such products and services also find customers in the majority of world markets that face similar market constraints.

Mahindra & Mahindra, a $17 billion diversified business house, drives structured innovation through open innovation programmes and frugal engineering. Their philosophy of innovation is as follows:

> *'We pride ourselves in overcoming complex challenges "without" enough capital, technology, or skilled human resources. Our ability to deliver more with less is fundamental to who we are.'*

Many other Indian companies share this philosophy without explicitly mentioning it, and have frugality in their DNA. Frugal innovation needs to be differentiated from 'jugaad' (the Hindi word for a quick and short-term fix). It does not mean a low-cost, low quality solution but one that serves the required needs of a customer with minimum impact on resources.

Most advanced economies have ceded this competitive advantage as their access to resources, and customer expectations, have grown over the past decades. Frugally engineered products from emerging markets can pose a serious challenge to established players in advanced economies (termed 'reverse innovation') with increasing resource consciousness and the unbridled rise of complexity.

What we are also seeing in emerging multinational corporations from India is their ability to learn from an international market and apply it to their global operations. For instance, Godrej, a leading conglomerate, has used its learning from its Indonesian and Argentinian markets, which have similarities with the Indian one to develop new hair care products. It has then used its scale of operations in India to offer these products at an affordable price. This utilization of synergies from similar markets leads to collaborative innovation between emerging economies.

Innovation Led by Start-ups

Much has been written about the start-up scene in India. A combination of a young and digitally native population with the third largest internet community globally after China and the US (which it is estimated to overtake this year), and a far from saturated market for goods and services has driven billions in global capital into India. India is home to the third largest number of technology start-ups globally, ahead of China and Israel. It has eight 'unicorns' (companies with valuations of $1 billion or more in less than ten years of being founded) to Europe's nine. Investors poured in more than $5 billion into the Indian start-up sector in 2015.

The days of stratospheric evaluations of 'me-too' start-ups with no innovative product or business model, aided by low-cost capital from the anaemically growing advanced economies, are thankfully over. The tightening of capital flows has led to a focus on start-ups beyond e-commerce into education, healthcare, infrastructure, etc. which make a significant value addition to people's lives and thereby have a more sustainable revenue model. Some of these like Mitra Biotech (offering personalized cancer care), and Druva (offering mobile and cloud data protection) are expanding beyond the Indian market into the rest of Asia and even the US.

The frugal nature of Indian innovation is at work in start-ups as well. An example is that of Ideaforge, a drone making start-up that replaces expensive and heavy zoom cameras with normal ones equipped with an advanced software for a digital zoom, thereby creating one of the cheapest and lightest drones in the world. It has a market share of more than 90 per cent in India and is busy making plans to expand beyond the Indian market. The lack of basic infrastructure and resource constraints will force India to innovate in the digital space, and start-ups funded by international (and increasingly domestic) capital promise a continuation of the growth momentum in the coming years.

Weaker Links

The success stories of innovation in India are not without hitches. Almost all our respondents pointed out the weak educational system in India that fails to impart a sound basic education for the masses. Yes, there are clusters of high quality teaching and research, but this is more an exception than the rule. Even at the top universities, traditional academic excellence is valued more than creativity and innovation.

Additionally, the centres of excellence are disconnected from the problems of the majority of the population who are lower on the socio-economic scale, and thereby are unable to leverage innovation for a more inclusive society. The cooperation between industry and academia also leaves a lot to be desired. The gap between what is taught at university and what is needed by industry is so wide that most of the new recruits are not employable and have to be trained by their companies.

Indo-German Cooperation

The potential for cooperation between Germany and India in innovation is tremendous. Germany, as a high-technology-driven economy, needs to preserve its technological edge to sustain its economy. Given its demographic change, it is becoming increasingly difficult for it to find enough technologists and researchers to keep its industries at the cutting edge. Since Germany is not a natural destination like the US or the UK for migration of highly qualified professionals, it needs to collaborate with countries that have a large talent pool of scientific workers.

Thus India is an ideal partner in this endeavour. Leading German multinationals like SAP, Siemens and Bosch have recognized the opportunity and have scaled up their presence in India; most of them already have their largest R&D centres outside Germany in India. What is missing in India is the Mittelstand, the small- and medium-scale enterprises that are typically family owned. Many Mittelstand companies are technology leaders in their fields but are facing challenges in attracting the next generation of talent to maintain their technological leadership.

With the emerging markets, which have a young population, overtaking the advanced economies, the economic dynamism is already shifting.

To understand these markets and to develop products and services for the markets of tomorrow, organizations need to build a significant presence in these countries and develop strong partnerships with local stakeholders. India, with its social and economic diversity, is a microcosm of what most emerging markets are, and thus offers a proving ground for those venturing in.

Another field of deeper collaboration is Indo-German academic research. There are already excellent initiatives in this area, such as the Indo-German Science and Technology Centre (IGSTC). The IGSTC, which aims to foster innovation through R&D networking, and to solve global problems through joint knowledge pools, is the first centre of its kind that Germany has co-created with another country. Even though this initiative is heartening, there is very little university-to-university collaboration between India and Germany.

The number of Indian students in Germany is about 11,500, much less than the 100,000-plus Indian student community in the US. The number of partnerships and dual-degree programmes which Indian universities have with the US, the UK, Australia and Canada far exceed those with Germany. Such partnerships would enable a free flow of researchers between India and Germany, fostering a better understanding of their respective research academic structures and research networks.

India and Germany already have a strong basis for cooperation in the field of innovation. With a focused approach and a comprehensive strategy, this cooperation could be taken to a much higher level. Enhanced cooperation would benefit their respective economies and societies, and help in tackling global challenges like climate change, sustainable development and food security.